Musical Childhoods of Asia and the Pacific

A Volume in
Advances in Music Education Research

Series Editors:
Linda K Thompson, *Lee University*
Mark Robin Campbell, *State University of New York at Potsdam*

Advances in Music Education Research

Linda K Thompson and Mark Robin Campbell, Series Editors

Diverse Methodologies in the Study of Music Teaching and Learning (2008)
edited by Linda K. Thompson and Mark Robin Campbell

Research Perspectives: Thought and Practice in Music Education (2009)
edited by Linda K. Thompson and Mark Robin Campbell

Issues of Identity in Music Education: Narratives and Practices (2010)
edited by Linda K. Thompson and Mark Robin Campbell

Musical Childhoods of Asia and the Pacific (2012)
edited by Chee-Hoo Lum and Peter Whiteman

Musical Childhoods of Asia and the Pacific

edited by

Chee-Hoo Lum
National Institute of Education
Nanyang Technological University

and

Peter Whiteman
Macquarie University

Information Age Publishing, Inc.
Charlotte, North Carolina • www.infoagepub.com

Library of Congress Cataloging-in-Publication Data

Musical childhoods of Asia and the Pacific / edited by Chee-Hoo Lum and Peter Whiteman.
p. cm. -- (Advances in music education research)
ISBN 978-1-61735-774-9 (pbk.) -- ISBN 978-1-61735-775-6 (hardcover) -- ISBN 978-1-61735-776-3 (ebook) 1. Music--Instruction and study--Juvenile--Asia. 2. Music--Instruction and study--Juvenile--Pacific Area. I. Thompson, Linda K. II. Campbell, Mark Robin.
MT3.A78M88 2012
780.83'095--dc23

                                                        2012000589

Printed in the United States of America

CONTENTS

CHAPTER 1

CHILDREN AND CHILDHOODS

Chee-Hoo Lum and Peter Whiteman

THE CONCOURSE OF CHILDHOOD

Childhood. We have all had our distinctly individual experiences of this complex and diverse phase in our lives bound by sociocultural-historical contexts. Of the plethora in existence, no two notions of childhood are the same. Childhood is at once ephemeral and enduring. Decidedly pluralistic, it is a temporary phase for children but a permanent yet flexible construct for human cultures. By the very nature of human development, childhood is something that we traverse. It is something through which we pass as individuals, albeit with far-reaching, lifelong influence, yet it is a permanent state of affairs for our wider cultures, profoundly influenced by us as we pass. What it means, what it does, and the influences it exerts are wildly varied through time and across borders.

DIVERSE CHILDHOODS

Chinese philosopher and reformer Confucius (551 B.C.–479 B.C.) once said, "Respect the young. How do you know that they will not one day be all that you are now?" (Kinney, 1995, p. 12). Childhood is a much-treasured part of the life process within the Chinese family and as the child grows and develops, he or she should be carefully guided by parents and

Musical Childhoods of Asia and the Pacific, pp. 1–9
Copyright © 2012 by Information Age Publishing
All rights of reproduction in any form reserved.

the community to successfully *"chen ren* (become a man)." The Chinese child is typically brought up with his or her parents impressing upon the child to always respect and obey his or her elders and to have a sense of filial piety. While many Chinese parents see childhood as a time distinguished by few connate merits, they have profound admiration for the potential of children's intellectual and moral capabilities, which must be realized through education and development (Kinney, 1995).

Within Indian society, the "image of the young child revealed an innocent being, immersed in an atmosphere of love, appreciation, and indulgence extended by the older members of the family and community" (Gupta, 2006, p. 111). Gupta goes on to say that this concept is aptly illustrated in "palna-posna," a Hindi phrase commonly used to describe the raising of children, "the meaning of which includes a combination of the concepts of cradling, nurturing, and protecting" (p. 111). She explains how the young child in India is never thought of as a blank slate but "considered to be a gift from God: energetic, mischievous, charming, lovable, intelligent, competent, playful" (p. 113). Even as adults, most Indian children perpetuate strong familial bonds, caring for parents into old age, with strong interdependent relationships (Gupta, 2006).

In present-day Japanese society, "the importance of being with others, the pleasure of being with others, the acquisition of "social skills" to facilitate acceptance by others, are themes that Japanese adults never fail to emphasize in dealing with children from a very young age" (Chen, 1996, p. 120). A fundamental concern of Japanese adults in dealing with children is that children should never be left alone unaccompanied and that someone should always be assigned to be with them. Chen maintains that there is also a strong conception of anticipating "what a child may feel and then to accommodate to what is needed is characteristic of Japanese adults' attitudes in socializing their children" (p. 122). Fundamentally, children are brought up to cultivate *monono aware wo shiru* (to have the capacity of knowing the pathos of things) and to sympathize and empathize with the weak (Chen, 1996).

Traditional Aboriginal childhood was a short period in someone's life, with relative freedom, the end marked with ritual initiation around the time of puberty (Fryer-Smith, 2002). Thousands of decades ago, prior to white settlement, learning in Australia was indeed firmly ensconced in a sociocultural realm. Children learned through stories about the land and observing and emulating older, knowledgeable others to whom they were close (Parliament of the Commonwealth of Australia, 1985).

While there needs to be a constant review of culturally situated experience in a fast-paced world of technology and media that influences social changes, an understanding of the relevance of childhood in particular cultures (in this instance of Asia and the Pacific) will provide a deeper critique "to the tension between innovation and conservation in the generation of solutions to age-old and brand-new traditions" (Kakar, 1981, p. 182). We must admit there are commonalities as well as differences in the lives of children not just as individuals but across different cultural settings and only through addressing these situated experiences in varied geographical locales can we be informed about the appropriateness and usefulness of intended research methodologies that will serve to modify and re-evaluate theoretical and philosophical constructs thought initially to be applicable across wide domains.

DIVERSE MUSICAL CHILDHOODS

"Children learn the role of music within their society simply by living in their culture, and the musical grammar they develop is a direct result of what sounds come into their ears" (Campbell, 2006, p. 433). As they grow, children are developing a sense of their musical heritage, for it is apt to be their own soundscape of live and mediated expressions. Their inventions of a musical nature derive from this musical sound-surround (Campbell, 2006).

There is an increasing interest over the last two decades in early childhood and childhood music education research toward the investigation of contexts with which children engage in music, making sense of the social, cultural, and historical worlds that situate children's musical experience and learning (Kerchner & Abril, 2009). Context is significant because it puts "children in their 'real-life' dimensions of talking about and 'doing' music" (Campbell, 1998, p. 9). Understanding contexts inform music educators of what children already have in their musical palette: of repertoire learned from home and the community, of skills developed through music lessons from instrumental teachers and technological gadgets, and of uses and function from enjoyment to religious associations.

Children learn music of their own heritage and of children's culture from a very young age. They are "musically enculturated so as to reflect the local facets of their homes, families, and neighborhood communities. They are trained and entrained, educated and schooled, according to national policies and cultural preferences" (Campbell, 2006, p. 415). As McPherson (2006) reiterates, "any conception of music must encompass the ways in which children mature musically as a result of enculturation, training, and education" (p. vii). Understanding contexts is vital for music educators as it "affects both what is taught and how it is taught" (Bresler, 2007, p. viii).

We have come a long way from Moog's (1968/1976) classic longitudinal study of children's musical development, with greater emphasis in recent research work on the complexities with which music and musicking (Small, 1998) happens. Tafuri (2008), for instance, following the line taken by Moog's study, conducted a longitudinal study of children (birth to age 6) with intent in seeking out children's musical development in the context of musical activities organized and conducted by the researchers and the continued musical activities that parents would conduct in the home, within "a family environment that had plenty of musical stimulation, and the parents would accompany them with encouragement and praise as they grew" (p. 25). Studies in recent years have also looked at infants' interaction with their caregivers (Ilari, 2009), of how infants "learn music behaviors as a special kind of human cultural activity" (Malloch & Trevarthen, 2009, p. 183), family (Custodero, 2009) and media influences on children (Campbell, 1998; Gaunt, 2006; Lum & Campbell, 2009; Marsh, 1999), school or music program influences (Abril, 2009; Humpal, 2009; Valerio, 2009), and children's engagement in play and playground games (Marsh, 2008), among other considerations of environmental and social factors. Edited collections (e.g., Smithrim & Upitis, 2007) also point to a diverse range of researchers who have sounded out the significance of play and the body, social mediation, and slowing down pedagogy and going deep into understanding children's music-making processes (Young, 2003). As Boynton and Kok (2006) stressed, "engaging with music as a child cannot be equated with exclusively sonic experiences … children absorb behavioral norms and cultural values within a process that has often been termed 'enculturation,' or more recently, 'musical socialization' " (p. xii).

> In examining setting and situations of music learning by young people across cultures, comparisons may be made of the strategies employed by children in the process of knowing music well enough to be able to perform it, to create it anew, to understand its meaning. As they live, children learn, and many are keen to know the music that suits them and their view of the world--as well as to reflect the musical values of adults who are influential in shaping their cultural identities. (Campbell, 2006, p. 432)

This book serves to provide a glimpse of children's engagement in, with, and through music within Asia and the Pacific region. Through various methodologies, a range of researchers (music educators, musicians, ethnomusicologists, and sociologists) have ventured into the realm of musical childhoods: musical childhoods that comprise children's musical growth and development at home, in schools and within their community that are contextually different in many ways, providing added views of and reflective thoughts on early childhood and childhood music education practices and products.

In Chapter 2, Downing takes us on an ethnomusicological journey to Indonesia as she examines social change and gender issues surrounding children's gamelan ensembles in Bali. Readers are privileged to learn about the place and importance of physical learning in children's acquisition of musical knowledge and skills, and are treated to images of girls in gamelan ensembles. Although women's gamelan is becoming more common, those ensembles that include women and girls are often seen to be of lesser value than their male counterparts. With some documentation from the children's viewpoint, this chapter tests boundaries of embodied learning and gender.

Through "singing maternally" and "speaking autoethnographically" in Chapter 3, Mackinlay provides a particularly personal reflection on motherhood and methodology. Without motherhood, the notion of childhood is hypothetical at best, yet rarely have mothers and their musical worlds been closely assayed. In this chapter, the author uses her personal relationships and experiences with her two sons as the basis for giving an account of the locations and roles of mothers and musics. We hear about mothering and musicking and are apprised of the fact that mothers are "painfully absent" from the music education literature. The autoethnographic lens that Mackinlay chooses to employ provides an intensely personal and detailed interrogation of the undeniable importance of mothers and their musics.

In Chapter 4, we get to "hang out" with Britney and Raihan. In so doing, we are welcomed into the musical lives of two Melayu (Malay-Muslim) families with 1- to 11-year-old children in Singapore. In this ethnographic case study, Lum provides insight into the musical lives of Melayu children in Singapore, with accounts of the rich yet diverse musical engagements of two families. While some musics could be seen as innately on a collision course with Islam, this study serves to fortify the importance of our consideration of place and context when undertaking research in our field. We are charged with opening up conversations among those involved, to ensure that children's music education is realized in a state of optimal opportunity with regard for individual interpretations of what music can mean in children's lives.

Kim takes readers on a journey of Ki-ak-mu ("artistic integration" in Korean) in early childhood. In Chapter 5, she unpacks the notion of concept-based integration, where a particular concept is the germinal point for curriculum decision making. Readers are apprised of what a concept-based integrated arts curriculum is and how young children respond. Children's responses were generally positive, with evidence of concepts formed in music and movement experiences transferring to other arts domains. It seemed that parents, on the other hand, found integration to be a somewhat challenging notion.

Predicating education with the belief that "every child is smart" and that intelligence is indeed a plural concept, Chapter 6 invites readers into the world of children's musics in a Multiple Intelligences (MI) school in Manila. Costes-Onishi presents us with a case study of how children's musical intelligence is nurtured through traditional musics of the Philippines in the early years of school. Through a frank and candid account from an ethnomusicologist, we are exhorted to ensure that music learning encompasses not only contextually dependent extra-musical aspects but musical ones as well. We are introduced to the notion of "educating for understanding," exposed to a particular school's approach to this, and offered insight into whether the goal of musical understanding is really achieved.

In Chapter 7, Adachi explores the music learning of Japanese children by probing Music for Moppets, an introductory music program for preschool children. Firmly resisting the urge of some to engage young children in rote, decontextualized music learning, the program is informed by backward task analyses based on an expert student pursuing an advanced degree in music. From these case studies, spontaneous musical play, often taking place in the home, emerges as an important lynchpin in children's musical lives. Strong evidence is presented for the manner in which structured learning in the Music for Moppets program can be integrated with spontaneous musical play at home. Readers are introduced to young children who, through their spontaneous musical play, demonstrate clear potential to become independent learners without the need for explicit parental guidance.

Whiteman and Campbell's report of children's conceptualization of "music" in Chapter 8 is firmly founded in the traditions of the new sociologies of childhood and values children as active agents in their learning. Not satisfied with adult conceptions of a domain that can feature prominently in early childhood programs, they armed children with digital cameras and invited them to take photographs of "music" with a view to discovering what this concept really meant to the children. Using the photographs as stimulus for discussion with the children, a range of conceptualizations was uncovered; from the completely sonic to the completely functional. The authors offer a suggestion for how this approach and the information gleaned could be used to inform the curriculum decisions that are made every day in early childhood learning environments.

Lee reports on an exploration of young children's free musical play in Chapter 9. Undertaken in two Taiwanese contexts, 2- to 6-year-old children were observed in their interactions around music learning centers. They played instruments, created rhymes, sang songs, and moved. Their invented songs were in some ways reminiscent of earlier findings of studies of musical play. The observations of children musicking in various social combinations provide support for the provision of musical opportunity in forms that acknowledge the social nature of the children.

In Chapter 10, Onishi and Young offer a rich narrative recount of a 15-year-old violinist's struggle for quality music education from early childhood in Burma/Myanmar. While access to a Western art music education is a *fait accompli* for some of us, this would not have been the case for Phong Phong were it not for his parents, their engagement with music in their formative years, and their persistence in providing opportunity for their son. We hear about the trials and tribulations surrounding Phong Phong's becoming a violinist and are reminded of the crucial role that the sociopolitical context plays in the musical nurturing of young people.

Ambasta and McLeod's case study of the family of Ustad Kadar Khan forms Chapter 11. Explicating the oral tradition that surrounds the study of North Indian classical music with a guru, readers find out about the four elements of mastery and the crucial role of the family in the child's music education. We are told how music learning experiences are tailored to the individual person and context, and that music and movement can be inextricably entwined. Listening is presented as an element of paramount importance in children's musical learning, as is the immersion in musical attitudes and life over technical concerns. As with many other studies in this volume, the rich social context and relationships that enshroud musicking are strongly and critically influential.

This collection of work straddles geographic locations and methodological paradigms. We hope that this diverse collection provides readers with inspirations and aspirations to continue to explore and unpack the diverse worlds that are contemporary musical childhoods of Asia and the Pacific and beyond.

REFERENCES

Abril, C. R. (2009). Pulling the curtain back on performance in the elementary school. In J. L. Kerchner & C. R. Abril (Eds.), *Musical experiences in our lives: Things we learn and meanings we make* (pp. 93–112). Lanham, MD: Roman and Littlefield Education.

Boynton, S., & Kok, R. -M. (Eds.). (2006). *Musical childhoods and the cultures of youth*. Middletown, CT: Wesleyan University Press.

Bresler, L. (Ed.). (2007). *International handbook of research in arts education. Part one*. Dordecht, The Netherlands: Springer.

Campbell, P. S. (1998). *Songs in their heads. Music and its meaning in children's lives*. New York: Oxford University Press.

Campbell, P. S. (2006). Global practices. In G. E. McPherson (Ed.), *The child as musician: A handbook of musical development* (pp. 415–438). New York: Oxford University Press.

Chen, S. -J. (1996). Positive childishness: Images of childhood in Japan. In C. P. Hwang, M. E. Lamb, & I. E. Sigel (Eds.), *Images of childhood* (pp. 113–127). Mahwah, NJ: Lawrence Erlbaum Associates.

Custodero, L. A. (2009). Musical portraits, musical pathways: Stories of meaning making in the lives of six families. In J. L. Kerchner & C. R. Abril (Eds.), *Musical experiences in our lives: Things we learn and meanings we make* (pp. 77–92). Lanham, MD: Rowman & Littlefield.

Fryer-Smith, S. (2002). *Aboriginal benchbook for Western Australian courts*. Carlton, Victoria, Australia: Australian Institute of Judicial Administration Incorporated.

Gaunt, K. D. (2006). *The games black girls play: Learning the ropes from double-dutch to hip-hop*. New York: New York University Press.

Gupta, A. (2006). *Early childhood education, postcolonial theory, and teaching practices in India: Balancing Vygotsky and the Veda*. New York: Palgrave Macmillan.

Humpal, M. E. (2009). A community music program for parents and children with and without special needs. In J. L. Kerchner & C. R. Abril (Eds.), *Musical experiences in our lives: Things we learn and meanings we make* (pp. 59–76). Lanham, MD: Rowman & Littlefield.

Ilari, B. (2009). Songs of belonging: Musical interactions in early life. In J. L. Kerchner & C. R. Abril (Eds.), *Musical experiences in our lives: Things we learn and meanings we make* (pp. 21-38). Lanham, MD: Rowman & Littlefield.

Kakar, S. (1981). *The inner world: A psycho-analytic study of childhood and society in India*. New Delhi: Oxford University Press.

Kerchner, J. L., & Abril, C. R. (Eds.). (2009). *Musical experiences in our lives: Things we learn and meanings we make*. Lanham, MD: Rowman & Littlefield.

Kinney, A. B. (Ed.). (1995). *Chinese views of childhood*. Honolulu: University of Hawaii Press.

Lum, C. H., & Campbell, P. S. (2009). "El Camaleon": The musical secrets of Mirella Valdez. In J. L. Kerchner & C. R. Abril (Eds.), *Musical experiences in our lives: Things we learn and meanings we make* (pp. 113–126). Lanham, MD: Rowman & Littlefield.

Malloch, S., & Trevarthen, C. (2009). Musicality: Communicating the vitality and interests of life. In C. Trevarthen & S. Malloch (Eds.), *Communicative musicality: Exploring the basis of human companionshi* (pp. 1–12). Oxford, England: Oxford University Press.

Marsh, K. (1999). Mediated orality: The role of popular music in the changing tradition of children's musical play. *Research Studies in Music Education, 13*, 2–11.

Marsh, K. (2008). *The musical playground: Global tradition and change in children's songs and games*. New York: Oxford University Press.

McPherson, G. E. (Ed.). (2006). *The child as musician: A handbook of musical development*. New York: Oxford University Press.

Moog, H. (1976). *The musical experience of the preschool child*. London: Schott & Co. (Original work published 1968)

Parliament of the Commonwealth of Australia. (1985). *Aboriginal education. Report of the House of Representatives Select Committee on Aboriginal Education*. Canberra, ACT: Australian Government Publishing Service.

Small, C. (1998). *Musicking: The meanings of performing and listening*. Hanover, NH: University Press of New England.

Smithrim, K., & Upitis, R. (Eds.). (2007). *Listen to their voices: Research and practice in early childhood music*. Toronto: Canadian Music Educators' Association.

Tafuri, J. (2008). *Infant musicality: New research for educators and parents*. Surrey, England: Ashgate.

Valerio, W. H. (2009). From the teacher's view: Observations of toddlers' musical development. In J. L. Kerchner & C. R. Abril (Eds.), *Musical experiences in our lives: Things we learn and meanings we make* (pp. 39–58). Lanham, MD: Rowman & Littlefield.

Young, S. (2003). Time-space structuring in spontaneous play on educational percussion instruments among three- and four-year-olds. *British Journal of Music Education, 20*, 45–60.

CHAPTER 2

EMBODIED LEARNING OF MUSIC AND GENDER IN BALINESE CHILDREN'S GAMELANS

Sonja Lynn Downing

Fifteen young girls of a newly formed Balinese gamelan (traditional percussion-based music) ensemble sit expectantly at their instruments, tentatively tapping their mallets on the bronze gong-chimes. Their teacher, Ni Wayan Mudiari,[1] sits down in front of one instrument and plays a short series of notes. She indicates for the children to repeat what she has just played. Most of the children pick up the patterns quickly, but one of the drummers is having trouble. Mudiari sits down behind her, grasps both the girl's hands in hers, and beats out the rhythm, allowing the girl to experience the correct pattern with her own body.

In some respects, this interaction is typical of musical learning situations in Bali, particularly during rehearsals of children's gamelans. It exemplifies the strong physical aspect within the learning and teaching processes, where musical knowledge is embodied in the musician. Because gamelan music is often interpreted as portraying a particular gendered character, the pedagogical process also allows for ways of learning and embodying gender concepts. However, because of the gender of both the teacher and the children in the above anecdote from October

Musical Childhoods of Asia and the Pacific, pp. 11–35
Copyright © 2012 by Information Age Publishing
All rights of reproduction in any form reserved.

2006, this rehearsal demonstrates notable changes occurring in gamelan music education and transmission. The small number of women who teach gamelan music is gradually increasing. Additionally, in the last decade, a few gamelans have developed where girls are allowed and encouraged to play.[2] In this chapter, I explore the relationship between the learning of gender concepts and behaviors, and the learning of gamelan music. Within contexts of gamelan rehearsals in Bali, gendered ways of movement and behavior are explicitly and implicitly taught, challenged, and reformulated at a young age. This study has significant implications for music education research and practice as it indicates the importance of the role of physical learning in the acquisition and internalization of musical knowledge and skill, as well as the significance of how these methods relate to gender identity in childhood. It also demonstrates the benefits of combining methodological approaches from ethnomusicology and the sociology of childhood.

Though some ethnomusicologists studying gamelan and other Indonesian musics are interested in the transmission process of musical repertoire, knowledge, and competence (Brinner, 1995; Herbst, 1997; Weiss, 2006), rarely has any focused on this process in childhood. Colin McPhee had an interest in children's participation in gamelan music in the 1930s; however, aside from his involvement with the "Club of Small Men" in the village of Sayan (McPhee, 1938/1955), we know little about the history of children's gamelans in Bali. In the field of ethnomusicology, increasing attention is being given to music participation and its relation to gender construction and performativity, but seldom have ethnomusicologists focused on this in the context of children's participation.[3] Looking to children in the context of learning gamelan in Bali is crucial to understanding gamelan transmission and pedagogy. A focus on girls' experiences and how this pedagogy may change with their emergent participation helps to illuminate the relationship between gender and music education, and strengthens intersection of gender studies and ethnomusicology. The following interpretations are based on my research in Bali between 2003 and 2007—including interviews with young musicians, teachers, family members, and associated community leaders—and my experiences participating in the Çudamani Girls' Gamelan near Ubud and in women's gamelans in Denpasar.[4]

Depending on the available resources and interest within a community, boys as young as about 7 years old may begin formally learning to play gamelan, usually within their village. Those who are talented and motivated might join the adult village group directly, or after some informal private study at home. In some regions of Bali, village organizations or private families form ensembles whose membership consists only of children and youth, usually within roughly 7 to 17 years of age, as an extracurricular activity, as feeder groups for adult ensembles, for tourist performances, and/or to compete in gamelan festival competitions. Children's gamelans are modeled on adult gamelans, and usually perform pieces also included in the repertoire of adult groups, though they may play these with slower tempos. Though children's ensembles are growing in number and visibility, girls seldom are allowed or encouraged to join.

Adult women have been active in gamelans in village, temple, festival competition, and local governmental contexts since the late 1970s and early 1980s, and women's gamelans have become numerous in the last decade. However, a strong hierarchy remains, where women's groups are usually considered inferior to men's groups in terms of playing speed, dynamic range, and technical clarity. Despite usually performing on *gamelan gong kebyar* instruments, which many people associate with a Balinese masculine aesthetic of loudness, boldness, and speed, women are often taught and seek to perform in manners appropriate to Balinese ideals of feminine behavior and physical movement, the characteristics of which include softness, sweetness, and gracefulness (Bakan, 1997/1998; Downing, 2010; Susilo, 2003; Willner, 1997).[5]

Many female musicians in Bali indicate that one reason women do not seem to play as well as men is that they did not begin to learn until they were already adults. My research has focused on the few gamelans in Bali where young girls are learning instrumental music, either alongside boys or in girls-only ensembles. Close examination of the teaching and learning process offers insights into how these girls are negotiating expected behavior and movement styles within a context that historically has been male-dominated and reveals how an emphasis on physical learning and appropriate repertoire choice have the potential to offer a flexible space for girls to learn.

BALINESE GAMELAN PEDAGOGY

The embodiment of knowledge is a significant and necessary component of learning music in Bali. Studies of oral music transmission within music traditions that do not use notation in teaching often focus on cognitive processes, but kinesthetic learning is crucial in Balinese gamelan. Everyone in Bali whom I asked about the teaching and learning processes stressed the importance of learning through physical movement, and most talked about the need to understand the "feeling" of the music.[6] I Ketut Pradnya is the director of Sanggar Pulo Candani Wiswakarma, a private music and dance studio in the town of Batubulan that includes several genres of mixed-gender children's gamelans. He referenced Balinese religious knowledge, relating the combination of logic and intuition to the structure of any other dualism in Bali, that is, something does not make sense or become whole without its opposite. He told me that through yoga practice as well as through the performing arts, his members learn to combine and seek a balance between rational thought and intuitive feeling, and that this increases the students' sensitivity within traditional arts participation (K. Pradnya, personal communication, September 8, 2006).

Ida Ayu Arya Satyani, a Balinese gamelan and dance performer and teacher, has a pedagogy and understanding of the learning process that is heavily influenced by her father's stern teaching methods and his grounding in the scholarly study and practice of Balinese Hindu yoga. She and her three sisters teach music and dance at Sanggar Maha Bajra Sandhi, a private studio that includes a large mixed-gender children's gamelan in the Denpasar region directed by their father, Ida Wayan Oka Granoka. During an interview with Satyani at her home in Batubulan, I asked her how she goes about teaching the "feeling" of the music to her students. She explained that it is a long-term process, saying, "It needs repetition, and lots of experience. The point is, after a long time, after you are old, have aged, then you will know the feeling" (I. A. A. Satyani, personal communication, May 24, 2006). She made it clear to me that the emphasis on physical learning and movement was in addition to, not at the expense of, intellectual learning and cognition. She described how her father's philosophy of integrating yoga within her family's cultural arts programs for children and youth helps to connect the body and mind:

> All of this memorization uses thinking first, but in my experience, as long as I am thinking like that, the feeling is difficult to attain. You have to just let it flow. That is why my father teaches us *yoga asana*, with breathing and concentration. Within the arts, the knowledge of music does not mean that we throw out logic in favor of feeling. Instead, the logic is brought into the heart. (I. A. A. Satyani, personal communication, May 24, 2006)

Anthropologist Thomas J. Csordas explained the learning process as active participation and interaction with the world via the body. Echoing Pradnya, Csordas (1993) wrote, "I think it is not difficult to conceive of intuition as embodied knowledge" (p. 147). He proposed a theory of embodiment, applicable here, as "a phenomenology of the body that recognizes embodiment as the existential condition in which culture and self are grounded" (p. 136), emphasizing the importance of embodiment in understanding both the individual and broader societal beliefs and practices.

These philosophies are put into practice in several different ways in Bali. While employing all aspects of what Timothy Rice (1994) called an aura-visual-tactile pedagogy, what Tomie Hahn (1996) called kinesthetic transmission, and what Kyra Gaunt (2006) called kinetic orality, many teaching techniques used today in children's gamelans stress physical experience. The most striking technique is used often if the children have no prior experience, and especially if they are having difficulty with a technique or part. A teacher may sit or stand behind them, grasp their hands, and move them for the student, as shown in Figure 2.1[7] and described in the beginning of this chapter. In this way, the student actively assimilates kinesthetic musical knowledge through a simultaneously receptive and participatory experience.[8] This teaching method by physically touching, holding, and molding a child's body is an old one in Bali. Several musicians with whom I spoke recalled learning only this way from elderly dance and gamelan masters. Gregory Bateson and Margaret Mead (1942) documented this method, not just in instrumental music, but also in daily life practices. Mead (1955) wrote, "Children learn from the feel of other people's bodies and from watching, although this watching itself has a kinesthetic quality" (p. 43).

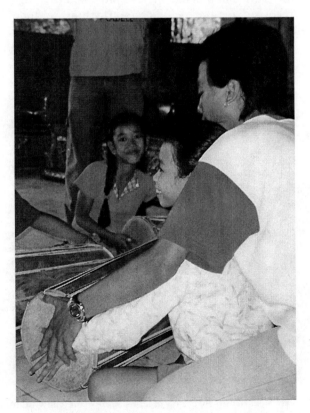

Figure 2.1.   I Made Widana teaches Candra on *kendang* (2003).

Other teaching methods do not involve physical contact; although, as Mead noted, they do rely on visual attention to the teacher's physical movements. One common method is to demonstrate the music directly on an instrument. Usually a teacher will sit in front of an instrument across from a student and play the parts, little by little, for the musicians to repeat (see Figure 2.2). A related method is to indicate pitches or rhythms with hand, head, or other bodily gestures and signals without using an instrument. The teacher may make head or hand gestures to show when to strike the gong. He or she may also indicate to players of the lower instruments which keys to strike. In a gong kebyar ensemble, the jegogan and calung (larger metallophone) instruments each have only one octave, which spans five keys. A teacher will hold up one hand, fingers outstretched, each finger and thumb symbolizing a respective key, pitches 1 through 5. The teacher will show the melody by pointing to the appropriate finger signaling the pitches of the melody. Once an ensemble becomes more experienced and is comfortable with playing techniques and the players have embodied a sense of pitch and rhythm, teachers may give new parts by singing the melodies and rhythms, shifting from a visual and kinesthetic focus to an aural one.

Figure 2.2.   Dewa Ketut Alit Adnyana teaches Kadek and the Çudamani Girls' Gamelan. I Made Karjana teaches in the background (2006).

These methods involve what Csordas (1993) described as "somatic modes of attention," developed from John Blacking's (1977) concepts of "shared somatic states" and "bodily empathy" (p. 10), and defined as "culturally elaborated ways of attending to and with one's body in surroundings that include the embodied presence of others" (Csordas, 1993, p. 138). On the learning process, Csordas wrote that there is, as seen in the teaching and learning methods above, "a somatic mode of attention associated with the acquisition of any technique of the body, but that this mode of attention recedes into the horizon once the technique is mastered" (p. 139). Close and conscious attention to one's body recedes once, as Satyani stated, "the logic is brought into the heart." Building on the works of Campbell (1991, 2004), Marsh (2008), Schippers (2010), and Solís (2004) studying the effectiveness of adapting indigenous music pedagogies into classroom contexts, I think attention to physical learning and the embodiment of knowledge, such as described by Pradnya, Satyani, and Granoka, may be effective in other contexts of music learning beyond gamelan.[9]

It is important to note that this kinesthetic watching and learning can occur even before students begin formal training. Children in Bali, and especially in southern Bali and the Ubud region, and especially those in musical families, often begin to pick up elements of gamelan playing long before they join an organized rehearsal. Children and babies see gamelan performances at the many temple ceremonies that occur. Young children are often allowed to sit in their parents' laps during rehearsals. Before or after rehearsals, or during temple ceremonies when the gamelan is not being used, children often play individually or in small groups on the instruments, imitating what they have seen their parents or other community members doing. In this way, they have a chance to try out the instruments and to get a feel for them before ever being formally instructed. Barbara Rogoff (1993) coined the term "guided participation" to use instead of terms like "rearing" or "socialization" to describe children's participation with adult guidance in social activities (p. 254). This is a useful term for how children learn many domestic tasks, though what I have described might more precisely be termed "unguided participation," as children's musical exploration is merely permitted in a safe space where adults are present but are not directing the children. In past decades and in some regions of Bali, girls were not allowed or encouraged to try out instruments in this way (W. Mudiari, personal communication, May 23, 2006), but musician, dancer, and scholar Emiko Saraswati Susilo (2003) observed that girls were permitted to try out instruments in the Pengosekan village by the late 1990s. I observed this continuing in this decade (see Figure 2.3).

Figure 2.3.   Young children try out low melody instruments during the musicians'
break at a temple ceremony in Pengosekan (2006).

Once children do join a gamelan ensemble, they are often taught to
play in ways deemed appropriate to their gender. This gendering is especially clear with adult ensembles; many instructors teach women's ensembles simplified repertoire and with different methods than they use for
men's ensembles (Downing, 2008; McGraw, 2004; Willner, 1997). Several
teachers at Sanggar Çudamani have experience teaching both boys and
girls. Sanggar Çudamani is a music and dance studio in Pengosekan village near Ubud, co-directed by I Dewa Putu Berata and Emiko Susilo, and
includes one of the only all-girls gamelans in Bali, as well as ensembles for
boys and men. I separately asked Berata and two other male teachers, I
Made Widana and I Dewa Ketut Alit Adnyana, if they had experienced
differences between teaching boys and girls. Widana answered that he
adjusts his teaching approach according to two main variables he observes
between girls' and boys' gamelans: discipline and ability. He said the girls
are better with the former, the boys with the latter, and that he is more satisfied teaching a disciplined ensemble.[10] Widana told me,

> From my experience, the girls are very enthusiastic about learning, and if
> you tell them to do this or don't do that, they will comply. The boys are not
> disciplined enough, but they can play faster than the girls. But sometimes,
> they are oppositional or their playful spirits come out, and they do not want

to behave until I yell "Quiet!" and then they will quiet down. After just a few minutes, they will be making noises again, like ducks. Again, "Quiet!" and I'll hit the drum "*Pang pang pang*!" and only then are they quiet. (personal communication, May 11, 2006)

Adnyana emphasizes the importance of creating a positive atmosphere when teaching girls. "Our voices convey encouragement, especially in teaching beginners: 'Yes, you can, good, good, that's good, again, again, again'," he demonstrated to me using a kind and gentle voice. Humor is a key teaching strategy Widana and Adnyana both use in order to aid such a positive atmosphere. Adnyana told me, "You have to joke around a little bit. If we are too tense, they will get stressed. Then, if you tell them to come the next day, maybe they won't come" (personal communication, April 28, 2006). Adnyana tells jokes and uses funny voices to make the children laugh. The benefit, he said, is that the students will be relaxed and therefore more able to pay attention to the next musical directions he gives.

According to Berata, the biggest factor in children's ability is not gender, but experience. He said that age matters slightly, but that experience matters more, even with adult ensembles. Adult groups with little or no playing experience, Berata told me, are the same as children's gamelans with little or no experience. He has observed that children learn technique faster, "maybe because their minds are emptier than adults," and that adults learn technique more slowly "because their hands are beginning to get stiff." However, Berata said, adults' knowledge and understanding deepens faster (personal communication, August 14, 2006). His brother and composer I Dewa Ketut Alit concurred, stating that children can play technically as well as adults, though they may not have the same depth of understanding (personal communication, September 28, 2006). While teachers may not necessarily choose the same approach, attention to these issues are crucial to developing appropriately thoughtful and challenging teaching methods and curricula.

LEARNING GENDER THROUGH REPERTOIRE AND MOVEMENT

I have discussed methods of teaching common in the context of Balinese children's gamelans. What is taught is another important matter in terms of how children must negotiate socially deemed-appropriate gendered behavior. This includes specific repertoire, choreographed ensemble movement, and individual movement style. The first two aspects are taught directly and explicitly by teachers, while the latter is generally picked up individually by watching others. All of these components of playing gamelan ensemble music are directly related to the gender, age, and personality of the musicians, though in ways that depend on interaction between teachers and students. Girls' and mixed-gender gamelan ensembles in Bali are challenging the current norms of men, boys, or women playing gamelan. This new type of membership requires teachers to address a variety of choices concerning appropriate characteristics of music, and requires children, particularly girls, to cope with conflicting perceptions about their gender identities. Negotiations of character, style, and gender allow these groups to actively resist and contradict ideals of appropriate gender behavior, as well as challenge and expand how genres of gamelan music themselves are gendered.

There are multiple and conflicting conceptions of childhood in Bali. In the Balinese language, children are referred to literally as "small women" (*istri alit*) and "small men" (*lanang alit*) and are often given adult-type tasks around the home. In contrast, national Indonesian notions include the view that children are amusing objects "for adults to play with" (Shiraishi, 1997, p. 58). Because of the lack of a single idea of child-likeness and because they may hold differing ideological views of children, teachers have varying approaches to the question of what is appropriate repertoire for young musicians. Some teachers seek to match the genre, style, and ascribed character of the music to the assumed qualities and abilities of the gender and age of their members. For example, Ni Ketut Suryatini, female composer and professor of instrumental music at the Indonesian Arts Institute (*Institut Seni Indonesia*) in Denpasar, has composed new pieces for children's groups that she considers appropriate to what she sees as children's high energy levels, playfulness, and basic technical abilities. In an interview with her, she noted that often children's gamelans performing in festivals and competitions are given pieces that are technically very difficult. While Berata and Alit described children's high technical abilities, Suryatini does not agree with an approach that pushes children too much (personal communication, May 8, 2006).

Other teachers encourage their members to be flexible to learn and perform a wide variety of musical styles. The directors of Sanggar Pulo Candani Wiswakarma and Sanggar Maha Bajra Sandhi, mentioned above, deliberately do not limit their choices of repertoire for their respective children's ensembles. Pradnya tells the teachers he hires to teach the children the most difficult and complicated pieces first, so that the students learn to be patient with the learning process. Satyani and her father compose music that they view as technically appropriate to children's abilities; their group includes some of the youngest performing musicians I have seen in Bali, at 5 and 6 years old. However, the philosophical and religious symbolism in their music and dance compositions is among the weightiest and most solemn I have seen performed by any large group of any age in Bali, seemingly contradicting ideas of children's gamelan performances as light and playful. For example, in 2006, Sang-gar Maha Bajra Sandhi participated in a full daylong set of rituals and performances based on several ancient genres of Balinese music to com-memorate the 100-year anniversary of the royal mass suicides in Badung in the face of Dutch colonialism.

Berata holds that children's ensemble teachers or coaches should choose pieces that fit with children's character, such as basic ceremonial pieces (lelambatan), or dance pieces composed in the 20th twentieth or twenty-first centuries. He also suggests pieces with vocal parts because, he said, children are not yet malu (shy or embarrassed) about singing, whereas audiences regard adult gamelan members' singing as humorous. Berata composed a piece called "Suluh," for gamelan and vocals, for the Çudamani Girls' Gamelan. Taking advantage of the group's use of Çuda-mani's seven-tone gamelan semarandana instruments, Berata composed it in the slendro mode, rather than the more common selisir, to give the girls a chance to start becoming familiar with different modes.[11] Through this piece, he said, "I want to them to show softness, even though they can play loud" (personal communication, August 14, 2006). Acknowledging their ability to play beyond their supposed gendered characteristics, he still aims to teach them to perform characteristics of an ideal Balinese femininity.

Alit has taught and written pieces for several children's gamelans in the Ubud area. He said that while he feels that a difference in character between men and women is felt strongly in Bali where the division of labor can be stark, he does not think that the arts should be limited or forced in any way with regard to gender. Alit acknowledges, however, that we do not know how things will be in the future. He notes the current ten-dency to keep boys and girls separate, but said that since women's groups are growing and are improving their technique, feeling, and musical lead-ership, they may become prominent in 10 or 20 years. As for children, Alit does not write music for a specific "children's character." He said to me, "We in Bali do not have anything specific for children. Why must we make music specifically for children? Why can we not give them freedom to play any music?" (personal communication, July 31, 2006). Despite these various choices, the teaching methods are similar in each group, with a heavy emphasis on physical learning and bodily understanding before intellectual processing.

Understanding the feel of gamelan music involves one's physical movements, underscoring Pradnya's, Satyani's, and Csordas's emphases of the role of the body in learning. Once musicians are comfortable enough with a new piece of music to the point of having a good under-standing of the "feeling" of the music, they may play with a certain style of physical expression, called gaya.[12] Gaya is often used to indicate cues for dynamic, tempo, or section changes, or merely to communicate energy to the rest of the ensemble (D. M. Berati, personal communication, August 27, 2006; W. Mudiari, personal communication, May 23, 2006). Individual gaya is used primarily by the *ugal* (lead metallophone) and *kendang* (drum) players who give these cues (Tenzer, 2000, p. 105). The particular style or degree of extra movement depends on the piece, the genre, the performance context, and the individual musician. Musicians learn gaya by watching other musicians and develop their own personal style over time.

Styles of movement even outside the realm of the performing arts are often gendered. Judith Butler has drawn a connection between movement and gender and stated that gender itself is "a corporeal style" (1988, p. 521). Lynette Parker (1997) noted that learning to be a boy or a girl in Bali involves embodying a specific gendered *gaya*, where boys are more active and outgoing and girls are more passive and restrained; these bodily styles parallel those in gamelan performance. She noted that since the 1970s, however, girls' participation in sports and other activities have created more situations in which "bodily style is open for negotiation" (p. 506). While adult women's gamelan performances have often reinforced a sense of feminine *gaya* as soft and restrained, I propose that girls' and mixed-gender gamelans are opening opportunities for girls to develop more nuanced senses of *gaya*.

Such opportunities are not opening easily, however. Children, young teenagers, and women often do not play with much *gaya*. Ni Luh Trisna Dewi, a 19-year-old member of the mixed-gender children's gamelan at Sanggar Pulo Candani Wiswakarma and, at the time of this research, one of the only two female students majoring in instrumental music at the Indonesian Arts Institute in Denpasar, said she wishes that she could play with more *gaya*. She said that it is better to play with *gaya* so that the musicians are more enthusiastic. However, she feels constrained by the lack of *gaya* of the group, as the many female members of Sanggar Pulo Candani Wiswakarma are "hesitant to move their bodies like that," and she is not comfortable being the only one to play with *gaya* (L. T. Dewi, personal communication, May 16, 2006).

Csordas's (1993) "somatic modes of attention" is a helpful way to describe how gamelan players are intensely aware of each other's movements and moods so that they respond to each other nearly instantaneously. As children learn gamelan, they are aware of both their teachers' movement styles as well as those of their fellow musicians. Deborah Wong wrote, "Recent theory suggests that bodies are socially constructed, often through performance ... and that the performative reality of such interpretations [of gender and sexuality] is often deeply contradictory" (2004, p. 163). Such contradictions can be seen in the tensions that may arise, as styles of movement are not consistent across various groups of people with whom the gamelan students interact. For example, Dewi is aware of her teachers' *gaya*, but perhaps is more acutely aware of, and feels a greater need to mirror, her fellow members' lack thereof.

Because of the contradictions in what is taught and adopted, children must negotiate how they embody physical aspects of both music and gender knowledge, and styles may be gradually adopted or resisted individually. In embodying musical knowledge and gender concepts through learning gamelan, one's gendered identity is not static, nor are the concepts of gender. To better understand this negotiation process, I draw on Australian scholar Glenda MacNaughton's (2000) model of poststructuralist identity formation from her research on gender in early childhood, paraphrased here: (1) There is no one, single, fixed gender identity to be learned; (2) a child is an active player, but not a free agent; (3) a child receives many messages from many sources; and (4) interaction with others is central (p. 28). Through interaction with their peers, fellow musicians, family members, and their gamelan teachers, girls in children's ensembles address multiple messages regarding how best to behave and perform as a child or as a girl. Many of these interactions, in particular during gamelan rehearsals, are physical and kinesthetic in nature.

In addition to questions of individual style and choice of repertoire, coordinated group movements also may contribute to the learning of appropriate movements per assumed gendered character of the musicians. Depending on the context of an upcoming performance, a gamelan teacher or composer may synchronize the movements of the gamelan members' hands, heads, bodies, and mallets into a sort of group choreography. Since about 2003, this has become increasingly popular in competition performances for men's and especially boys' ensembles, which use sharp, angular poses and energetic movements (N. Windha, personal communication, October 8, 2006). At Sanggar Çudamani in 2006, Berata's brother I Dewa Putu Rai added some movements and singing for the girls' gamelan in a composition by I Nyoman Windha, called "Gita Giri Jaya." The original piece, written during Windha's residence as Guest Music Director at the American-based Gamelan Sekar Jaya, included a section in which some of the members perform *kecak*, a type of rhythmic vocal chant. *Kecak* in Bali is rarely performed by women, and the teachers at Çudamani did not teach it to the girls. This left a few long sections of music where the *gangsa* (metallophone) and *reyong* (gong-chime) players sat silently, not playing. Always inventive, the teachers added a melody for the girls to sing to fill the musical space. Then Rai and Berata added choreographed movements. The Çudamani teachers encouraged the girls to move in such a way that was specifically feminine, using arm and hand positioning and head movements common to *legong* and other

Figure 2.4.   De Ayu in a refined female dance pose (2006).

Figure 2.5.   The Çudamani Girls' Gamelan rehearses choreography for "Gita Giri Jaya" (2006).

refined female dances (see Figures 2.4 and 2.5). Through teaching this choreography, the teachers were kinesthetically transmitting gendered ideas about how girls should move and behave on stage and how femininity is embodied and performed.

While the girls already knew these movements well from studying dance, some of them were reluctant and resistant to move in such a way in the context of playing instrumental music. When I asked a small group of Çudamani Girls' Gamelan members how they thought of the choreography in "Gita Giri Jaya," 13-year-old *ugal* player Komang[13] told me, "I don't like it. It feels forced to dance that way" (personal communication, May 24, 2006). If the teachers were not paying close attention in rehearsal, the girls would often not do the movements at all. Moving in such an overtly choreographed way and being recast as dancers did not seem appropriate to them in the context of playing instrumental music. Their resistance indicates a tension between their teachers' perception of them as young children, whose feminine dance movements would be appropriate on stage, and their own perception of themselves as young women, and in this context, as musicians, not dancers. The girls have been fairly vocal in telling the teachers what they like or dislike since a young age, but they knew they ultimately had little choice in this context of preparation for a major performance at the Bali Arts Festival in Denpasar. Eventually, they became comfortable with the choreography by the time of the Arts Festival performance, and Wiwik, one of the *gangsa* (metallophone) players, told me specifically that she enjoyed doing the choreography, saying "It is good with the dance movements. It makes the piece more interesting" (personal communication, May 24, 2006). This process illuminates the strength of the influences on how these girls embody concepts of an idealized Balinese feminine gender.

Each point of MacNaughton's model can be seen clearly here. There are competing ideas of appropriateness, and no single idea of femininity. These girls are active in resisting the movements given the chance, though they are not free to act at their individual will. They receive many messages from different sources, in this particular case the message about how to perform in a feminine manner from their teachers, peer messages from within the ensemble about not standing out, and outside-of-gamelan peer accusations of lack of femininity because of gamelan participation. Peer and student-teacher interaction shape how these messages are conveyed and received as the girls are constrained by the potential for being reprimanded by teachers, or embarrassed by not following their fellow members.

Women and girl musicians often perform Balinese femininity through the particular repertoire, slower tempos, less precise damping (a technique involving stopping the sound of each key with the left hand before or as the next key is struck with the right hand so that the pitches do not overlap), restricted individual *gaya*, and occasionally fluid and graceful choreography they employ on stage or in temple ceremony performances (Downing, 2010, p. 63). These embodied notions of musical femininity are transmitted and reinforced through kinetic orality, but rather than peer-to-peer transmission, as Gaunt (2006) describes in her own research, these ideas are taught directly by (usually) male teachers and learned indirectly through watching others' performances live or on television. However, rather than perpetuating an already established sense of identity, a sense of Balinese girlhood is being dismantled and recreated through girls' participation in children's gamelans, and through their own mediation between teachers and peers regarding repertoire, technique, and styles of movement.

CONCLUSION

By examining the experiences of Balinese children and gamelan teachers, I have illustrated how the interactive and dynamic process of studying gamelan involves the embodiment and negotiation of concepts about gender. Csordas (1993) has offered ways to theorize the importance of embodied perception and understanding through and of the body; similarly, the teaching philosophies and methods of several Balinese music teachers show the importance of learning through physical experience. Csordas highlighted the significance of embodied knowledge, which describes the result of combined methods of learning gamelan by which musical knowledge enters the body. Since gamelan playing is gendered in complex ways, complex notions of gender behavior and identity enter the body along with musical knowledge and gendered movement, in the form of individual styles or choreographed ways of playing.

Through this learning process, MacNaughton (2000) noted that children have varying degrees of flexibility in terms of what notions of gender behavior to adopt and reproduce or contradict. The case study of the Çudamani Girls' Gamelan learning choreographed movements, and other young female musicians' unfulfilled desire to play with *gaya*, demonstrates ways of addressing identity constructions. Within this process, children learn to embody musical knowledge by getting the feel for specific gamelan pieces, melodies, and rhythmic patterns. When ideas about gender are contested, women and girls often find themselves constrained by notions of appropriate gender movement and behavior. This brings out tensions where embodying femininity contradicts musicality. It also shows tension between competing ideas of femininity, such as the Çudamani girls being told to move like refined, feminine dancers, while not wanting to be perceived as standing out from their peers.

This chapter has addressed gender construction in practice, through the physical process of embodying music and associated styles of movement. As this is a process that takes place over long periods of time, children may increasingly add their own ideas to the mix. Girls are balancing what they are given and taught from their teachers; influences from peers, family, and the media; and their own musical desires through time. Thus, these constructions and negotiations of what it means to be feminine, masculine, young, adult, and musical happen in practice, where gender concepts are addressed personally and interactively through a dynamic, long-term process of embodying music and gender together. Ethnomusicologists interested in music transmission would do well to pay attention to the experiences of children and to heed the work of scholars studying children learning music. In line with current scholars such as Campbell (1991, 2004), Marsh (2008), and Schippers (2010) who are working in the intersection of ethnomusicology and music education and espouse looking to indigenous music pedagogies for ways to develop music education in schools, I hope my work contributes to the growing understanding and broader utilization of effective pedagogical methods employed around the world.

RESEARCHER'S REFLECTION

Heading to Bali with a background in ethnomusicological fieldwork methods, I quickly found that this training was incomplete for doing research with children. I adapted standard ethnomusicological methods to make them more appropriate and effective in working with children, in ways that parallel some child-centered approaches from the sociology of childhood. While neither ethnomusicologists who work with children nor most childhood sociologists mention looking to children themselves to develop research methods, the methods I have found to be the most helpful and satisfying to all involved were initiated by children themselves.[14]

Childhood sociologists are concerned with the inherent hierarchy in the child-researcher relationship, where children may see the researcher in a position of authority or higher social status due to his or her adult status and may therefore alter their behavior when the researcher is present. William Corsaro (1985) suggested mediating this hierarchy by taking what he calls a reactive approach, responding to children's actions, but not dictating the interactions. I took this approach with regard to positioning myself in the context of observing children's rehearsals. It was members of the Çudamani Girls' Gamelan themselves who first invited

me to fill an empty seat in 2003, and allowed me to play and learn alongside them in their regular rehearsals. Jonathan McIntosh (2006)
addressed the child-researcher hierarchy Corsaro noted by allowing the
children he worked with in Bali to be in a position as his teacher and even
manipulator. I, however, agree more with Ki Mantle Hood's (1960) views
on bimusicality aiding research than McIntosh's perspective, and feel that
the fact that I was studying gamelan and Indonesian language greatly
facilitated my interactions and participant observation with child musicians in Bali. Once the Çudamani girls saw that I could keep up with and
not burden their rehearsals, they frequently plugged me into whatever
seat was left open by an absent member. Not playing would not only have
been a missed opportunity, but it would also have been potentially rude.[15]
Rehearsing with an incomplete gamelan is undesirable, and so if a non-
member can fill in, as long as they are not musically disruptive or incom-
petent, they should play along. Eventually, any absences of mine from
rehearsals drew sharp reprimands from some of the girls, who came to see
me as a functioning member of their gamelan or, at least, as a necessary
placeholder. This offered me a unique perspective on the daily workings
of one of the very few all-girls' gamelan ensembles in Bali.

Asking for people to participate in interviews steps considerably
beyond the bounds of a reactive approach as an interview is a formalized
interaction initiated by the researcher. However, I aimed to be as accommodating to the children's wishes as was possible regarding how, where,
and when we conducted the interviews. It was the girls, ages 10–16 at the
time, who came up with the idea to do group interviews.[16] The girls came
in groups of two to five, some with their friends and others with their
younger sisters or cousins. After much trial and error, I found that rather
than open-ended questions, asking the girls specific questions about
events, such as particular performances or the preparations leading up to
them, were the most successful in opening fruitful and informative conversations.

One of the most brilliant interview moments was when *reyong* (gong-
chime) player Imut turned the tables and began interviewing me. We had
wrapped up everything I had wanted to discuss with her and her friend
Sak De. Imut jumped up and said, "Now, I want to ask!" (personal communication, May 22, 2006). She asked me why I, too, like to play gamelan.
Sak De joined in with a few questions, and between the two of them, they
asked about my preference for Balinese gamelan or Western music, my
experience studying Balinese dance, and my life goals. This moment
reminded me of the importance, as Michelle Kisliuk (1997) wrote, of letting interviewees get to know me and not just the other way around
(p. 27). It was also important for Imut and Sak De to express their power
in the interview process.

Figure 2.6.   Ratna and friends play hand-clapping games during down time at their dance rehearsal. Photo by Komang, age 9 (2005).

Figure 2.7.   Two of the teachers of the Çudamani Girls' Gamelan: I Dewa Made Guna Arta (top) and I Made Karjana (bottom). Photo by Imut, age 13 (2006).

While documentation by video and/or audio recording have been standard techniques within ethnomusicology methods (Hood, 1971; Nettl, 1964), their use in research with children has been contested (Graue & Walsh, 1998, pp. 116–117). Still, I did take photographs of rehearsals and performances, and occasionally handed my camera, upon request, to some of the children to add to the documentation. The girls who used my camera have contributed some of the most illuminating photos, which allow the viewer a glimpse into the girls' worlds, such as the girls' interactions with each other during downtime before and after rehearsals (see Figure 2.6), as well as perspectives of their gamelan teachers (see Figure 2.7). It also allowed them to have control over the ethnographic gaze on themselves as well as to turn the gaze back onto the researcher (see Figure 2.8). This shift in positioning and control furthers Corsaro's aim to dismantle the child-researcher hierarchy.

Additionally, the audio and video equipment sparked interest among the children, and many wanted to listen to themselves after the interview, or watch the videos I had made of their rehearsals and performances (see Figure 2.9). Often, their responses to the recordings, photographs, or videos elicited valuable information about their experiences and opinions of

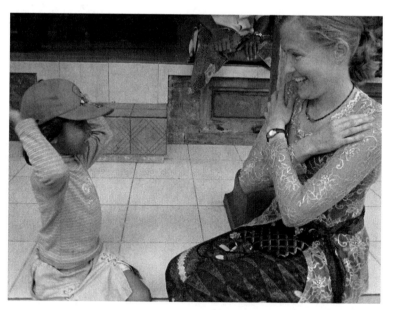

Figure 2.8.   The author learns hand-clapping games from Ayu. Photo by Candra, age 12 (2006).

Figure 2.9.   Wiwik, age 9, and Candra, age 9, review video recordings of their rehearsals on the author's video camera (2003).

what had just happened, offering me versions of Ruth and Verlon Stone's (1981) "feedback interview."

In my research, I found that a combination of methods from ethnomusicology, such as bimusical participant observation, and the sociology of childhood, such as methods from Corsaro, offered the most effective and appropriate approaches. Having children direct at least some of the interactions and documentation methods resulted not only in the richest research results, but also in the most meaningful fieldwork experiences. Ethnographers would do well to encourage more participation by children in the research process. I look forward to seeing the exciting work that such intergenerational research collaboration produces.

NOTES

1.   *Ni* or *I* are Balinese honorifics for women and men, respectively.

2.   See Downing (2008, 2010) for further details on emerging all-girls' and mixed-gender children's gamelan ensembles in Bali.

3.   Notable exceptions include John Blacking's (1967, 1985) research on Venda girls' initiation songs and dances, Carol Merrill-Mirsky's (1986) study of girls' hand-clapping games in the 1980s, Kyra Gaunt's (2006) research with black girls in America, and Amanda Minks's (2008) research on Nicaraguan Miskitu children's song games.

4.   This research was funded by a Fulbright-Hays Doctoral Dissertation Research Abroad grant, a grant from the Pacific Rim Research Program, and a UCSB Humanities/Social Sciences research grant. I am eternally grateful to the children and their teachers and family members who welcomed me into their musical and daily lives in Bali. Interviews were conducted in Bali in the Indonesian language, and all translations into English are my own.

5.   *Gamelan gong kebyar* ensembles are the most common in Bali among men's and women's ensembles alike; see Tenzer (2000) for detailed information on this genre of Balinese gamelan.

6.   Some teachers I spoke with used the Indonesian term *rasa*, and others used the English word *feeling*. See Weiss (2006) for a (Javanese-centered) discussion of *rasa* and gamelan music.

7.   All photos were taken in Bali by the author, except where otherwise noted.

8.   See Campbell's (1991, p. 213) diagram of receptive and participatory experiences through three modes of learning music.

9.   Schippers (2010) and Harnish (2004) both discuss teaching and learning Balinese gamelan music beyond Indonesia, though Schippers does not address the primarily physical aspects of learning, and both focus on teaching gamelan at the university level rather than on contexts for teaching children.

10.   This stance contrasts with Balinese composer I Ketut Suandita's experience a decade earlier that teaching boys is easier than teaching girls (Bakan, 1997/1998, p. 69), possibly indicating a recent shift in attitudes toward teaching girls.

11.   Though Andrew McGraw (1999/2000) noted, in his history of the newly developed and increasingly popular seven-tone gamelan semarandana (also spelled semara dana), that symbolic meanings of different modes are variable and often ambiguous, Michael Bakan quoted performer and scholar I Wayan Dibia, suggesting that playing in *slendro* would make the masculine-gendered *gamelan beleganjur* more appropriate for women to play (Bakan, 1997/1998, p. 79).

12.   In the Indonesian language, *gaya* generally means style, form, or manner (Echols & Shadily, 1989), but Balinese musicians often use the term specifically to mean style of bodily movement.

13.   All children in this chapter are referred to by their nickname only.

14.   A few childhood sociologists have begun to discuss involving children in the research process; see Alderson (2000) and Jones (2004).

15.   Timothy Cooley (1997) took this a step further, citing Anthony Seeger?s research with the Suyá people of the Amazon, and noted that often partici-

pation becomes not just a privilege but also a duty. In the context of the Çudamani Girls? Gamelan, I found this to ring true.

16.   See Graue and Walsh (1998), Mayall (2000), and Kellett and Ding (2004) for further discussion of the benefits of conducting group interviews with children.

REFERENCES

Alderson, P. (2000). Children as researchers: The Effects of participation rights on research methodology. In P. Christensen & A. James (Eds.), *Research with children: Perspectives and practices* (pp. 241–257). London and New York: Routledge Falmer.

Bakan, M. (1998). From oxymoron to reality: Agendas of gender and the rise of Balinese women's gamelan beleganjur in Bali, Indonesia. *Asian Music, 29*(1), 37–85. (Original work published 1997)

Bateson, G., & Mead, M. (1942). *Balinese character: A photographic analysis*. New York: New York Academy of Sciences.

Blacking, J. (1967). *Venda children's songs: A Study in ethnomusicological analysis*. Johannesburg, South Africa: Witwatersrand University Press.

Blacking, J. (1977). *The anthropology of the body*. London: Academic Press.

Blacking, J. (1985). Movement, dance, music, and the Venda girls' initiation cycle. In P. Spencer (Ed.), *Society and the dance: The Social anthropology of process and performance* (pp. 64–91). Cambridge, England: Cambridge University Press.

Brinner, B. (1995). *Knowing music, making music: Javanese gamelan and the theory of musical competence and interaction*. Chicago: University of Chicago Press.

Butler, J. (1988). Performative acts and gender constitution: An essay in phenomenology and feminist theory. *Theatre Journal, 40*(4), 519–531.

Campbell, P. S. (1991). *Lessons from the world: A cross-cultural guide to music teaching and learning*. New York: Schirmer Books.

Campbell, P. S. (2004). *Teaching music globally: Experiencing music, expressing culture*. Oxford, England: Oxford University Press.

Cooley, T. J. (1997). Casting shadows in the field: An Introduction. In G. F. Barz & T. J. Cooley (Eds.), *Shadows in the field: New perspectives in ethnomusicology* (pp. 3–19). Oxford, England: Oxford University Press.

Corsaro, W. A. (1985). *Friendship and peer culture in the early years*. Norwood, NJ: Ablex.

Csordas, T. J. (1993). Somatic modes of attention. *Cultural Anthropology, 8*(2), 135–156.

Downing, S. L. (2008). *Arjuna's angels: Girls learning gamelan music in Bali* (Doctoral dissertation). Retrieved from Proquest Dissertations and Theses database. (UMI No. 3319878).

Downing, S. L. (2010). Leading girls in gamelan: Agency and gender negotiation in Bali. *Ethnomusicology, 54*(1), 54–80.

Echols, J. M., & Shadily, H. (Eds.). (1989). *Kamus Indonesia Inggris: An Indonesian–English dictionary* (3rd ed.). Jakarta, Indonesia: Penerbit PT Gramedia.

Gaunt, K. D. (2006). *The games black girls play: Learning the ropes from double-dutch to hip-hop*. New York: New York University Press.

Graue, M. E., & Walsh, D. J. (1998). *Studying children in context: Theories, methods, and ethics*. Thousand Oaks, CA: SAGE.

Hahn, T. (1996). Teaching through touch: An Aspect of the kinesthetic transmission process of nihon buyo. In *The body in dance: Modes of inquiry, paradigms for viewing artistic work and scientific inquiry. Proceedings of the Congress on Research in Dance*, pp. 77–85.

Harnish, D. (2004). "No, not 'Bali Hai'!": Challenges of adaptation and Orientalism in performing and teaching Balinese gamelan. In T. Solís (Ed.), *Performing ethnomusicology: Teaching and representation in world music ensembles* (pp. 126–137). Berkeley: University of California Press.

Herbst, E. (1997). *Voices in Bali: Energies and perceptions in vocal music and dance theater*. Middletown, CT: Wesleyan University Press.

Hood, M. (1960). The challenge of "bi-musicality." *Ethnomusicology, 4*(2), 55–59.

Hood, M. (1971). *The ethnomusicologist*. New York: McGraw-Hill.

Jones, A. (2004). Involving children and young people as researchers. In S. Fraser, V. Lewis, S. Ding, M. Kellett, & C. Robinson (Eds.), *Doing research with children and young people* (pp. 113–130). London: Sage.

Kellett, M., & Ding, S. (2004). Middle childhood. In S. Fraser, V. Lewis, S. Ding, M. Kellett, & C. Robinson (Eds.), *Doing research with children and young people* (pp. 161–174). London: Sage.

Kisliuk, M. (1997). (Un)doing fieldwork: Sharing songs, sharing lives. In G. F. Barz & T. J. Cooley (Eds.), *Shadows in the field: New perspectives for fieldwork in ethnomusicology* (pp. 23–44). New York: Oxford University Press.

MacNaughton, G. (2000). *Rethinking gender in early childhood education*. London: Paul Chapman.

Marsh, K. (2008). *The musical playground: Global tradition and change in children's songs and games*. Oxford, England: Oxford University Press.

Mayall, B. (2000). Conversation with children: Working with generational issues. In P. Christensen & A. James (Eds.), *Research with children: Perspectives and practices* (pp. 120–135). London: Routledge Falmer.

McGraw, A. (1999/2000). The development of the "gamelan semara dana" and the expansion of the modal system in Bali, Indonesia. *Asian Music, 31*(1), 63–93.

McGraw, A. (2004). "Playing like men": The cultural politics of women's gamelan. *Latitudes, 47*, 12–17.

McIntosh, J. (2006). How dancing, singing, and playing shape the ethnographer: Researching children in a Balinese dance studio. *Anthropology Matters, 8*(2), 1–17.

McPhee, C. (1955). Children and music in Bali. In M. Mead & M. Wolfenstein (Eds.), *Childhood in contemporary cultures* (pp. 70–98). Chicago: University of Chicago Press. (Original work published 1938)

Mead, M. (1955). Children and ritual in Bali. In M. Mead & M. Wolfenstein (Eds.), *Childhood in contemporary cultures* (pp. 40–51). Chicago: University of Chicago Press.

Merrill-Mirsky, C. (1986). Girls' handclapping games in three Los Angeles schools. *Yearbook for Traditional Music, 18,* 47–59.

Minks, A. (2008). Performing gender in song games among Nicaraguan Miskitu children. *Language and Communication, 28,* 36–56.

Nettl, B. (1964). *Theory and method in ethnomusicology.* New York: Free Press of Glencoe.

Parker, L. (1997). Engendering school children in Bali. *Journal of the Royal Anthropological Institute, 3*(3), 497–516.

Rice, T. (1994). *May it fill your soul: Experiencing Bulgarian music.* Chicago: University of Chicago Press.

Rogoff, B. (1993). *Guided participation in cultural activity by toddlers and caregivers.* Chicago: University of Chicago Press.

Schippers, H. (2010). *Facing the music: Shaping music education from a global perspective.* Oxford, England: Oxford University Press.

Shiraishi, S. S. (1997). *Young heroes: The Indonesian family in politics.* Ithaca: Cornell Southeast Asia Program Publications.

Solís, T. (Ed.). (2004). *Performing ethnomusicology: Teaching and representation in world music ensembles.* Berkeley: University of California Press.

Stone, R. M., and Stone, V. L. (1981). Event, feedback, and analysis: Research media in the study of music events. *Ethnomusicology, 25*(2), 215-225.

Susilo, E. S. (2003). *Gamelan wanita: A study of women's gamelan in Bali* (Southeast Asia Paper No. 43). Manoa: University of Hawaii, Center for Southeast Asian Studies.

Tenzer, M. (2000). *Gamelan gong kebyar: The art of twentieth-century Balinese music.* Chicago: University of Chicago Press.

Weiss, S. (2006). *Listening to an earlier Java: Aesthetics, gender, and the music of wayang in Central Java.* Leiden, The Netherlands: KITLV Press.

Willner, S. (1997). *Kebyar wanita: A Look at women's gamelan groups in Bali.* Paper presented at the annual meeting of the Society for Balinese Studies, Denpasar, Bali, Indonesia.

Wong, D. (2004). *Speak it louder: Asian Americans making music.* New York: Routledge.

CHAPTER 3

SPEAKING AUTOETHNOGRAPHICALLY AND SINGING MATERNALLY

Elizabeth Mackinlay

INTRODUCTION

Small footsteps pad quietly into our room. I lift my head to one side and see that it is my 3-year-old son Hamish. My next instinct is to look at the clock and the time reads 3:13 A.M.

Musical Childhoods of Asia and the Pacific, pp. 37–56

Figure 3.1.   Waking from sleep.

I struggle to wake from my deep slumber but try to focus quickly on what-ever it is that is troubling my baby. "The Grinch was here Mama, he was coming to get me," his tiny voice breaks as he whispers the horror of his dream with tears in his eyes and a trembling lip. The infamous green Dr Seuss character who steals Christmas from the Who's in Whoville has visited him in his sleep and Hamish is terrified. I slide my legs out of bed and gen-tly take his hand in mine. "Come on, darling," I whisper, "Mama will take you back to bed." Hamish nods his head and we walk quietly back to his room. As he climbs into bed I ask him, "Would you like Mama to sing you a song? To chase your memories of the Grinch away?" Hamish nods his head and my heart almost breaks to see the tears well in his baby blues at the mere mention of the monster's name. I pull his cotton blanket over him and snuggle close to him. I begin to softly croon one of our favorite Evermore songs: "Goodnight, goodnight my love, goodnight my only friend. Even though the day is over, goodnight is not the end." As I sing, I stroke his forehead and the calm and intimate reverie this creates takes me back to another time and place when I was a young girl, laying in my bed petrified of the demons I believed hid in the dark. My mother would sing to me and her hand would brush my hair, hoping that her sweet voice and tender touch would erase the memories of my dream and send me back to sleep. Hamish's tears become my own as I remember the overwhelming feeling of safety, warmth, and love my mother's song gave to me as a child. My voice becomes choked with emotion as I continue to sing. The peaceful and relaxed look on Hamish's face as his eyelids slowly close tells me that in this moment, I have become a mother like my own through song. (Journal entry and sketch, October, 2, 2008)

In this chapter, I continue to "sing maternally" and "speak autoethnographically" to explore the potential of autoethnographic research methodology and writing practices to unmask and understand the musical worlds of mothers. The ways that music becomes mothering, like so many other things associated with maternal worlds, is hidden behind the mythical and private walls of domestic bliss that Western society has constructed for us. Despite women's invisibility as mothers in public,

> most women have been mothers in the sense of tenders and carers for the young, whether as sisters, aunts, nurses, teachers, foster-mothers, stepmothers.... For most of us a woman provided the continuity and stability—but also the rejections and refusals—of our early lives and it is with a woman's hands, eyes, body, voice, that we associate our primal sensations, our earliest social experience. (Rich, 1976, p. 12)

The inherently personal yet social nature of mothering invites me to consider the potential of autoethnography to explore the relationship between music and mothering. In autoethnographic method and writing, a scene is set, a story told, intricate connections are woven, experience and theory are evoked and then ruthlessly let go (Holman Jones, 2005, p. 765). All of the balls that have been juggled fly into the air and both performer and audience stand waiting with baited breath to see how they might fall. Autoethnographic methods place emphasis on reuniting the personal with the physical, emotional, mental, social, and cultural dimensions of everyday life (Ellis, 2004, p. xix). It works to hold self and culture together (Holman Jones, p. 764). Using my personal narratives and reflections, poetry and sketches, in this chapter I will explore the ways in which autoethnographic methods can be applied, migrated, and extended into the area of early childhood music education through the autoethnographic lens and pen of myself as a mother who sings to her children. I ask you to sing your own song as you read this chapter—as a mother, or a person who has experienced a mother's song as a child or through your own children—so that together we may both come to understand how and why our "personal accounts count" (Holman Jones, 2005, p. 764).

MEETING MOTHERING THROUGH AUTOETHNOGRAPHY

My particular way of seeing mothering is colored by my personal experiences and the relationships with my two sons, Max and Hamish. Everything I am and all that I do as a mother is intimately linked with the other mothers in my life—my own mother, her sisters and aunties on my father's side, cousins of my own generation, close friends who are also mothers, and the ever present memories of my grand- and great-grandmothers. The intergenerational link between myself as mother and other women as mothers who are part of my life means that mothering is always already personal, and unmasking yourself as a mother is a potentially risky kind of exposure. Will people judge you as a "good enough" mother? Will your failings as a mother shine too brightly under the spotlight? Or will readers see beyond the dirt and dust to the extraordinary love you hold for your children?

It becomes slightly more comfortable for me when I step into those areas of vulnerability through the lens of autoethnography. I wonder what it is you want and need to know about autoethnography as a research practice. Do you need to know that autoethnography is on the left of a continuum in social science where a realist approach is positioned on the right and creativity at the opposite end? Should I tell you that autoethnography is intimately linked to the development of postmodern forms of ethnographic writing? Perhaps the word "postmodern" will scare you away. Let me try again. Combining *auto-* (self) with *ethno-* (culture) graphy allows us as researchers to engage in a social science practice that is artful, poetic, and empathetic and makes space for us to "keep in their minds and feel in their bodies" (Ellis, 2004, p. 30) the complexities of lived experience. I have always found a certain kind of freedom in autoethnography to add "impressionistic and interpretative" dimensions to the ways that social scientists typically seek to think about the world (Ellis, 2004, p. 30). In this way, autoethnography is undoubtedly an aesthetic type of "post"-academic prose that makes use of narration, characterization, and storylines to write intimately in first person about private lives, relationships, and connections between people across time and emotional experiences. I feel like I need to justify my use of autoethnography further. Would it help if I told you that autoethnography is accepted academic practice for those on the left in social science and for those of us who believe that "we cannot move theory into action unless we can find it in the eccentric and wandering ways of our daily life"? (Pratt, as cited in Holman Jones, 2005, p. 763). The work of Stacey Holman Jones (1998, 2005), Carolyn Ellis (1995, 2004) and with her partner Art Bochner (1996), and Laurel Richardson (1997) are powerful examples of autoethnography and their voices are everywhere in this chapter—as silent witnesses and at times speaking loudly alongside mine.

I wanted to ask my colleague and friend Carolyn Ellis—the grandmother and definitely the trendsetter of this approach—to assist me in drafting this description of autoethnography but she regrettably declined. She was busy teaching a theory and methods class with her partner in crime Art Bochner at the University of Florida in Tampa. I thought about asking Lucy Green to write with me because I like the critical approach she brings to our work as women in music education, but she too has just started another new semester of classes and students. However, on the upside, I am really pleased that you have joined me as my reader. Autoethnography is, after all, an attempt for writers and readers to have an intimate connection through words on the page. You will hear me speaking directly to you and do not be at all surprised if I ask from time to time for guidance on the ways we can embrace the personal, emotional, musical, intersubjective, and embodied nature of our mothering work through theoretical musings. Although she could never replace my learned and much loved colleagues in autoethnography and music education, I asked Ms. Autoethnography to assist me in positioning this paper methodologically (see Figure 3.2).

Ms. Autoethnography looks fabulous, doesn't she? She's wearing a number of different guises and tonight she is wearing a colorful costume of many different textures, colors, and cuts. Her dress is a subtle lavender blend of elegant and exploratory poetry. A pair of red chunky but somehow feminine playlet shoes ground her attire firmly to everyday life. Her hat is carefully and lovingly woven with several identities and patterned with a number of e-mail conversations aimed at braving and confronting the cold truths of positivist thinking. Her outfit is completed by some spectacular bling around her neck and on her fingers to emphasize the twinkle and sparkle of that "a-ha" moment, which often happens when we stop to wonder at our world, who we are in relation to it, and to each other. She hopes that her unique sense of fashion enables a scene to be set, a story told, intricate connections woven, experience and theory evoked, and then ruthlessly let go (Holman Jones, 2005, p. 765).

I asked Ms. Autoethnography earlier how she felt about the clothes she would be wearing tonight. She gave a hearty laugh and replied that her clothes reminded her of a juggling act where any number of balls are

warm
woollen
hat to brave the cold

* more bling for
that extra
sparkle!

lavender dress
(just gorgeous!)

heart of bling

sensible red shoes

Comfortable, waterproof,
suits all terrains, shiny
buckle, nice!

Figure 3.2.   Ms. Autoethnography.

thrown high into the air, and both performer and audience stand giddy and waiting with baited breath to see how they might fall. Ms. Autoethnography warns, however, that this style is not to everyone's taste. While she places emphasis on reuniting the personal with the physical, emotional, mental, relational, social, and cultural dimensions of everyday life in her outfit (Ellis, 2004, p. xix), she urges others who wish to emanate her unique sense of fashion to be wary of the sometimes careless slippage into autobiography that can happen when we stand in front of the mirror too long. It is easy to become self-obsessed and forget the central goal of what Ms. Autoethnography does—that is, to observe the self observing so that we can come to a better understanding of the phenomena we began gazing at in the first place.

So, how did you find Ms. Autoethnography? Did you like her clothes and motivations? Is she your kind of girl? I wanted to bring her along with me to demonstrate the method she so proudly wears on her body and how this research method is useful and perhaps even desirable for our purposes as researchers who are interested in the everyday worlds of mothers. Autoethnography allows us to open that usually tightly shut Pandora's box of emotion, engagement, locatedness, and ethics that come hand in hand with the experience of mothering, the performance of song, the interrelationships we form with our children as mothers through singing, and the ways we choose to describe, narrate, and define mothering and motherhood—whether we like it or not.

MOTHERING TODAY

I feel so tired I can barely concentrate. My hands shake as I reach to pour hot water into my tea—the cup that I so desperately hope will bring me back to some semblance of life. Wondering whether my baby will sleep long enough for me to drink it, I sigh heavily as I stir one teaspoon of sugar into my tea. My eyes are scratchy, my head aches, my neck is sore, and my back feels bent out of shape from the three breast-feeds my baby needed last night. I think I know why sleep deprivation is used as a form of torture—it's the lack of sleep that really cripples you and limits your capacity to feel … well, to feel normal. Still dressed in my pink dressing gown and fluffy slippers, I drag my feet and myself into the living room. I flick on the television and absent-mindedly flick through the *Woman's Day* lying on the coffee table. A picture of Sarah Murdoch, the famous former Australian supermodel now married to a media magnate, grabs my attention. The caption reads "Murdoch–Sarah talks about babies and why she wanted an all-natural covershoot." Blonde hair, blue eyes, red lips, and white teeth look back at me and I am curious as to what she might have to say about motherhood—what I am really wondering, of course, is, did she have days like today as a first-time mother when she was not sure anymore who she was, whether what she was doing as a mother was right, or even whether she was a good enough mother? I read the article quickly, scanning for anything she might have to say about the joys as well as the tribulations of being a mother. I am dismayed to find that most of the article is about her achievements outside of her life as a mother, the things that she does when she walks away from her children and leaves them in the care of a nanny, her assistant, or her mother. What is "normal" for Sarah Murdoch is clearly not the same as "normal" for me and I realize that I am foolish to even think of mothering today as a particular kind of "normal."

Perhaps the most normal thing about becoming a mother, I think wryly to myself, is that nothing can prepare you for the ways that your life is about to change. For many women today, becoming a mother is one of the most defining moments in a woman's life. However, hand in hand with the great joys of first-time mothering often comes great sorrow, anger, frustration, pain, confusion, and constraint. Increasingly, women experience motherhood as a crisis as they attempt to enact and embody many different familial, social, cultural, and moral discourses about mothering and motherhood (Miller, 2005, p. 13). A mother today tries to balance her attempt to conform to the romanticized and imagined constructions of motherhood she grew up with as a girl, with the reality of her daily experiences and life as a mother (Hanigsberg & Ruddick, 1999). I can remember a conversation I had not long after my first baby was born with Anna, a woman who attended the same new mother's group as me at the local child health center. I felt as though I was looking in a mirror when our eyes met and talk between us began easily. "Do you know what, Liz?" Anna asked me quite philosophically. I shook my head. "It's all smoke and mirrors—all bloody smoke and mirrors!" I looked at her quizzically, unsure of what she meant. "I wanted this baby so much, but none of them told me—not my mother, my aunties, or even my own sisters! All they bloody well did was take me shopping, buy me coffee and carrot cake, fill my cupboards with pretty clothes for the baby—who turned out to be a boy anyway—and look past me with knowing glances at one another. None of them told me!" I am still confused. "Oh Liz, did anyone tell you it would be like this? The sleepless nights, producing and being milked like a cow, dry retching over full nappies, not to mention the nonexistent sex life! I don't even know who I am anymore—I used to be a successful business woman and now I can't even make my own bed—where have I gone, Liz? Where?" The sad and lost look on Anna's face stayed with me throughout the remainder of the day and I can still picture her now. Her story illustrated to me that women today are no longer "thoroughly at home with being at home" (Maushart, 1997, p. 10; see also Bergum, 1997) and instead are primed for achievement, to want and expect to have it all at once—career, house, husband, children, and happiness (Hays, 1996; Hewlett, 2002; Peters, 1997). For many women, the reality of bringing a life into this world disrupts this picture-perfect image of an ideal woman (Le Blanc, 1999).

Once her baby turned 9 weeks old, Anna did not come back to our mother's group. She e-mailed me to say that she had returned to full-time work and her baby was now in child care 5 days a week. I heard many of the women in our group "*tsk, tsk, tsk*" about Anna's decision, but I admired her for being brave enough to remove the "mask of motherhood" we had all become so good at wearing, and act upon what *she knew* in her heart of hearts was the right thing to do for her own health and well-being as a woman and that of her baby. Was Anna's way of coping with the shift in her identity from manager to mother "normal"? The answer is of course yes and no. I am sure that many first-time mothers reading about Anna's decision may feel a sense of connection with her feelings of hopelessness and failure, but perhaps also disconnection in regards to needing to return to a prebaby lifestyle and identity, and I would bet my life that the tension between them has built a wall of guilt too high to see over.

Each woman's experience of motherhood is uniquely their own and one in which they alone try to make sense of. I am not sure now how I made sense of my new identity as a mother but perhaps a retelling of my experience will help me to see myself becoming a mother more clearly. I fell pregnant with my first child at age 29—much older than when my mother, her mother, and her grandmother had given birth to their first children. I had moved to Brisbane in Queensland, Australia, to begin my career as a university lecturer in 1997 and none of the significant women in my life lived within a 1,000-kilometer radius of me—my mother Lyn resided in the south of the country in a small town called Ballarat, my older sister Sally in the capital city of Australia, and my mother-in-law Jeannie in the northern town of Darwin. As a relatively young female in academia, I found myself isolated professionally as a pregnant woman— the swelling belly of a woman did not fit easily, readily, or comfortably within the hallowed walls of lecture theaters nor behind the desk and under tables at faculty meetings (Acker & Feuerverger, 1996). Many of the people who I considered my friends at university were either too young to be remotely interested in birth and babies or relishing their role as grand- mothers. When my baby boy Max arrived, I found myself alone—com- pletely alone from the women I so desperately needed near me—and at home with a new baby. I did not know why he cried so much, why he wanted to feed so often, and why he wouldn't sleep. I madly leafed through the pages of all the books about pregnancy and motherhood I had bought prior to giving birth to find solutions, answers—anything that would calm my baby and my growing sense of failure. I stopped trusting my own mothering instincts and wanted an expert on mothering—Mir- iam Stoppard (2005), Kaz Cooke (1999), Robin Barker (2001)—to tell me what to do. When I spoke to my mother or sister on the phone, I would smile bravely through my tears and hope that the loneliness I felt behind my mask of motherhood would remain unheard and unseen.

One of the baby gifts that Max was given by a close friend of mine was a small board book called *Hush Little Baby* by Sylvia Long (1997a). This well-known lullaby is revised by Long to focus on the joys of nature and the environment rather than material possessions, each page revealing a tender scene as a mama bunny lulls her baby bunny to sleep by enlisting a parade of bedtime wonders—the beauty of a hummingbird in flight; the magic of a harvest moon; the reassurance of a parent's hug, all these and more. (Long, 1997b)

The tune of *Hush Little Baby* is a favorite of mine and I adored the sentiment behind the new words, so decided to learn it and sing it to Max at bedtime. When I first began to sing, his baby blue eyes fixed on mine and his crying quieted. I found myself beginning to smile as I sang and as the song ended, I could see Max become lost in that magical moment between waking and sleep. I gently kissed his forehead and walked out of the room, my fingers crossed behind my back in a desperate plea for him to stay asleep. My wish was answered and Max slept soundly until his next feeding time. I can remember the amazement, elation, and joy I found in knowing that the music I loved singing was something I could also use in my performative role as a mother. Music enabled me to find myself and my voice as a mother, and singing to my children has since become a much loved aspect of my relationship with Max and Hamish. The songs I sing as a mother help to define, ground, and nurture me as a mother and a woman in all my guises. In so many ways, singing to my boys became a type of pedagogy of everyday life for me—a means by which I learned how to be a mother and who I was as a mother.

MAKING MOTHERS VISIBLE IN EARLY CHILDHOOD MUSIC EDUCATION[1]

I wonder then, where are mothers positioned in discourses of music education and what importance is given to the necessity to teach mothers how to sing for their own well-being and the health of their relationship with their children? I quickly retreat to the shelves of the university library to search. I find that early childhood education sources place emphasis on the significant role of mother-as-teacher (e.g., Scott-Jones, 1987, p. 22), so much so that the lines between teaching and mothering are blurred (Collins, 1998, p. 92) and the boundaries between the two roles are unclear (Claesson & Brice, 1989, p. 3). O'Reilly, Short, and Porter describe this duality as reflective of a mother's "preservative" love, that is, a "commitment to preserve, grow, and train the child to take her/his place in society" (2005, p. 5). I stop reading and pause for a moment to take in what I have read. The positioning of mothering and teaching as "woman's work" and the feminization of music per se engenders a sense of confidence that I will find a mother's voice in discussions of teaching and learning music.

In a 1917 paper titled "Message to You, Mother Music Lover," Helen Ware was one of the first to write about the relationship of mothers to music. The message she wanted to give to mothers came from the words of Clara Schumann, who is reported by Ware as declaring that "First and last, the mission of music is to aid us to create in the home a pure and ennobling atmosphere" (p. 22). Ware asserts that this "beautiful senti-ment" must be impressed upon all American mothers and emphasizes that "the music education of the child is a grave necessity to every home ... for verily, 'A home without Music is but a stack of bricks and mortar' " (p. 22). The linking of motherhood to music education is evident here, but again, we see the focus of a mother's musical activities as valuable and noteworthy when directed outside herself to her children.

I turn the pages of more recent texts in music education to search for a different depiction of her (e.g., Campbell, 2004; Elliott, 1995; Jorgensen, 2003). My fingers skim down lists of indexes to the letter M and I look for words like "mother," "motherhood," "mothering," and "maternal". My face frowns—they are not there. I realize with dismay that here, too, alongside other music disciplines, mothers are painfully absent. Despite the value attached to a mother singing for the development of her child, the way that a mother herself experiences, relates to, and renders mean-ingful the social and musical moment of singing to her baby remains silent and hidden in academic discourse. Here we can see the historical legacy of white patriarchy at play, which hands mothers in relation to music a double bias. Women are devalued women in the private/domestic/ reproductive sphere (de Beauvoir, 1997; Landes, 1998; Ortner, 1997), and the tradition of singing to children is located firmly within the sphere of "little music traditions" and considered trivial and profane. While it is true that some feminist scholars in new musicology such as Citron (1993, pp. 63–65) and Fried Block (1994) have discussed the role of women as mothers, these partial revelations come hand in hand with the histories, works, and lives of their child prodigies. A mother's voice is largely excluded from the Western music canons because the songs she sings are performed within the domestic worlds and everyday lives of women. As this realization dawns on me, the lamenting voice of Crittenden (2002) rings in my ears, "All of the lip service to motherhood still floats in the air, as insubstantial as clouds of angel dust. On the ground, where mothers live, the lack of respect and tangible recognition is still part of every mother's experience" (p. 2).

I have saved the work of Lucy Green (1997), *Music, Gender, Education* until last and as I hold her book in my hand, I notice the image on the front cover: a woman is pictured seated playing a piano while nursing a child on her lap. Taking us back to a time past, the woman and child featured in this picture appear serene and at peace, and their expressions remind me of a mother's love and warm embrace. I cannot help but think about and be encouraged by the significance of this representation as discourse—a mother making music with her child is positioned as the first image we see in a discussion about music, gender, and education. I am not disappointed. Green goes on to assert that women's role in music education has been considerable; indeed, women have dominated as music teachers in all countries "which provide systematic institutional and private music education, throughout the twentieth century" (p. 48). Like Citron, she further asserts that a mother's role in music education cannot be underestimated. In this domestic realm of motherhood, Green tells us that a woman fulfills her maternal and musical duties in ways that "affirm patriarchal definitions of femininity" (p. 48). By singing serenely in private to her sleepy baby, a mother becomes all that is expected of her publicly and through her music, the mask of motherhood becomes embodied. I read on and catch myself smiling as I hear Green speaking in her own voice as a mother:

> The strength and beauty of this womanly custom strike me when I remember my own maternal grandmother singing a lovely hymn-like wordless lullaby to me when I was a child, the same song my mother always chose and to whom her mother must therefore have sung it; which I sang to my children and which, when my daughter's other grandmother was dying, was the song the little girl spontaneously chose with which to wish her farewell. It is not because of mere whim that I have reverted to personal anecdote in order to illustrate this practice: its history is of course, unwritten. (p. 48)

Green's personal reflections remind me of the writings by ethnomusicologist Bess Lomax-Hawes, one of the few women in this discipline to write about the social practice of singing to her children. After interviewing African American singer Bessie Jones, Lomax-Hawes (1974) recalls:

> And then I remembered singing my own babies to sleep. I happen to know quite a number of lullabies myself (and I come from a lullaby-singing family); but the song that always seemed to "work" best—my stand-by old reliable in times of stress—was the Protestant hymn "I am bound for the Promised Land." (p. 141)

Lomax Hawes reflects further about the paradox of motherhood in Western society and remarks,

> No wonder American mothers sing to their babies—and more especially, probably, to themselves—about separation and space and going very far away. I always found myself that rocking a baby to sleep was kind of a sad thing to do-not miserable or tragic or irksome—just a little bit sad, somehow.... The American lullaby is—on one of it's deeper levels, a mother's conversation with herself about separation. And as such, one of its most pro-

foundly supportive functions is to make the inevitable and inexorable payment of our social dues just a little less personally painful. (p. 148)

While the personal stories of Green and Lomax-Hawes provide rich narratives about a mother's musical experiences, Drinker (1948/1995) turns to history and cultures outside her own to find the musical voices of mothers. Positioning lullabies as women's work, she states that the songs a mother sings to her children are one of the largest groups of women's songs. The lullabies of Dyak women, Hottentot mothers, women in Greenland, and Pygmy[2] mothers are all cited by Drinker as high points of musical achievement where the "whole of the singing is marked by the deepest feeling in the voice.... A bewitching charm lies in the ... mother's lullaby tones which she hums as she rocks her child. She sways her body and croons a simple song" (Thalbitzer, cited in Drinker, 1948/1995, p. 46). Reflecting further about the importance of the musical work of mothers, Drinker positions women as the keepers of traditional lore, re-creators of the musical heritage of the past, and composers of new rhythms and new melodies. For Drinker, mothers and women as singers hold the key to bringing back "in a great fertilising flow" into today the music of tomorrow (p. 53). Together, the words of Ware, Drinker, Lomax-Hawes, and Green position the musical work of mothers as essential to their identity as women and in relation to the musical worlds of their children. Their words at once fill me with hope and despair—the strong statements and pleas of these four women for recognition, support, and action for mothers as music makers and music educators span 100 years, with little variation in their agendas. The musical worlds of mothers appear to have vanished beneath the struggle for women today to be "perfect mothers," the overwhelming sense of guilt and failure many mothers experience when they cannot sustain performance of the multitude of motherhood myths, and the continued devaluing of mothers and mothering work by our society today.

SINGING OUR MOTHER'S SONGS, TEACHING OUR DAUGHTERS TO SING: TALKING ABOUT MUSIC AS MOTHERS IN MY FAMILY

I can still see the tears in her eyes as she tells me about the night before her mother died. Its Christmastime and my Auntie Florence and I are standing by the kitchen bench reminiscing about festive seasons past when her mother (my grandmother) was still alive. We talked about children, football, and somehow I find myself telling Auntie Florence about the latest project I am working on: music and mothering. "Actually, Auntie Florence," I hesitate slightly. "I was wondering if I could maybe interview you sometime about your life as a musical mother and any memories you might have about Nana singing?" Auntie Florence doesn't say anything for a moment and I frown, worried that maybe I have asked something I shouldn't have. When she speaks, her voice is choked with emotion:

> I visited Mum in Melbourne Hospital the night before she died. I don't remember how we got into talking about singing but Mum wanted to sing to me. I wrote down the words while I was with her as she sang it through:
>
> Little bird you are welcome what news do you bring
> From our mother one word and tell us and sing
> A kiss and a letter I bring you today
> If you have something better I'll take it away
> Take one word to our mother and that is our love
> Fly away gentle bird, Fly away gentle dove.
>
> How it popped into her memory I don't know as it was one I never remember hearing before and she said she sang it to all of us.

Tears begin to fall down my Auntie's face as she is taken back to that moment: "It was a very special sharing time—I didn't know that it would be the last time ever that I would be sitting talking with her. She died that very same night. Even though I don't remember her singing especially to me, I have that last memory." My Auntie is now sobbing and I put my arms around her and cry with her. Eventually we pass one another a tissue and make a promise to meet soon to remember and talk some more about her mother and herself as a mother through music. Our next meeting, however, takes place not in person, but via e-mail.

From: Liz Mackinlay

To: Florence Fahey
Sent: Tuesday, August 18, 2008, 4:56 PM
Subject: Re: Back on the Net

Hi Auntie Florence,

Thanks so much for your lovely e-mail awhile ago—I'm sorry I didn't get back to you sooner—I really don't know where the time goes sometimes.

It will be great to meet up with you if we can arrange it when I come down to visit Mum and Dad. In the meantime, maybe I could e-mail a few questions about music and mothering to you and we could do some virtual chatting? What do you think?

Love always, Beth x

From: Florence Fahey

To: Liz Mackinlay
Sent: Thursday, August 20, 2008, 8:56 PM
Subject: Re: Music questions

Hi Beth,

Sounds like a good idea to do some chatting via e-mail if that will work. Enjoy the warm weather up north, wish I could join you.

Love, Auntie Florence

From Liz Mackinlay

To: Florence Fahey
Sent: Thursday, September 10, 2008, 12:00 PM
Subject: Re: Music questions

Hi Auntie Florence,

That's great that we can chat on e-mail. I hope you don't mind, but to get the ball rolling, I've popped in these couple of questions:

1. What are your earliest and most powerful memories of Nana singing to you as a child? What did she sing?

2. You mentioned at Christmas a few years ago that Nana had asked you to sing to her as she was slipping away from us. Would you be able to remember that moment? What did she ask you to sing? Why do you think she asked? What happened to her and to you while you were singing?

Thanks, Auntie Florence—you're an angel!

Love always, Beth x

From Florence Fahey
To: Liz Mackinlay
Sent: Thursday, September 27, 2008, 2:12 PM
Subject: Re: Music questions

Hi Beth,

Finally have some time to sit at the computer and get the music info off to you. My earliest memories of Mum singing to us was when my brothers were little—Peter, Malcolm, and Keith. She always sang around the house doing her housework and there was always lots of singing around the piano, mainly on weekends—no time during the week. Music was always a big part of our lives as we had the wireless but of course no TV, and the love of music was really nurtured in us. The songs she sang to the boys were the same ones she said she sang to me. The main one was this Lullaby—

> Go to sleep my baby, close your pretty eyes,
> Angels up above you peeping at you deary from the skies,
> Great big moon is shining, stars begin to peep,
> Time for little piccaninnies to go to sleep,
> Piccaninnies time to go to sleep.

She'd also sing about the babes in the wood who died. It was a sad song—Malcolm and Keith would go to sleep and I'd go off and cry:

> Now my dears don't you know that a long time ago,
> There were two little children whose names I don't know
> They were carried away on a bright summer's day
> And left in the woods so I've heard some folk say.

(A couple of verses I've forgotten)

> And the robins so red when they found they were dead,
> Gathered strawberry leaves and all over them spread.
> And all the day long, in the branches so strong
> They would sit and would sing and this was their song—
> Poor babes in the wood, poor babes in the wood
> Now don't you remember poor babes in the wood.

I always sang to my kids—the same songs Mum sang to me including the action songs - This is the way the farmer rides etc. When the grandchildren appeared the same songs were sung to them. They had their favorites and Luke was still wanting a song at bedtime when he was getting quite big. Their special songs were Jesus loves me, Away in a Manger, Doggie in the Window. I always felt honored that Sam and Luke would want Grandma to sing their bedtime song to them. Because I was with Paul and Tracey for so many months after Mitch was born, I sang to him for hours to get him soothed and settled. Mitch loves music now and I can still entertain him that way now. Things like this make you realize how important these times become in your life. Many memories came flooding in as I was writing this down—things that I hadn't thought of in years—even brought on some tears—happy ones and some sad ones too.

Be in touch with you again soon,

Love to all,

Auntie Florence

It is some time before I realize that I have read and reread Auntie Florence's e-mail a number of times over, wanting to capture, experience, and remember all of the details and memories she has shared with me about music in her life as a daughter, mother, and grandmother. The music and mothering script she has written speaks volumes to me about the centrality of songs and singing to her experiences of motherhood—watching her own mother sing to music while doing housework, singing around the piano as a family with her mother at the center, songs to soothe in the dark hours of night, and singing as love relationships between mothers and children, and grandmothers and grandchildren. It has been too easy (and convenient) to think of these musical moments as insignificant in their simplicity and everydayness—as nothing more than the part and parcel of the domestic work and lives of women. Yet I cannot help but see the image of Auntie Florence's face as she told of her mother singing once more to her just before she passed away and I know that the musical moments I have described here cannot be carelessly dismissed. My Nana chose to sing to her only daughter the moment they last laid eyes on one another—a lullaby bonded them together in death just as it had joined them as mother and child at birth. The musical gift of security, belonging, and identity my grandmother gave to her daughter, Auntie Florence has in turn given to her own children and grandchildren—music has sustained and continues to nurture her in her multifaceted role as a mother.

REFLECTIONS: A MOTHER SINGS HER SONG IN A LETTER

Dear Reader,

I hope that you have enjoyed reading my discussion of music, mothering, and autoethnography. I use the word "hope" because I am not entirely sure who you are—perhaps you are a mother, you may be a music educator, a teacher working in the context of early childhood education, or even an ethnographic researcher—or perhaps none of these labels accurately describe you. My intention was to show, by way of example, what autoethnographic method is and how it can be usefully applied to our understanding of the intimate link between mothers, early childhood, and music education.

The early childhood context I have placed in full view of my camera is not in any way a new scene to discourses of music education; however, the angle, light, and contrast placed on it when I look through the lens with the eyes of a mother creates a different kind of picture—one that I might not have noticed or considered important before. This is the power of autoethnography—new ways of seeing, listening, speaking, and singing about the experience of motherhood can be opened up when we listen, look, and learn from the everyday-extraordinariness of a woman singing to her baby. Thanks for taking the time to listen to my story and I look forward to hearing yours if and when we meet in person.

Yours in motherhood,

Liz

NOTES

1. This section of the chapter first appeared in the Australian *Kodály Bulletin* and is reprinted here with full permission.
2. Please note that these are the terms that Drinker uses to refer to these cultural groups, some of which are not in usage today (e.g., "Efe" is the preferred term over "Pygmy").

REFERENCES

Acker, S., & Feuerverger, G. (1996). Doing good and feeling bad: The work of women university teachers. *Cambridge Journal of Education, 26*(3), 401–422.

Barker, R. (2001). *Baby love: Everything you need to know about your new baby* (Rev. ed.). Sydney: Pan Macmillan Australia Pty Ltd.

Bergum, V. (1997). *A child on her mind: The experience of becoming a mother.* Westport, CN: Bergin & Garvey

Campbell, P. S. (2004). *Teaching music globally: Experiencing music, expressing culture.* New York: Oxford University Press.

Citron, M. (1993). *Gender and the musical canon.* New York: Cambridge University Press.

Claesson, M. A., & Brice, R. A. (1989). Teacher/mothers: Effects of a dual role. *American Educational Research Journal, 26*(1), 1–23.

Collins, A. (1998). Mothers as teachers—Teachers as mothers. In S. Abbey & A. O'Reilly (Eds.), *Redefining motherhood: Changing identities and patterns* (pp. 92–102). Toronto, ON, Canada: Second Story Press.

Cooke, K. (1999). *Up the duff.* Ringwood, Victoria, Australia: Penguin.

Crittenden, A. (2002). *The price of motherhood: Why the most important job in the world is still the least valued.* New York: Henry Holt.

de Beauvoir, S. (1997). *The second sex* (H. M. Parschley, Ed. & Trans). London: Vintage Press.

Drinker, S. (1995). *Music and women: The story of women in relation to their music.* New York: The Feminist Press at the City University of New York.

Elliott, D. (1995). *Music matters: A new philosophy of music education.* New York: Oxford University Press. (Original work published 1948)

Ellis, C. (1995). *Final negotiations: A story of love, loss and chronic illness.* Philadelphia: Temple University Press.

Ellis, C. (2004). *The ethnographic I: A methodological novel about autoethnography*. Walnut Creek, MA: AltaMira Press.

Ellis, C., & Bochner, C. (Eds.). (1996). *Composing ethnography: Alternative forms of qualitative writing*. Walnut Creek, MA: AltaMira Press.

Fried Block, A. (1994). The child is the mother of the woman: Amy Beach's New England upbringing. In S. Cook & J. S. Tsou (Eds.), *Cecilia reclaimed: Feminist perspectives on gender and music* (pp. 107–133). Urbana: University of Illinois Press.

Green, L. (1997). *Music, gender and education*. New York: Cambridge University Press. Holman Jones, S. (1998). *Kaleidoscope notes: Writing women's music and organizational culture*. Walnut Creek, CA: AltaMira.

Hanigsberg, J., & Ruddick, S. (Eds.). (1999). *Mother troubles: Rethinking contemporary dilemmas*. Boston, MA: Beacon Press.

Hays, S. (1996). *The cultural contradictions of motherhood*. New Haven, CT: Yale University Press.

Hewlett, S. A. (2002). *Creating a life: Professional women and the quest for children*. New York, NY: Miramax Books (Hyperion).

Holman Jones, S. (2005). Autoethnography: Making the personal political. In N. K. Denzin & Y. S. Lincoln (Eds.), *The Sage handbook of qualitative research* (3rd ed., pp. 763–791). Thousand Oaks, CA: SAGE.

Jorgensen, E. R. (2003). *Transforming music education*. Bloomington: Indiana University Press.

Landes, J. (1998). Introduction. In J. Landes (Ed.), *Feminism, the public and the private* (pp. 1–20). Oxford, England: Oxford University Press.

Le Blanc, W. (1999). *Naked motherhood: Shattering illusions and sharing truths*. Milsons Point, NSW, Australia: Random House Australia.

Lomax-Hawes, B. (1974). Folksongs and function: Some thoughts on the American lullaby. *Journal of American Folklore*, 87, 140–148.

Long, S. (1997a). *Hush little baby*. San Francisco: Chronicle Books.

Long, S. (1997b). *Hush little baby. Sylvia Long's children's books*. Retrieved January 16, 2012 from http://www.sylvia-long.com/hush1.htm

Maushart, S. (1997). *The mask of motherhood: How mothering changes everything and why we pretend it doesn't*. Milsons Point, NSW, Australia: Random House Australia.

Miller, T. (2005). *Making sense of motherhood: A narrative approach*. New York: Cambridge University Press.

O'Reilly, A., Porter, T., & Short, P. (2005). *Motherhood: Power and oppression*. Toronto, ON, Canada: Women's Press.

Ortner, S. (1998). Is female to male as nature is to culture? In J. Landes (Ed.), *Feminism, the public and the private* (pp. 21–44). Oxford, England: Oxford University Press.

Peters, J. K. (1997). *When mothers work: Loving our children without sacrificing ourselves*. Reading, MA: Addison-Wesley.

Rich, A. (1976). *Of woman born: Motherhood as experience and institution*. New York: W.W. Norton.

Richardson, L. (1997). *Fields of play: Constructing an academic life*. New Brunswick, NJ: Rutgers Press.

Scott-Jones, D. (1987). Mother-as-teacher in the families of high- and low-achiev-
  ing low-income Black first-graders. *Journal of Negro Education, 56*(1), 21–34.
Stoppard, M. (2005). *Conception, pregnancy and birth* (Rev. ed.). London: Dorling
  Kindersley.
Ware, H. (1917). A message to you, mother music lover. *Music Supervisors Journal,
  4*(2), 22–24.

CHAPTER 4

HANGING OUT WITH BRITNEY[1] AND RAIHAN[2]

The Colorful Musical Lives of Malay/Muslim Children in Singapore

Chee-Hoo Lum

IMPETUS

We have an inclination towards sounds, melodious voices. But we have to channel it properly. The arts are something Man needs in life. The person who lives without the arts is one who is hard-hearted and shallow. (Ustaz Syed Abdillah Ahmad on *Music & Islam*)

Several years back when I taught music in a local primary school, the recorder was introduced in instrumental playing to Primary 3 (age 9) to 6 (age 12) students. Students were required to have a recorder and bring it to class during music lessons. I would often encounter situations where students would forget to bring or lose their instrument at some point. In one particular incident, after reminding a student several times about bringing the recorder, I decided to give her parents a call and to my surprise, the father sternly remarked that he had no intention of buying the

Musical Childhoods of Asia and the Pacific, pp. 57–74
Copyright © 2012 by Information Age Publishing
All rights of reproduction in any form reserved.

instrument, came directly to the school to speak with the principal, and took his child out of music class permanently. I was totally taken aback and did not understand at that time why the child's parents would deprive her of music lessons. The principal eventually disclosed to me that while the parents had no objection to their child participating in singing in music lessons, they firmly asserted that playing an instrument was not something they wanted the child to do, citing religious reasons for their decision. This incident left a deep impression on me and sparked my curiosity in gaining a better understanding of the varied social and religious contexts with which music can happen in the lives of Melayu (Malay/Muslim) children in Singapore.

INTRODUCTION

Popular observations and anecdotal evidence suggests that when it comes to arts and sports, the Malays (in Singapore) have a natural talent to excel. Acclaimed master potter Iskandar Jalil says, "Most of us would say that the Malays are gifted in the arts. We have Pak Zubir Said, Haji Ahmad Jaafar, P. Ramlee, Anita Sarawak, Najip Ali..." (Rahman, 2002, p. 187).

The term Melayu (Malay) "has more to do with political classification than anthropological definition ... refer[ing] to people of Austronesian stock from Malaysia, Singapore, Eastern Sumatra, Riau Islands, West Kalimantan, south Thailand and Brunei" (Hilarian, 2006b, p. 284). The Melayu people identify with each other "both socially and culturally by their religion, customary rites, language and in their music" (Hilarian, 2006b, p. 284). The Malays in Singapore make up about 14% of the country's population and form the majority of the Muslim population. Most Malays in Singapore are descendants of immigrants who came from peninsular Malaya, Sumatra, Java, and the other islands of the Indonesian archipelago. The majority of Malays in Singapore generally share a similar culture with those in Peninsula Malaysia.

The initial musical influences of the Melayu community in Singapore came primarily from the Hadhrami Arabs. These include the gambus lutes and the marwas percussion instruments as well as the dance genres of zapin and sharah of Arabian origin (Hilarian, 2006b, p. 285). Interestingly, the music and dance forms "performed by the Muslim/Malay community are a result of the transmission of Hadhrami Arab culture brought about through the spread of Islam" and the "gambus, marwas, zapin and sharah can be said to hold prestige with the Muslim/Malay community due to their 'Arabness' and links with an ever growing pan-Islamic ideology" (Hilarian, 2006b, p. 288).

BRIEF NOTE ON MUSIC AND ISLAM

Music has traditionally been one of the more controversial issues in the Muslim world. In Khalid Baig's (2008) inquiry into Islam's stance on music, he states clearly that a great majority of scholars declare prohibition (on music) and the few who do not have a consensus on the issue, also conclude that it is best to abstain:

> After all the arguments are considered, it is obvious that even if the object of dispute (music) is cleared of a judgment of prohibition, it is not cleared of doubt. And believers are the ones who stop in the face of doubt as made clear by the hadith: Whoever stayed clear of it protected his honor and his religion. And whoever wanders around a preserve is likely to fall into it. (Al-Shawkani, Nayl al-Awtar, cited in Baig, 2008, p. 275)

Singing, according to Baig (2008), also remains dangerous and most contemporary music is prohibited for several reasons:

> There is no doubt that in [their present] form these [music and singing] are mostly prohibited because they accompany prohibited things, lead to other prohibited things, distract from obligations, and waste money. (Al-Shawkani, cited in Baig, 2008, p. 276)

According to Shiloah (1995), the lawfulness of music has been debated since the first century of Islam (ninth century A.D.) and continues to this day. According to the great theologian, religious reformer, and mystic, Abu Hamid al-Ghazzali (1058–1111), in his authoritative work *Ihya' 'ulum al-din* (The Revival of Religious Sciences), which attempts to integrate Sufism and orthodoxy, he concluded that both statutory and analogous evidence indicate the admissibility of music. al-Ghazzali argued that

> music and singing are means of evoking what is truly in one's heart; under their influence the heart reveals itself and its contents.... In other words, the nature of music's influence on man very much depends on the basic intentions of the listener and the purpose for which music is used. (Shiloah, 1995, p. 43)

Evidently, there are no definite answers and the views of Islam on music remain contentious.

> In the context of Singapore, ethnomusicologist Larry Hilarian (2007) is of the view that the Malay/Muslim population considers music as vital and necessary in both secular and religious aspects. Music is perceived by many Malays as having a positive spiritual value, especially if it is used in a devotional way, with moral meaning in its song-texts. Most Malay Muslims in the

Malay world do not consider music to be sinful (haram); on the contrary, it is praiseworthy if used in the correct Islamic context. (p. 15)

It is in light of this "correct Islamic context" that I am interested in examining the role music plays in the particular lives of Melayu children. A localized understanding can then bring forth constructive discussions pertaining to education possibilities in the music classroom. I am mindful that the topic can be sensitive and anonymity of the subjects needs to be protected.

My initial access to subjects came by chance and subsequently sparked me to approach close Melayu friends and colleagues to gain access to other Melayu families with young children that would allow me to visit their homes, observe their children, and have informal conversations with parents, caregivers, and children about the musical influences and purpose of music in their lives. Two case studies are detailed in this chapter.

INNOCENCE IS BLISS?:
OF WOMANIZERS AND A DAMAGED HEART

I was tired from a day of jogging and swimming with Ben, Farhan and his young niece and nephews (Dzulkifli, age 11; Dalilah, age 6; and Dahari, age 5). We were on our way to drop the children off when Ben suggested driving them to Orchard Road[3] to look at the Christmas decorations and lights. We were subsequently stuck in a heavy traffic jam with rain pounding on the car windows. As we inched forward with the children dozing off, the driver (Ben) switched on the radio (tuned to FM 98.7), blasting the latest English popular hit songs. To my surprise, all three children came alive, singing and moving in unison to every single song that came on, from Britney Spears to Danity Kane. And so it goes:

> You're a womanizer, oh womanizer, oh you're a womanizer baby!
> You you you are! You you you are!
> Womanizer womanizer womanizer![4]

> Damaged, damaged, damaged, damaged! I thought that I should let you know that my heart is damaged, damaged, so damaged![5]

I was surprised, to say the least, as I listened and watched intently their MTV moves as they performed for me from the backseat of the car. They sang and moved in sync with the music and their melodic and rhythmic accuracy were uncanny. The researcher curiosity in me was stirred and I knew I had to find out more about the musical lives of these children. As

Danity Kane's "Damaged" drew to a close, Dahari (who spoke minimal English) turned to me and asked, "Uncle, what is damaged?" to which I smiled and made a mental note to myself that the younger children (Dahari and Dalilah) have probably no idea what the lyrics to most of these songs mean.

Subsequently, I managed to have many informal conversations with the children on several outings and visited the family where I was able to informally interview their parents and family members that were caregivers to the children. Audio and video recordings were also made during these sessions, including the children confidently singing, dancing, moving, and making funny faces unabashedly at the video camera.

LIVING WITH BRITNEY AND PETER PAN

I was drawn immediately to the family's karaoke room when I first entered the house. As a matter of fact, I could hear the powerful karaoke singing streaming from the windows of their fifth-level apartment from the ground floor lift landing even before I entered. It was Saiful, Dzulkifli's father, singing his favorite popular Malay tune from Peter Pan, an Indonesian pop rock band from Bandung.

Karaoke is a significant musical event in the household. It is a weekend affair, with the family gathering in the karaoke room singing and dancing away for hours on end. Saiful used to be a drummer in an amateur rock band in his teens and early 20s with his younger brother on the electric guitar. Although they disbanded due to work and family commitments, the two brothers still kept their musical ties through karaoke. As Saiful remarked, "I love to sing and I love music … so I converted one room into a karaoke room. Rather than go out and sing away, I would rather do it at home…. I will be the regular (singer in the karaoke room) plus my two younger ones" Saiful reported that before his younger brother got married,

> We used to sing every weekend until 4:00 A.M…. We sing English, Malay rock songs, like from the Eagles, Scorpion, Deep Purple, R.E.M., and INXS. The Malay ones will be more to what is popular. Right now, I sing Peter Pan and Radja (Indonesian rock band) and their music is getting better. Previously we followed Malaysian rock bands but now we've moved to Indonesia because to me the music (of the Malaysian bands) are not as powerful as before. Now (referring to the Indonesian rock bands), the beat is more like the dancing beat and I prefer that kind of music.

Saiful is always the one who will begin the karaoke session at home. According to him, "When I start (singing karaoke), everybody will want to start." It seems the children have taken to the singing as well, as they select their favorite songs and sing with ease to the karaoke tracks using the microphone, turned up to a raging decibel level.

During the week, both parents are working and the children are cared for by relatives. Dahari stays with grandma from Mondays to Fridays, only spending the weekends at home. Dalilah and Dzulkifli are cared for by their aunt (who lives a block away from them) and cousins (Suriati, age 18, and Suhailah, age 14) until their parents return from work in the late evenings.

Suriati plays a significant role in Dalilah's love for popular media and culture. Suriati has been an active dancer since her secondary school days, being in traditional Malay dance and switching to contemporary pop, jazz, and hip-hop in the last few years. As she proudly proclaimed, "Basically I think it is in the genes, from my grandmother (who used to be a professional dancer in Malay traditional genres)!" Suriati explained how she formed a hip-hop dance group:

> through meeting people through the radio cause there is this program called "Hook Out" on FM 98.7 and that is how I met people and until now, I'm still active in dancing, ... the group consists of 8 people ... two guys that are 13 and the rest, a Chinese girl that is 24 years old this year...we do hip-hop dancing and now try to incorporate jazz and all those 60s dancing ... we like to watch *Grease*.

Suriati aspires to be the next "big thing" in the dance industry. Her goal in the next few years is to save up enough money to go to America and pursue an undergraduate degree in economics while seeking auditions and opportunities for dance roles in the media industry. Suriati and her group members "use the community centre dance studios or multi-purpose hall for practice ... we practice around three times a week, depending on everyone's schedule ... we start at 1:00 and finish around 7:00 ... not singing, just dance."

Suriati is an avid radio listener. She says, "I think radio influence[s] and conquers the mind and then from there I know this song is nice (refers to how she picks her songs for choreography). I will get a friend to remix the song for me." Suriati would then put together a medley of the latest pop hits on the Billboard charts (many times doing her own basic sound editing sequences), choreograph the steps, and teach it to her fellow group members. Suriati's inspiration of late comes from the Pussycat Dolls, "so most of the dance steps will be like very 'exotic' " (imitating the Pussycat Dolls that she watches on MTV). She also incorporates jumpstyle in her choreography; dance instruction videos by Patrick Jumpen that she watches on YouTube. Her group has competed in annual hip-hop dance competitions and performed for paid gigs in different corporate or wedding functions.

Dalilah, who hangs around Suriati every day of the week, follows everything that Suriati does. And as Suriati whole-heartedly declared,

> I sparked their interest in dance 'cause they always follow me to my practices.... It's like monkey see monkey do 'cause they are still young.... So whenever I say today there's a new dance step and they will be like, Yeah! (shout with joy). I want to train them (Dalilah and her youngest sister Sofia, age 6 years) so that they can be part of the group in the near future.

Suriati does not just encourage but puts serious time into teaching the girls hip-hop moves every day. She described her process: "I will start by simplifying the steps for them, let them practice with the music repeatedly until they are familiar before moving on to the next stage." They (Suriati, Dalilah, and Sofia) dance every day in Suriati's room as well, full-length mirror included. Suriati explains that she also encourages the girls to think and come up with their own dance steps:

> sometimes I would show them videos and tell them this is nice or that is nice.... We will talk about dance, I don't want it to be just my choreography, I want them to like the steps as well, so that's why I ask them, "Do you have any dance steps for me?" So that they can choreograph their own dance later.

The girls are currently working on a remix medley consisting of Britney Spears's "Womanizer," Pussycat Dolls' "When I Grow Up," and Danity Kane's "Damaged." Being a critical observer of Dalilah and Sofia's progress, Suriati noted,

> They are still trying to dance, although there are some crookedness (not getting some of the dance steps), but so far I think there is potential ... like they can set up their own group (eventually).... I think they can go far with it (because of their interest) and I hope the interest doesn't stop there.

It is no wonder that Dalilah and Sofia are so familiar with current popular music repertoire and their lyrics as they are repeatedly exposed to the music while practicing, making it a truly embodied learning experience. Dalilah and Sofia became a huge influence on Suhailah as well, teaching her the dance steps after learning them from Suriati. Dalilah's parents felt that the great interest in dance, other than influences coming from Suriati, was triggered by the *High School Musical*[6] craze influenced by their schoolmates, which prompted them to choreograph, sing, and dance.

Thoughts of being a professional dancer have crossed Suriati's mind but her mother has sounded her objections, maintaining that "There are a lot of boundaries. My mother discouraged me 'cause she is a professional dancer (Malay traditional dance) last time ... she always performed in hotels when she was younger then she found that it's not a very good influence." Suriati tries very hard over the years to hide the fact that she is actively dancing from her father:

> My father's side is more conservative cause they are more religious.... They always want us to be religious teachers, so do not allow us to wear short skirts or have dance classes, they say it's kind of immoral.... So far when I have performances, I won't tell the other side [father's side of the family].... I tell them I am no longer into dancing 'cause I don't want my grandfather to nag at me ... because my grandfather is like a religious teacher last time.... They always think like "punk" songs are immoral, actually we just listen for amusement only, we don't really follow their tradition.... So like they want only those religious songs like those talking about what Islam is all about.... To them, like these songs (popular music), they gain no respect.

Particularly because hip-hop dancing involves a lot of "suggestive" movements and Suriati's choreography tends to come directly or modified from MTV videos that she has seen,

> we follow the trend, so tends to be more sexy ... he [Father] will buy the CDs ("Nashid"[7]) and he will open [switch it on] in the car and we all are forced to listen to it, no choice.... Maybe for my generation, we are not into traditional dance and all [religious music].

The other significant musical influence in Dalilah's and Dahari's life is Dzulkifli and Saiful. Dzulkifli has been with the cheerleading squad in his primary school for about 2 years and has taken a liking to cheerleading as he gets to experiment and learn about different break-dance and hip-hop moves taught by the instructor. His mobile phone is loaded with Linkin Park songs and he often sings with his fellow male cheerleading mates along with the mobile device. Linkin Park is also one of Saiful's favorite pop groups.

As the family travels in the car, Saiful likes to put on CDs of Linkin Park and also pop singers such as Rihanna, including mixed dance tracks. As Saiful describes,

> Mostly in the car because I will fetch the kids everyday and so when I on (switch on) the music, they keep on listening ... like Linkin Park, also those pop bands like Rihanna, like my girl she likes Rihanna ... more to the popular, sellable ones. They are very energetic and they keep singing and don't seem bored and I don't stop them. They will just follow the music. If I like the song, I will sing with them.

Dzulkifli also uses his Sony-Ericsson phone to create mixed dance tracks and will on occasion ask his parents what they thought of his creation. Jamilah, Dzulkifli's mother, in an encouraging tone, had the following response: "Sometimes I don't want to disappoint him, like it's not very nice, so I ask him to try again." Jamilah would also encourage in her own way, the children's artistic pursuits: "I rent dance movies (like the cheerleading movie *Step It Up*) for them to watch, they like the dance steps ... only like musicals, they will be very attracted."

Musical development for Dalilah, Dahari, and Dzulkifli were thus incidental, not something that the parents actively planned for but when interest was shown, the parents were encouraging and supportive, as indicative in their candid remarks:

> I play the music, I didn't ask them to sing but suddenly they just started singing! They are really energetic, they keep singing and they don't seem bored, so I don't stop them because it is music, you know ... and when I like the song, I will sing along with them.

> And then the (elder) brother, he's into dancing ... he also participated in the Malay dance. I was surprised, I didn't know he was in the Malay dance 'cause I don't know how to do it.... I was surprised to find out that my child can really dance, I never really told them to but they did it on their own.

Dalilah, Dahari, and Dzulkifli's parents termed themselves as modern, contemporary Muslims. Through our conversations and interactions, they have expressed that they are perfectly fine with their children pursuing their musical interests, be it Britney Spears or Linkin Park, just like they enjoyed singing and listening to music themselves. To Saiful and Jamilah, music has significance in not just entertaining but bonding everyone in their household.

ON WESTERN CLASSICAL MUSIC AND THE MALAY SILAT

Janah and I were classmates in college and we majored in music and math. She was an avid trumpeter and played in the college symphonic band. Her main instrument was the piano and I recall her wonderful rendition of Chopin's "Barcarolle Op. 60" in our final-year recital. The class also remembered Janah's involvement with the silat (Malay martial art form) as she comes from a strong family lineage of this age-old tradition and competes internationally, winning numerous awards. Janah subsequently taught music in the public secondary school system for 10 years before leaving the service to look after her two daughters (Aisha, age 1; Aida, age 2). The musical lives of Aisha and Aida were of interest to me given their mother's musical interests and active involvement in Western classical music and traditional Malay arts and culture. Organizing to visit their home was relatively simple and straightforward; literally a phone call away, providing easy access to the girls and family members, where I was always greeted with a warm welcome.

Janah and Sharil (Janah's husband) met because of their common interest and passion for silat. Janah comes from a family of silat masters beginning with her grandfather and Sharil is a well-known figure in the silat world. Both Sharil and Janah continue to be very involved in the martial art form and have started *Tapat Suji*, a silat club in Singapore, teaching children to young adults. As Janah pointed out,

> What attracted me initially was the music and seeing people perform with the music, doing the movements.... Originally from the Malay culture and to a certain extent, the Muslim culture ... there are prayers before we start.

Aisha and Aida have been enculturated into the silat culture since birth as Janah would bring them to practices and performances, which occur quite regularly throughout the year. During these performances, there would typically be other musical performances that would include traditional Malay music and dance. Aisha and Aida are thus surrounded by this rich cultural soundscape, which might prove impactful to their growing musical and artistic interests. The club has made Aisha and Aida sets of silat uniforms, which they wear during performance days. As Janah rightly proclaimed, "They are in the company of people who do it [silat] twice or three times a month, they follow us to silat practice!" She professes:

> being a musical person myself, I guess they started their musical education right when they were in me, in the womb ... I sing a lullaby [to them in my womb] right before I sleep and sing to them when I wake. I just make it [the songs] up.

The family home has no shortage of musical instruments. The piano sits comfortably in the living room, with the guitar, kulintang, gendang, child-sized kompang, and maracas all within easy reach for the children. According to Janah,

> Aisha loves the drums, all sorts of drums as long as she gets to play kompang and the gendang. She can identify what the guitar is 'cause whenever the uncle (Janah's younger brother) comes over, she will ask him to play. She identifies the piano as well.

When Janah was still teaching in school, she would occasionally bring the girls with her to band practice. Janah observed that "they will meddle with the percussion, they will look and watch ... pretty well-behaved, just walking around and observing." The television, DVD, and CD player provide the main music source for the children. Aida, at age 2, has already learned to operate the DVD player, putting in her favorite DVDs from the CD sleeves. As Grandma remarked, "She decides what she wants to watch!"

Janah has a habit of singing regularly. She says, "I love to sing when I do work and you know how kids like to imitate what adults do? My daughter is like that [imitating her singing]." Thus, Aisha and Aida are oftentimes surrounded by music and as Janah further explained,

> because we are involved in silat, we like to attend cultural shows ... like Malay traditional performances and dancing and acting, like a musical ... what I am surprised with is they can actually sit through the whole performance, observing, and she [the younger one] goes along with the music has pretty good timing.... She will start dancing and singing.

Janah is aided in this musical endeavor by her husband. The parents create spontaneous songs "to distract the kids when traveling." They also "play music [in the car and at home] that they are familiar with, DVDs like the *Arabic Alphabets* ... and *Barney* or *Thomas the Train*." The *Arabic Alphabet* DVD is essentially a karaoke disc that teaches children to identify the Arabic alphabet through song. Through constant exposure and repetition, Aida, at the tender age of 2, has memorized all the songs on the 90-minute DVD. While she is still unable to pronounce the alphabets accurately, Aida can sing every song with correct pitch and rhythm, along with the appropriate actions and movements portrayed in the visuals. According to the parents, they want the children to be familiar with the alphabet at an early age so that it can assist the children in reading and learning about the Qu'ran as they attend religious classes. The DVD was bought in Malaysia on a relative's recommendation. The *Barney* DVDs present songs that teach about colors, animals, and various other themes that the children enjoy watching and singing along with as well.

Grandma professes to be a fan of musicals, "I know the songs from my generation, musicals like *Mary Poppins*, *My Fair Lady*, at that time there were lots of musicals, Julie Andrews." She would often substitute the words of tunes with the children's names to lull them to sleep, "like *The Rain in Spain*, I will just use their names ... I make the words as I go along, there's no permanent type of, no fixed lyrics." And as Janah remarked, very often "they sing themselves to sleep ... like kitty cats!"

Another favorite activity for Aida is listening and singing to Disney songs. Janah has acquired a picture book cum sing-along CD that consists of lyrics to theme songs from various Disney animation productions. Aida loves to hug her Tigger (tiger plush toy from *Winnie-the-Pooh*) as she flips through the songbook while the music is being played on a portable CD-player. It was clear to me while observing Aida that although she did not comprehend the lyrics, she was sensitive to the mood and expression of the song, singing ever so gently in soft and tender moments and changing dynamics and pace as the song swells and subsides. Aida was also able to pick out the general contour of pitch and rhythm as indicative in the musical example. I was particularly impressed with Aida's ability to sense the rubato in the music and ended the song in synchrony with the accompaniment. Aida was also able to pre-empt the next song on the CD and flipped to the exact page before the music even began.

In studies focusing on children's ability to sing in tune, Welch (2008; Welch, Sergeant, & White, 1998) proposed a model of development divided into four phases, beginning with children focusing on the words of the song rather than the melody and singing with restricted pitch range and melodic phrases, to no significant melodic or pitch errors in relation to relatively simple songs from the singer's musical culture (Welch, 2008, p. 317). It would seem that Aida's singing would fall into the fourth phase proposed by Welch, which would be rather atypical for a 2-year-old. Aida's singing abilities have also developed beyond that observed in Tafuri's (2008) study of 2-year-old children. Tafuri noted that the children "often stopped after a few phrases ... but some of them at the age of two years and two months could sing songs with three complete verses and sing in tune, although the pronunciation of the words was still imprecise" (p. 64).

In speaking with grandma (Janah's mother) about the children and Janah's involvement in music, I sensed that musicking happens every so often in the home. Here are a few summary quotes that I gathered from our conversation on grandma's views of music and Islam:

> Basically from what I've heard from the religious teachers, music is allowed in Islam except that there are restrictions. For example, women should not sing in public because the voice of a woman is what we say "aurat" [what cannot be displayed].... There are some instruments that are not allowed in Islam.... I know [some types of] drums are permissible. And also, music that [brings you into a trance], and of course music with satanic elements. That's why they are not agreeable to heavy metal 'cause they feel there are elements that are not good for the soul.... For me, I don't go for the hard rock and metal music. For us, it is basically ballads, the normal, usual classical, maybe sentimental songs.... I feel my children are well aware of all these [unhealthy influences in terms of certain lyrics] elements and sometimes they just listen for enjoyment to know what is out there. They might just listen to it for pleasure or whatever.... Actually in Indonesia, one of the ways that they spread Islam was through music. So, you know, they cannot say that Islam does not allow music but there are restrictions.... For children, below puberty where they are still considered without sins, that (singing) is

still allowable. But once they reach puberty, they have to observe the restrictions. Because to me in an Islamic way, we should pursue all kinds of knowledge. Music is also a form of knowledge and I have a few relatives who are in the music world [professional musicians].

Music features prominently in the lives of Aisha and Aida. Janah, being musically trained, sings to them constantly and the home environment is filled with musical possibilities from the wide range of instruments available to the music CDs and DVDs of Disney medleys and Arabic alphabet songs. They are also in touch with the traditional Malay arts, being in the heart of silat and surrounded by music and dance. In my encounters with Aisha and Aida at home and in the "field," it was quite clear that musical experiences are carefully framed and selected for learning and sometimes entertainment purposes. Grandma's religious views on music have clearly been modeled through Janah, who in turn has beautifully translated that love of music as knowledge to Aisha and Aida.

IMPLICATIONS

Looking at guidelines on the permissibility or forbiddance of music, we go back to its practice and effects. If we don't use [music according to] Islamic ways or practices, it's forbidden. The effects are vice and sin. But if the practice is correct, and there is no vice, but only ordinary entertainment, or if it can bring someone closer to religion, then there is no problem. (Syed Abdillah Ahmad on *Music & Islam*)

The pervasive and rich musical environment provided by the two contrasting Melayu families leave poignant thoughts about their children's colorful musical lives. Perhaps the controversy and debate involving music and Islam is not such a jarring warning sign after all when one looks at the particular musical lives of these Melayu children in Singapore. Naturally, in a different context and a different locale, the scenario could be very different. It would seem from these two case studies that music is significant in these children's lives with wide variations of course in the selection of genres and styles of music. As personified in each family's religious stance on music, "There is considerable debate among Muslims regarding the permissibility of music (or certain types of music) in Islam.... Muslims identifying a greater religiosity with, among other things, a prohibition on music or particular forms of music" (Adely, 2007, p. 1671).

In Adely (2007) and Herrera's (2000) conversations with Muslim students in Jordan and Egypt on issues of permissibility of music in Islam, it was clear that "no one is certain what is forbidden or what is accepted which is why students are in a constant state of discussion and interpretation of these issues" (Herrera, 2000, p. 160). An understanding of the particular interpretations such as those highlighted in the above-mentioned case studies would open up constructive conversations for students and music educators that are contextually meaningful, grounded in actual experience.

It is clear from the encounters with these children that technology and the media fuel their musical interests and oftentimes provide them with creative ideas and learning possibilities. As Roberts and Foehr (2008) pointed out,

> The label "Media Generation" fits today's young people. More than any past generation, they have access to a wide, and still expanding, array of media--in their homes, in their rooms, and, with the emergence of minia-turization, in their backpacks and pockets. They devote more time to media than to any other single activity with the exception of sleep. (p. 30)

The parents are able at this stage in the children's lives, if they choose, to some extent control what comes to the eyes and ears of their children. This is evident in the types of media and technological exposure selected or left free to children's consumption in the two families. But one has to admit that media musical influences are abundant and all around and it would really be up to the children to discern which they choose to listen to or engage in as they grow older.

Looking back at my impetus to undertake this study, what have I learned from Aisha (age 1), Aida (age 2), Dahari (age 5), Dalilah (age 6), and Dzulkifli (age 11) is each individual child is engaged in music with great enthusiasm at home, singing and dancing wholeheartedly from Disney tunes to the latest hits on the pop charts. Each individual family has their own religious (Islamic) interpretation of what music can mean in their lives. Since music is readily accepted and celebrated in the household, it should also be part of these children's learning experiences in school. A localized understanding of the musical lives of these children give legitimacy to me as a music educator to think about what should or should not be included in music lessons in respect of diversity, allowing for what Jorgenson (2003) termed as a particularistic approach to music education, drawing upon "cultural richness of the places in which it is conducted and provides a sense of connectedness of people to the places in which they were born and live" (p. 65).

RESEARCHER'S REFLECTION ON METHODOLOGY: ISSUES WITH GAINING ACCESS

The two case studies present a snapshot of my continual research in examining and reflecting on young Melayu/Muslim children's engagement in music within the Singaporean context. The entry point came from my encounter with the children of long-term friends and colleagues that proved to be significant in gaining better access, particularly since I was delving into a subject matter that can be seen as sensitive to some local Melayu/Muslim families. Subsequent contact with other Melayu families came through introductions from the same set of friends and colleagues, pointing to the significance of snowball sampling for this particular project.

Gaining access is oftentimes much harder then it seems. Along the way, I met with a few bumps. An initial interview set up with a close friend and her children failed to materialize because she had not anticipated after speaking with her husband that he would take issue with me speaking with her on religious views on music and conversing/observing their children in musical play. Subsequently, I decided not to pursue the interview. An enquiry through another close Malay/Muslim ex-colleague to speak with an Imam (religious teacher) also failed to materialize. According to my ex-colleague, the Imam was not comfortable conversing with me in English. Instead, she offered to pass me reading materials that speak to the topic of music and Islam instead. After several phone calls and e-mail exchanges, I did not receive any information and decided not to push for further contact.

It was also important for me to know that the children and parents were not guarded by my presence and were willing to share their views freely, ensuring that all participants were "willing to share everything, warts and all, with the researcher" (Janesick, 1994). This can only be achieved through prolonged engagement and an emphasis on the value of personal contributions, as suggested by Shenton and Hayter (2004). Prolonged engagement being "over time, any sense of threat that may accompany the researcher's presence will diminish and, with careful handling, erroneous associations which may be made between the investigator and authority figures will be revealed to be unjustified" while value of personal contributions refer to the researcher attempting to "to ensure that he or she is not wildly incongruous within the world of the participants or in terms of the culture of the organization in which he or she is operating" (p. 228). In my interpretation, prolonged engagement comes from my long-term friendship with the mothers and my continued interaction with their children. Born and bred in Singapore, I have a good understanding of the local culture, which qualifies me in the value of personal contributions. Since there is no general consensus on the stance of Islam on music, the descriptions and particular experiences of the musical lives of these children will allow a localized and intimate look at what music can mean for Malay Muslims in Singapore.

The other pertinent issue to point out is being a male researcher in the field. When observing children in their homes, I am always conscious to ensure that either one of the parents are within eyeshot of the children. I never step into the bedrooms of the children without explicit permission from the parents and likewise, one of the parents will have to be in the room with the children. In play encounters where I am invited to participate by the children, I will also be mindful of my proximity to them, ensuring any unnecessary body contact. While it seems almost clinical, these are necessary ethical concerns that I have to be mindful of as a male researcher working with young children. Admittedly because of these restrictions, the data collection process involving observations and interviews of the children may be compromised in terms of the presence of the parents and me in the natural setting. I have, however, found that a prolonged period of contact with the children seems to bring out better communication and diffuse the researcher and parental effect. This is often indicated through the children's interaction with me, for instance, the casual tone in their conversations with me or cutting in on conversations I am having with parents, often unabashedly urging me to play with them.

The use of the video camera and audio recorder in the nooks and crannies where the children "hung out" was a common sight for the children from the beginning of the research project. The intention was to allow the children to be desensitized to the audio and video equipment after repeated exposure. Pointing the video camera directly at camera-shy children while they were engaged in musical behaviors, however, had the potential to cause anxiety and often resulted in the children's refusal to be recorded. Other than recording at the periphery of ongoing musical behaviors, I devised a system of recording where children felt less intimidated when faced directly with the camcorder. Instead of holding up the camcorder at eye level, I used the LCD screen to focus on the recording while placing the camcorder at the level of the unraised hand. This level corresponded to the beltline, so was a good distance below the face, thus affording an opportunity to maintain eye contact. The camcorder was placed in record mode as I conversed with the child as he or she was engaged in musical activities. This appeared to reduce the child's anxiety significantly and in many instances, allowed me to record musical behaviors uninterrupted. The child could then choose to replay what was recorded and have the option of deleting or retaining the material.

Also, the children were free to take the video camera off my hands anytime they wished to film themselves, their siblings, parents, and any other subject matter during the recording process. Not surprisingly, many of them did and had a fun time filming themselves singing, joking, and so on. This helped to diffuse the artificial video-recording setting, making the video camera part of the children's play. While I acknowledge that the use of video can never be "invisible" to the children (Graue & Walsh, 1998) and that there was a tendency for some children to "act" while being recorded, it is in my opinion that the constant exposure and familiarity with the use of the video camera had reduced children's heightening of behavior as it became less of a novelty to them at this unobtrusive level.

NOTES

1. Britney refers to Britney Spears, the American singer.
2. Raihan ("Fragrance of Heaven" in Arabic) is a prominent Malaysian Nashid (see note 4) group.
3. Syed Abdillah Ahmad is the late Ustaz (teacher of religion), a much-respected teacher and Islamic scholar in Singapore. This quotation comes from a CD recording of a teaching on *Music & Islam* by the Ustaz and is translated into English from Malay by Rohaniah Saini. No known date was stated on the CD and within the content of the CD.
4. A clarification on the term "hadith" is given by Hilarian (2006a) in which he states, "There are two meanings to the term hadith. The first usage refers to the Arabic word that literally means to "communicate," "a story," "conversation," or "historical events." This word has been used 23 times in the Qu'ran. The second meaning is used more widely and it refers to the "sayings" of the Prophet. This latter meaning of the hadith is a compilation of over a thousand narratives of the Prophet that has been compiled and recorded by the Companions of the Prophet, between 100 and 150 years after his death. In some ways, an analogy can be drawn to the Gospels of the New Testament, which is also a collection of "sayings" of Jesus according to the teachings of the apostles" (p. 62).
5. Orchard Road is a road in Singapore that houses the main retail and entertainment facilities of the city-state.
6. "Womanizer" is a song performed by Britney Spears.
7. "Damaged" is a song performed by American R&B group Danity Kane.
8. *High School Musical* is a Disney-produced musical about two high school juniors from rival cliques.
9. "Nashid" is an Islamic-oriented song. Traditionally, it is sung a cappella, accompanied only by a *daff* (drum). This musical style is used because many Muslim scholars interpret Islam as prohibiting the use of musical instruments except for some basic percussion. A new generation of "Nashid" artists use a wide variety of musical instruments in their art. This has caused controversy among the Muslim community because of the vast range of scholarly opinions that exist on music in Islam (Shiloah, 2000). These range from absolutely no music and singing, to that of any musical instruments allowed so long as the subject matter is of an Islamic ethos.

REFERENCES

Adely, F. J. (2007). Is music haram?: Jordanian girls educating each other about nation, faith, and gender in school. *Teachers College Record, 109*(70), 1663–1681.

Baig, K. (2008). *Slippery stone: An inquiry into Islam's stance on music*. Garden Grove, CA: Openmind Press.

Graue, M. E., & Walsh, D. J. (1998). *Studying children in context: Theories, methods and ethics*. Thousand Oaks, CA: SAGE.

Herrera, L. A. (2000). *The sanctity of the school: New Islamic education and modern Egypt*. Unpublished doctoral dissertation, Columbia University.

Hilarian, L. F. (2006a). The folk lute (Gambus), and its symbolic expression in Malay Muslim culture. *Folklore Studies, 32*, 50–65.

Hilarian, L. F. (2006b). The significance of the Hadhrami Arab contributions and influences on Melayu music, culture and Islamic practices. In R. Statelova, A. Rodel, L. Peycheva, I. Vlaeva, & V. Dimov (Eds.), *The human world and musical diversity: Proceedings from the fourth meeting of the ICTM study group "Music and Minorities."* Bulgaria: Institute of Art Studies, Bulgarian Academy of Science.

Hilarian, L. F. (2007, August). *The migration of lute-type instruments to the Malay Muslim World*. Paper presented at the Music in the World of Islam conference, Assilah.

Janesick, V. J. (1994). The dance of qualitative research design: metaphor, methodolatry and meaning. In N. K. Denzin, & Y. S. Lincoln (Eds.), *Handbook of qualitative research* (pp. 209–219). Thousand Oaks, CA: SAGE.

Jorgenson E. R. (2003). *Transforming music education*. Bloomington: Indiana University Press.

Rahman, S. A. (Ed.). (2002). *In quest of excellence: A story of Singapore Malays*. Singapore: KepMedia International Pte. Ltd.

Roberts, D. F., & Foehr, U. G. (2008). Trends in media use. *The Future of Children, 18*(1), 11–37.

Shenton, A. K., & Hayter, S. (2004). Strategies for gaining access to organizations and informants in qualitative studies. *Education for Information, 22*, 223–231.

Shiloah, A. (1995). *Music in the world of Islam: A socio-cultural study*. Aldershot, England: Scolar Press.

Tafuri, J. (2008). *Infant musicality: New research for educators and parents*. Surrey, England: Ashgate.

Welch, G. F. (2008). Singing and vocal development. In G. McPherson (Ed.), *The child as musician* (pp. 311–329). New York: Oxford University Press.

Welch, G. F., Sergeant, D. C., & White, P. (1998). The role of linguistic dominance in the acquisition of song. *Research Studies in Music Education, 10*, 67–74.

CHAPTER 5

KI-AK-MU AS THE BASIS FOR INTEGRATED ARTS CLASS FOR KOREAN CHILDREN

Curriculum Construction and Application

Young-Youn Kim

KI-AK-MU:
KOREAN MUSIC EDUCATIONAL CONCEPT OF INTEGRATION

In a mural painting in a tumulus found in *Chipan* of *Koguryo* during the period of the Three Kingdoms (57 B.C. to A.D. 668), three ladies and two male dancers were portrayed accompanying a chorus. Historical record suggested that the man with a hat in the chorus seemed to be the conductor (Chosunilbosa, 1995). Also, the mural paintings of Tomb number three in *Anak*, located in the farther northern part of *Yalu* river (bearing the inscribed date of A.D. 357) depict several instruments like a zither, a lute, and a long vertical flute with three seated musicians accompanying a dancer (H. Lee, 1981). All of these wall paintings prove that music and dance coexisted during this time of old Korea and implies that music and dance integration are expected in Korean music education (Ahn, 1998; Y.

Musical Childhoods of Asia and the Pacific, pp. 75–99
Copyright © 2012 by Information Age Publishing
All rights of reproduction in any form reserved.

Y. Kim, 2002; H. Lee, 1981). A specific Korean terminology, *Ki-ak-mu* (in Korean alphabet Han'gul, 기악무), identifies individual syllables of the term to mean "instrument" (*ki*) or "talent" (*ki*), "music" (*ak*), and "dance" (*mu*). The word as a whole implies the need for artistic integration.

There is a historical record that reports that a musician as well as dancer named *Mimaji* who had lived in *Paekche* Dynasty during the Three Kingdoms period of *Koguryo, Packjae, and Silla* (57 B.C. ~ A.D. 668) in old Korea taught a mask dance named Ki-ak-mu to the children who lived in Japan (Doosan Chíulpíansa, 2007). In the *Silla* dynasty (up to A.D. 936), the word *Ak*, meaning music, always meant both performance in music and dance. Also, it was told that during the *Chosun(Yi)* dynasty (A.D. 1392–1593), the styles and repertoire of instrumental and singing performance and dance differed depending up the social classes in which each artist belonged but music and dance always coexisted without exception. This was called either *Ak-ka-mu* or Ki-ak-mu dance (Han, 2000). Within Korean music educational terminology, Ki-ak-mu is commonly quoted among Korean people in arts-related fields, which supports the notion of integrated arts. Thus, the thought of Ki-ak-mu stimulated this researcher's attention to the topic of integration in arts education for young children in Korea.

Integration is not a new research topic among early childhood educators and researchers in Korea, both within music and the visual arts. Previous research on curricular integration emphasized the integrative method but only from theoretical perspectives, with little attention to preschool conditions (S. Kim, 2008). Early childhood education scholars and practitioners will do well to consider concept-based integration in the arts from the following perspectives: What kind of educational elements should be integrated? In what practical ways does the teacher integrate the arts with other experiences and understandings? When and where should the integration be done? And what is the final goal of concept-based integration[1] in the arts for young children?

There are many questions regarding concept-based arts integration instruction for young children. According to previous research in Korea (M. Kim, 2007; Park, 2004), preschool teachers generally agree to a need for integrated arts, but they have reported that they have little knowledge as to how to develop it. In other words, there is lack of knowledge and skills about integration among the preschool teachers in practical teaching situations. Thus, a theoretical study on curriculum integration that pays tribute to stimulate educators' thoughtful focus on this topic is required, especially in the field of early childhood education.

From a review of related literature, it becomes clear that the focus be given to concept-based arts integration instruction (Y. Y. Kim, 2002; Y. O. Kim, 2008). The selection of a concept is the starting point of an early childhood teacher's educational philosophy and practice. The array of shared concepts in the arts need also to be considered by those working in early childhood education in conjunction with specialists in music, dance, drama, and the visual arts. Since a preschool is annexed to the college where this chapter author works as dean and professor, the professional opportunity was available for building an integrative early childhood curriculum with experts in the arts. Thus, an arts integration curricular model was developed for in-service early childhood teachers in arts integration based on the shared consensus among scholars in the arts area.

From past teaching experiences, the author found that integrated musical experiences have the potential to make children more emotionally sensitive to others. In communicating with people around them, such integration may help children to be creative cognitively, socially, physically, and emotionally. This global view of learning through connected experiences across subjects underscores the value of the integrated approach and brings teachers toward the goal of early childhood education (S. Kim, 2008; Y. O. Kim, 2008).

Thus, the purposes of this current chapter are multiple. First, to articulate a concept-based music, movement, and art-integrated curriculum for preschool children in Korea. Second, to apply this integrated curriculum to children in practical teaching settings. Finally, to analyze children's interests and responses from the facilitated integrated activities so as to provide preschool teachers with a better understanding of a concept-based integrated arts curriculum. This chapter focuses on the following questions:

- What is a concept-based integrated arts curriculum for young children?
- How do children respond as they experience the concept-based integrated arts program?

EARLY CHILDHOOD MUSIC EDUCATION IN KOREA

In the academic field of early childhood education, integration is considered to be an important and effective approach. Early childhood educators have often claimed that it is undesirable to isolate music from other subjects, such as literature, play, movement, and the visual arts (Jang, 2007; Y. O. Kim, 2008). Based on the notion of developing the child's whole personality as an educational goal, early childhood educators value the process-oriented approach when they design arts education curriculum. This implies that children's experience of the arts is educationally valuable regardless of the result of certain activities. Thus, attention to the integration of total experiences is strongly recommended by the national curriculum for young children in Korea (Korean Ministry of Education and Human Resources Development, 2007; Korean Ministry of Education, Science and Technology Development, 2008).

Recently, in the field of early childhood education in Korea, some aspects from postmodern approaches in educational thoughts have raised the value of social contexts of learning in equivalence with the educational content of lessons, besides the notion of developmentally appropriate practice that was proposed by the National Association of Education for Young Children (NAEYC). It is a well-known fact that until the late 1970s, psychologists engaged in child development research accentuated a Piagetian perspective with regard to children's general and musical development. However, postmodernists emphasized the importance of the teachers' understanding of children's individuality or good character through the understanding of the child's surrounding environment and cultural context (Bruner, 1995). Thus, teachers of young children in Korea should look into the social and cultural contexts of children's learning. Arts-oriented integration may help to develop an understanding of individual preschoolers in their developing years.

Music is an important part of a child's daily life (Nye, 1975). Specialists in early childhood music education can address the needs of cultural transmission not only through music but also through movement as espoused by Dalcroze's Eurhythmic teaching method. It is a well-known fact that Dalcroze, a piano pedagogy specialist, emphasized a music learning method through accompanied movement (Dalcroze, 1921). Andress (1989) and Metz (1989) declared that music should not be taught in isolation to young children. S. Lee (2007) mentioned similar findings from her study on the effects of integrating movement with Korean music. In the field of early childhood education, the integration of music with other subjects such as literature and social studies should be reconsidered by early childhood education specialists (Jang, 2007; Yang, 2008). Campbell and Scott-Kassner (2006) explained integration as occurring within music, within the arts, and in subjects across the curriculum, from math and sciences to social studies and the language arts.

In this study, integration is limited to the realm of the arts, especially music, movement, and a sprinkling of the visual arts. Teachers of young children need to know about the selection of age-appropriate repertoire, adequate teaching time, and spots for the efficient delivery of these activities with ease during the school day. So there is need for a case study with regard to knowing how children respond to and express what they know about aspects or characteristics of music from the activities derived from an arts-integrated curriculum involving music, movement, and visual art. In this study, integration in music and movement is more strongly observed and discussed than the integration of music with visual arts, although the researcher's initial attention was to all three areas of music, movement, and visual arts. Interestingly, the results of the study corresponded to the Korean arts educational philosophy of Ki-ak-mu.

MUSICAL CONCEPTS AND CHILD MUSICAL DEVELOPMENT

Over the last 20 years, music educators have been providing diverse musical activities in their approaches to teaching musical concepts such as rhythm and melody. These musical concepts are the framework for children's musical thinking and understanding. Musical concepts become central to the music educational content of a curriculum (Andress, 1989; Y. H. Kim, 1982; H. Lee, 2002). McDonald and Ramsey (1992) said that experiencing the various musical elements help children to understand musical concepts. They noted that teachers of young children are guiding their children to access various types and styles of music, and are instrumental in helping lead children to conceptualize music fundamentals and the interrelationships of musical structures and forms. Thus, it follows that music is a fundamental subject in early childhood education.

Campbell and Scott-Kassner (2006) addressed the major concepts and subconcepts of music in detail. According to them, major concepts of music to be introduced to children are rhythm, melody, form, timbre, dynamics, quality of expression, and texture, while beat, duration, accent, meter, and rhythmic patterns are the subconcepts or elements of rhythm. Their explanation continues that repetition, improvisation, and contrast are the subconcepts of form, while terms like "monophonic" and "polyphonic" are the subconcepts of texture, and "tempo" and "dynamics" are encompassed within the quality of expression. A recent study by Marsh (2008) mentioned the importance of integration by stating that when music activity is accompanied by movement, musical activity is enhanced and intensified. Thus, teachers need to know what musical elements are applied to their selection of teaching method and content.

Teachers of young children need to consider the children's musicality in light of broader educational notions: teaching amount, speed, and level applied to children in preschool settings. There are obvious differences from age to age. For example, 3-year-old children can control their singing voice and express pitch, loudness, beat, and tempo changes and they can express simple rhythmic patterns. However, children above 3 years of age form musical concepts and develop this ability more delicately and at an advanced level when compared to younger children (Haines & Gerber, 1992).

MOVEMENT CONCEPTS AND MOVEMENT DEVELOPMENT

Movement is a fundamental body experience and the instinctive body language that is capable of expressing one's emotion. Movement education is intended to build self-esteem through kinesthetic activities. The purpose of movement education is to develop the individual's capacity to use the body as a moving instrument (Laban, 1963; Y. Lee, 2004), particularly as a means of creative development. It is a well-known fact that movement helps children to recognize the relationship between their surrounding environment and the things around them so as to express their feelings and emotions with ease (Holt, 1988; Paek, 2005).

Just as in music education, the teacher's acquaintance with movement concepts and elements is also emphasized in movement education (Laban, 1948; Park, 2004; Pica, 1995). Major concepts of movement education are the body's power or effort, space, and the relationship among these (Laban, 1948; Pica, 1995). The body concept helps children to understand themselves, and can be divided into the "whole body" concept versus "body as parts." In movement expression, children can know about their bodies as an independent feature of themselves, and recognize how to express or control their feelings and thoughts through their bodies. For this reason, children need kinesthetic movement experience from an early age.

Akin to music education, under the major concepts of body, power, and space, there are subelements such as movement and nonmovement, gesture with whole or partial body, and forms in straight, curve, twisted, and contrast movements (E. Kim, 2004). The concept of space means both direction and location. The flow concept consists of two types: one allows quick stops and the other deals with moving forward. There is individual space one can reach and public space out of personal reach. People with a strong understanding of space can move without collision with others and perform fast movement with height (Laban, 1948). Also they can communicate and coordinate with partners or with props such as hula-hoops or exercise balls (Choksy, Abramson, Gillespie, & Wood, 1986). The concept of effort means appropriate moving in time. Power and flow are the subconcepts of effort (Laban, 1948). The concept of time includes tempo and appropriate rhythm of body movement, while the concept of power or weight means the degree of muscle tension when people change position or balance.

As explained, since there are many concepts related to kinesthetic activity, it is necessary for young children to experience these movement concepts through diverse movement experiences. Experiencing diverse movement allows children to begin with reflective movement to novice movement and then fundamental movement, and finally onto expert movement. Reflective movement is instinct, unconscious movement such as sucking, direct changing, and grasping. Usually, immediate movement protects a child from danger. Novice movement looks insecure at first and appears slightly more developed up to the age of 2. It includes grounding with elbow and hips, fingers, and knees or intended movement such as walking. Movement such as stretching hands or grasping things develops continuously from ages 2–7. During this period, children stretch, giggle, and jump in a rather secure posture and develop the ability to throw and grab a ball. But the expert movement develops past the age of 7 (Feldman, 2006) and the difficulty level of movement increases as the child gets older. For example, 4-year-olds are more secure and easy in their movement control ability compared to 3-year-olds. They begin to control movement tempo, performing jumps, turning around, and galloping without hesitation.

KI-AK-MU, EARLY CHILDHOOD MUSIC AND MOVEMENT INTEGRATION RESEARCH IN KOREA

Moog (1976) explained that the child has the ability of rhythmic expression through various types of kinesthetic movement. For example, 3-year-olds can move with balance while listening to music, and they demonstrate their walking ability with and without toes (S. Yu, 2001). Musically, 3-year-olds can play with the xylophone, stay with one foot on the balance bar, and move forward when they have another's assistance. They can perform singing and finger games at the same time, or sometimes make creative scenes with music. During this time, children are ready to follow the rules of singing games and movement, to verify the tempo, dynamics, and more. Children can modify music with movement easier in faster tempos than in slower ones (Campbell & Scott-Kassner, 2002). Thus, it becomes easy for children at this age to understand the concepts of time, space, power, and movement (Gordon, 1990; S. Lee, 2007; Lee & Lee, 1997).

There is considerable research on the integrative method of teaching within early childhood education in Korea. S. Kim (1995) conducted her research on the effect of movement on children's musicality development and reported positive relationships between these two variants of movement and musicality. Im (2001) advocated the importance of integrated program development as a way toward children's musical understanding. She reported that children showed strong interest in music-and-movement-integrated activities in their preschool class. She derived that a concept-based music and movement integration could help children's musical understanding overall. M. Lee (2001) reported that movement was the most appropriate way to express children's feelings and that

84.6% of the subjects in her study preferred the integration of music and movement activities to the isolated activity of music or movement. Shin (2005) conducted her research on the relationship between movement as applied to music listening and children's improvement of creative impulses. Park (2004) examined the relationship between music listening with movement and children's musicality and emotional quotient changes. They reported that there was a positive relationship between these variants. Recently, M. Kim (2007) conducted her research on music listening with movement and reported its positive effect on children's musical aptitude and creativity. From these research studies, it can be seen that research focused on the music—movement or music—art integration methods of teaching, but did not specify the aspects of music, movement, or visual arts that need to be integrated. Also, the paucity of research on concept-based arts integration in early childhood calls for the pursuit of questions on the topic.

A CASE STUDY: KI-AK-MU IN AN INTEGRATED ARTS CURRICULUM

This qualitative case study aimed to construct a concept-based music, movement, and arts-integrated curriculum for 4- and 5-year-old children and to apply this as a way of understanding young children's musical responses. Thus, this is a qualitative study in general but a case study specifically. According to Bresler and Stake (2006), qualitative research as a general term shares certain characteristics of noninterventionist observation in natural settings, highly contextual description of people and events, and validation of information through triangulation. The study focuses on a specific preschool annexed to a university in Korea. The integrated activities were provided by arts specialist teachers for fifteen 4- and 5-year-old children. Children were provided with lessons of individual movement, craft, and music each week. The researcher conducted participant observation of music lessons and nonparticipant observation for dance and craft lessons. Each lesson plan was designed by three faculty members: one from each of the departments of dance, arts, and early childhood education. They had regular meetings prior to each lesson. Discussion was focused on the shared concept of three different arts areas and the activity contents. These plans were applied to the children in every lesson. The data gathered from each lesson were analyzed by the researcher according to the child's interest in and responses (verbal and nonverbal) to the integrated musical activities. Field notes written by the researcher focused on children's response, interest level, and music behavioral features.

Descriptions from interviews with mothers and teachers were utilized for interpretation of the research results.

PARTICIPANTS

Participants in this study were 15 children: seven 4-year-olds (three girls and four boys) and eight 5-year-olds (four girls and four boys). The children were attending Forest Park daycare center annexed to Forest Park University in Busan, South Korea. Most children in Forest Park daycare were from middle-class families, and parents of children were seen as devoted to their children. Busan is the second largest city in Korea, a port on the southeastern coast of the Korean peninsula. The children were taught by three special teachers, faculty members and their assistants in music, movement, and visual arts from the various departments of dance, visual arts, and early childhood. The researcher observed each class every week and wrote journals from her observations while the faculty members, including the researcher, constructed the integrated arts curriculum and the three special teachers applied this curriculum.

PROCEDURE

This study was comprised of three stages. In the first stage, in order to build an integrated curriculum that was appropriate for 4- and 5-year-old children, several meetings were held involving three departments and three assistants from the departments of dance, visual art, and early childhood education. In each meeting, they worked together to construct an integrated arts curriculum with consideration of the shared concepts (e.g., loudness) of music, movement, and visual arts and the selected monthly early childhood curriculum theme (e.g., animals) recommended by the Korean Ministry of Education. The developmental characteristics selected from the review of literature both on music education and movement education were also reflected in the curriculum. The second stage was to apply this concept-based integrated arts curriculum to the preschool setting. This occurred over 15 weeks, from April 1, 2008, to August 15, 2008. There were 45 integrated arts classes during the research period. In the final stage, the features of children's interest in and responses to these arts-integrated activities were analyzed. The flow chart of the research procedure is in Figure 5.1.

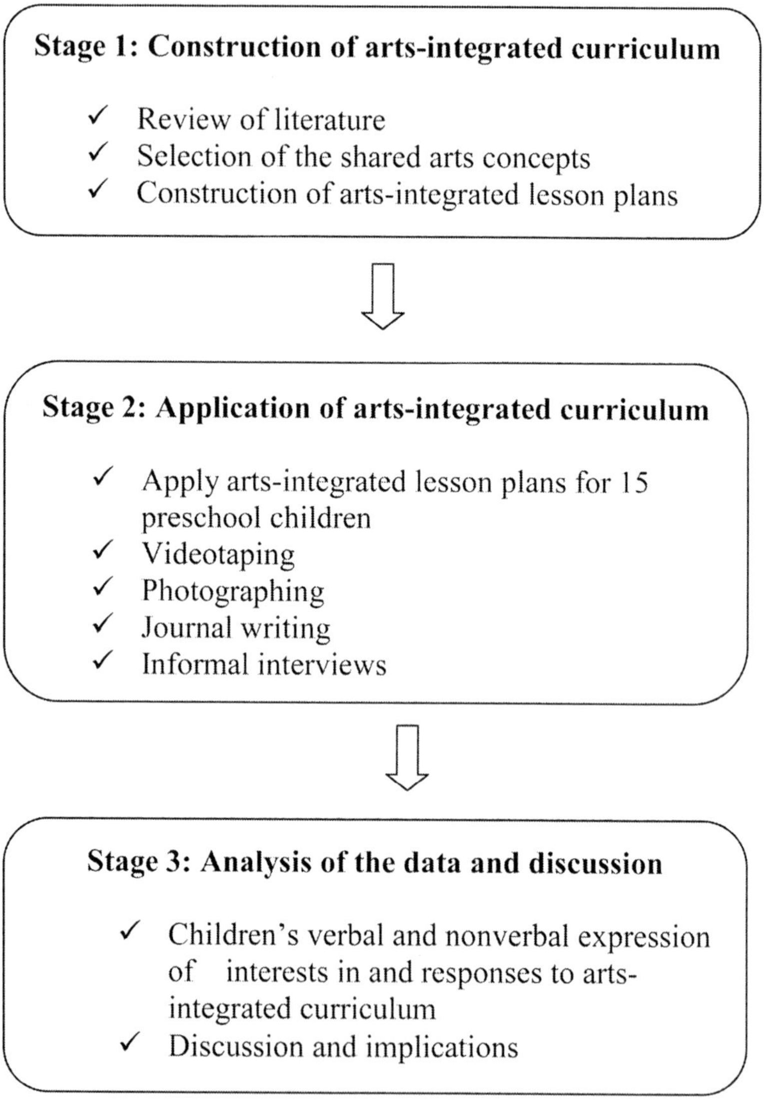

Stage 1: Construction of arts-integrated curriculum

- ✓ Review of literature
- ✓ Selection of the shared arts concepts
- ✓ Construction of arts-integrated lesson plans

Stage 2: Application of arts-integrated curriculum

- ✓ Apply arts-integrated lesson plans for 15 preschool children
- ✓ Videotaping
- ✓ Photographing
- ✓ Journal writing
- ✓ Informal interviews

Stage 3: Analysis of the data and discussion

- ✓ Children's verbal and nonverbal expression of   interests in and responses to arts-integrated curriculum
- ✓ Discussion and implications

Figure 5.1.   Research procedure.

DATA COLLECTION AND ANALYSIS

Data were collected via videotaping, photographing, and reflective jour-nal-writing; these procedures occurred during or following the observa-tion and informal interviews with mothers and teachers. Each lesson was observed and videotaped, and after each lesson, the researcher and teach-ers met to discuss the research and plan upcoming classes. Videotaping provides insight into interpersonal relationships and participants' social interactions (M. Lee, 2001, 2002). The recordings also made it possible for unlimited review of particular episodes to assist with the interpreta-tion of data. The researcher completed her journal-writing as soon as pos-sible after the observation of each class. The research was conducted over 15 weeks (April through August). During each week, there were three 50-minute lessons of music, movement, and visual arts in the mid-afternoon on Mondays, Wednesdays, and Thursdays.

As shown in Figure 5.2, the play room is rectangular in shape and spa-cious enough for 60 children. It has many small windows allowing fresh air to flow with ease. In the corner of the play room, there is a slide and a large toy house. Also there is one upright piano, CD players, projectors, and various rhythm instruments such as tambourines, rhythm sticks, tri-angles, and shakers, and activity aids such as *hansam* (a sleeve part of Korean costume). There are also rhythm cards and music scores in order to help children's understanding of musical knowledge.

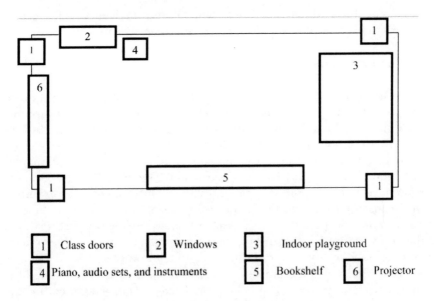

Figure 5.2. Map of playroom.

Participant as well as nonparticipant observation was conducted by the researcher during each lesson. For example, the researcher assisted teacher and children during musical activities but sat quietly during the visual arts activities. Each lesson followed the concept-based integrated arts curriculum, which was designed by the experts from the departments of dance, art, and music. During regular meetings, they determined the weekly shared concepts that were to be emphasized as well as the monthly theme derived from the Korean national preschool curriculum. Members of the team selected the activity content, which was spread across the three different arts areas. Videotaping and photographing were undertaken by assistants who are in-service classroom teachers of Forest Park daycare center. The researcher completed journal writing from the observations of each class. The data were analyzed according to the children's interests in and responses to the integrated arts curriculum. Children's verbal and nonverbal expression denoting their interests and responses were categorized and coded. For example, when a child said "Teacher, can we jump up when the words *Aeich'wi* ("Ah-choo" in English) comes up?", this expression was coded as children's positive response and is explained in detail later in this chapter.

RESULTS

Results of this study are reported in two parts: curriculum construction and curriculum application (with children's interests and responses).

Curriculum Construction

An integrated arts curriculum was constructed with consideration of the shared concepts of music and movement and the selected monthly early childhood curriculum theme recommended by the Korean Ministry of Education. In addition, the developmental characteristics selected from the review of literature both on music and movement education were also reflected in the curriculum construction. The team of area specialists subscribed to the shared musical and movement elements. For example, they consented that tempo in musical concept corresponds to time in movement concept and loudness relates to power, while contrast relates to direction. Figure 5.3 shows the shared concepts of music and movement and their application to the construction of a lesson plan.

When the research team designed the integrated lesson plans, three things were targeted: the weekly curricular theme suggested by the Korean Government, the selection of shared music-movement concepts for the planned activities, and the consideration of children's perfor-

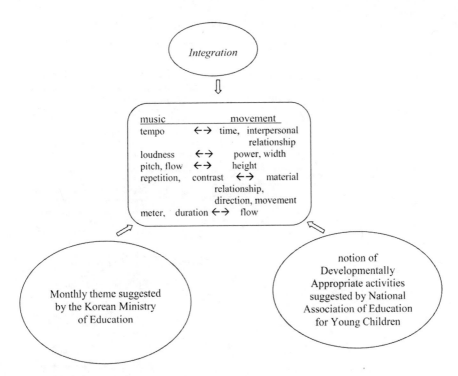

Figure 5.3. Correspondent integrated elements of music and movement.

mance ability. Table 5.1 is an example of a concept-based integrated curriculum applied over a period of 4 weeks during the month of July 2008. This lesson was designed for the 4- and 5-year-olds under the monthly theme of "Animal."

As a result of the application of the integrated curricular model, 4- and 5-year-old children exhibited high levels of interest in the concept-based music and movement learning. The musical activities allowed for integration of other expressions (i.e., voluntarily exploring and repetitively trying the activities with expression of the concept experienced in other classes). The lesson plan shown in Table 5.1 is further detailed in Table 5.2.

Table 5.3 is an example of a concrete, integrated lesson plan for the teacher's instant usage for children. This includes the class objective, the shared concepts of music and movement, and the teaching method.

As shown in Table 5.3, the application of the integrated arts curriculum consisted of three stages: opening, exposition, and closing. In the opening stage, children in the class are motivated by singing and rhythmic movement in order to destress and free up any tension, as well as to get ready for the main class. Usually this opening lasts for about 10 minutes.

Table 5.1.   Devised Arts-Integrated Curriculum

Monthly Theme	Animal			
Objective	From these integrated classes, children's creativity can be stimulated by imagination of the animal's movement. In movement that is related to the concept of power, children learn to fall down, roll and keep suspension. As muscle control develop through experience, children become sensitive to the ways of control and thus change their power deliberately. Also while they are making various poses of animals through clay art, children can experience joyfulness in the outcome of their effort at clay. In music class, the teacher may ask children to investigate the sounds in different parts of the body, and to transfer to the child nearby or create these sounds. From such activity, children become sensitive to the diverse sound sources in their surroundings.			
Month	# of Week	Shared Concept	Activity	Contents
6	1	Power/ Loudness & Dynamics/ Tempo	Movement: Visit the zoo	To imagine animal movement and expression of animal sounds
			Arts: Animal frame making *	To make giraffe shaped frame with a rolling clay panel
			Music: Peter and the wolf	To listen to the story of Peter and the wolf to learn about different instruments on the screen
	2		Movement: Animals in the prairie	To recognize movement of animals
			Arts: Pottery making *	To decorate the shape of sheep on the edge of a pot
			Music: Peter and the wolf	To remake the story with characters from Peter and the wolf. To decide on timbre and instrumentation
	3		Movement: Flying like birds	To use sharp and light power
			Arts: Animal world in fairy tales *	To draw animals on a farm freely on the paper as a group
			Music: Peter and wolf III	To sing the theme of the story. To play-act the theme of the story To make the properties of the characters from the story
	4		Movement: Deep and blue river	To experience flow of strong and soft power
			Arts: Animal vase making *	To make a vase with mold and decorate on the vase surface with animals
			Music: Ensemble	To play/act/move/sing in a music drama

* denotes visual arts class. Although the weekly schedule of the children's integrated arts class consisted of three class days of movement, visual arts and music, this discussion will limit to music and movement integration, because visual arts was weakly issued to children in this study. .

During the second stage of 35 minutes, children were asked to move freely to selected recorded music, according to the shared music and movement concept under investigation after learning and practice from the teacher's guidance. Then they move to the final lesson stage, playing mostly rhythmic instruments such as *Sogo* (small Korean hand drum) and shakers. The total class time was 50 minutes, but the timing remained flexible according to the children's moods and responses. To increase children's attention and interest, resources such as balloons, stickers, and ribbons were utilized in the class.

Table 5.2. Music and Movement Integrated Elements and Activity Applied

	Integrated elements		Activity
Rhythm	Duple Meter	Duple + Whole Body Things (Relationship)	To move body or things according to duple meter
	Duple Meter	Duple + Partial Body Whole Body	To move whole body or partial body according to duple meter
	Duration	Duration + Time	To move body or things according to duration change
Melody	Flow	Flow + Height	To move body high and low according to the tune flow
	Pitch	Pitch + Height	To move high and low according to the pitch
Form	Repetition	Repetition, Contrast + Relation	To move things according to the forms of repetition and contrast
	Phrase	Phrase + Direction Changing Movement	To change direction according to phrase. To perform changing movement
Timbre		Timber + Whole, Power	To perform body expressions according to the timbre of the instruments
Quality of Expression	Loudness	Loudness + Power	To move body or things according to loudness
	Loudness	Loudness + Width	To move widely or narrowly according to loudness
	Tempo	Tempo + Time	To move in an adequately tempo according to tempo
	Tempo	Tempo + Things (Relationship), Time	To move things adequately according to tempo
	Staccato/ Legato	Staccato/Legato + Flow	To move body and things according to single tone and consecutive tones

Table 5.3. Example of an Integrated Lesson Plan for Classroom Use

Activity	Toad, toad
Objective	1. to demonstrate duple rhythmic pattern with hand and foot 2. to move body joyfully variously on duple meter
Concept	·musical element–duple rhythmic pattern ·movement elements–whole body, relationship with things
Method	
Begin	① teacher sings first to children in a large group the song 'toad, toad' from the previous sand playing time. Teacher substitute the word 'toad' with each child's name so as to get the child's attention. - toad, toad, I will give you an old house, please give me a new house. Hey oo hey oo, will you bring buckets of water ② children sing along with the pictures in the story book 'toad' -Today is the day of house building for toads. The crawls gathered to hear this. Toad brings water, crawls pound ground... Toad and crawls are building a strong clay house together. ③ After reading a story, children sing with hand or knee clapping or move their head from one side to the other. -Do you know this song? You may move your head when you are singing. -What can you move other than your head while you are singing? -Let's sing with a hand clap and a knee tap and repeat the sequence? ④ Sitting one child in front of the other and sing while moving to the duple meter of the song. -move this way and that way while holding your partner's hands - What other ways can you think of moving ? -For example, it's possible for us to sit down and stand up. ⑤ Teacher approve and support children to move in different ways. -Look at .... S/he made this movement. That looks interesting. Let's do the same thing. ⑥ After finishing the activity, with as children's feelings about the singing and movement. -Hi .... what do you feel about this activity? -when were you most excited?
develop	
End	
Concerns	* To recommend all the children in class to participate to the activity

90

Curriculum Application

Video recordings, photographs, and journal entries were analyzed according to children's expressions, which indicated their interests and responses to the integrated movement and musical activities. The words and nuances from the children's verbal as well as nonverbal expressions indicated the children's interests and responses in the class. Their verbal and nonverbal expressions were categorized and coded. In this study, as Moorhead and Pond found in their Phillsbury Studies (1951), the social-personal context was seen to be highly relevant; some movements were developed first by one child and continued by that child or undertaken by others to form a series. Discourse analysis was used to investigate naturally occurring talk. Descriptions that symbolized specific actions or someone's feelings, such as "Let's jump on [particular words in song texts]," were underlined and examples of children's interests were also marked.

Children's interest. Children's responses were analyzed by verbal and nonverbal expression including gestures and facial expressions. Children voluntarily and repetitively demonstrated their expression with a smiling face. They were active in moving and singing prior to the teacher's invitation and then they enthusiastically volunteered what they did during free-play time. Following is an example of voluntary exploration described from the initiation and response by children and feedback from a teacher.

Child 1:   Teacher, what's this? (looking up at the teacher's face who is preparing for the music class)—(initiation)

Child 2:   This is *Poknami* song! Teacher, <u>can we jump up when the words *"Aeichiwi* ("Ah-choo" in English)" comes up?</u>—(response)

Teacher: Will you jump up at *"Aeichiwi"* ("Ah-choo" in English)? Would you show me?—(feedback)

Child 3:   <u>Let's jump like this, jump inside of tape marking 'personal space'</u>*. – (initiation)

Child 4:   (looking at the next child) <u>shall we jump holding hands?</u>—(response)

Child 3:   Okay, let's do it together, hold hands and jump.—(response)

Child 5:   <u>Teacher, I will crawl on the public space</u>*.—(response)

Teacher: Good job. Let's jump and move from inside to outside.—(feedback)

Some children already began to move and some children asked the teacher's permission to move. Then all the children were holding hands together, jumping to the beat and sang the song "Poknami." (Observation, June 16, 2008)

An excerpt from the researcher's fieldnotes indicates the progress made by the children in acquainting with the integrated concepts of the instruction.

As soon as the class starts for the children, they showed their instant responses of interest in the earlier class lessons by mentioning the focus terminologies of the shared concepts of movement and music, so that I recognized that they naturally acquire the shared concepts, which are the objective of this integrative class (refer * above). (Researcher's reflective journal, June 16, 2008)

The earlier description represents the children's active spontaneous response as they heard familiar songs, which they had learned in earlier lessons. Usually children in the class showed difficulty in expressing themselves. However, they participated in the integrated arts activity with joy and ease, and showed confidence during the activities. During the class, they seemed to recall their past instructional activity, and were able to repeat what they had expressed. Here is an example of a child who asked her teacher for a repetition of a past learning experience within the project, indicating her instructional desire to revisit the music along with some dramatic play.

Child: Teacher, please turn on the music of *Peter and the Wolf*.
Teacher: Why? For what?
Child: I want to play again the *Peter and the Wolf* drama with my friend *Eunsoo* (she shakes her tambourine).

Three to four children get together hearing the sounds of the tambourine and they ask the teacher to play the music from *Peter and the Wolf* on the piano. They then gathered around the piano and played instruments with vigor and volume. (Observation, July 18, 2008)

The children applied their experience of including loud sounds by using considerable physical strength while engaging in a craft activity involving earthen clay: pressing weakly and then with great strength to make clay animals. Just as in the movement activity in their music-making, children had continued to seek out ways to express strong and weak sounds while playing instruments.

Children's response. It was found that the 4- and 5-year-old children were able to construct various rhythmic movements in the feeling of duple meter, but they confused pitch with speed and strength. Children moved faster with energy with high notes, while slower and weaker with lower notes. However, the children seemed to understand the melodic flow of tunes quite well and expressed their recognition of these concepts with their correspondent high and low movements. Children enjoyed repetitive performances of movement as they listened to different types of music, and they showed their feeling for phrases by their changing directions and movement responses. Children were able to distinguish different types of sounds and expressed them using their bodies, but they focused more on searching for the sounds rather than expressing the sounds through movements. They made different forms of expressions, adjusting the space width or physical power in accordance with the strength and softness of the music. They controlled the speed of their movement according to the tempo of the music. Lastly, they clearly responded to staccato and legato and also offered physical expression according to the salient concepts of the musical excerpts. Following is a dialogue featuring a child's interest in singing with movement to music, both in a limited personal space and across a much larger public space. It is an example of voluntary exploration of a concept followed by feedback from the teacher.

Child 1: Teacher, shall we sing within the personal space today? – (initiation)

Teacher: What? Will you?—(feedback)

Child 1: No, let's start to sing within the personal space and move to public space.—(response)

Child 2: And then, return to personal space and sing like in the opera Magic Flute like this (aaa aaaaaaaaa a).—(response)

Child 3: Shall we raise our foot while we are singing? Look at me. See my high foot and see the lower one. It's fun to do. Sing up and sing down, up and down. Foot matches my song. I feel so good. Hey, I am the bird flying in the high sky over the cloud.—(initiation)

Teacher: What a wonderful discovery! I can see you are so much grown up because of singing this song.—(feedback)

The children then sang and hopped while holding instruments in their hands. Masking tape on the floor divided their personal space from their public space. (Observation, July 20, 2008)

From the above findings, it was concluded that children ages 4 and 5 actively participated in the integrated art—music—movement activity. They investigated and created various movement expressions utilizing the concept-related terminologies such as "personal space" and "public space."

This implies that children in this program demonstrated a high level of interest and understanding. Children actively responded verbally and non-verbally on staccato, and were more sensitive to that concept than to legato. They controlled their capacity to jump high and low. They made powerful long jumps, they crawled, they manipulated earthen clay in a strong and weakened, looser manner, and they decorated clay vases. They automatically changed any type of activity when legato music was replaced by staccato music. When they used instructional aids like ribbon or balloons, they adequately controlled the speed of the materials. This implies that they recognize the shared concepts of music and movement.

CONCLUSION

In the beginning of this program, most mothers seemed to dislike the structure of integrated arts classes. They wanted to see their child's development in dance movements like ballet and they asked teachers to teach musical instruments like the piano, violin, or harmonica to the children during the integrated arts classes. Some parents threatened to withdraw their children from the program in the beginning because they rarely saw their children demonstrate precise movement and instrumental playing at home after class. But a few mothers confessed that they liked this program because they thought that it would be possible for children to connect what they experienced in music class either into the movement or arts activity and vice versa, allowing the children to become more artistic. Such parents' responses motivated the researcher to carry on with courage.

Children gained a conceptual understanding of the arts through the integrated classes. They demonstrated their knowledge about music and movement concepts by frequent use of related terminology during their conversation with other children and teachers and seemed to grasp the concept of rhythm, including both duple and triple meter, and transferring this understanding into movement with ease. When they heard a song in duple meter, they created their own songs and improvised movements according to the created songs. They twisted their legs, crawled on the floor, turned in various directions, and then released and stretched out of the crawl. These types of responses show the children understanding the shared concepts, effectively utilizing these throughout the process of transition from music to movement. However, this was not always applied to art. The relationship between music and movement was typically strong while the application of concepts to art was often weak.

Children moved up and down according to the melodic changes. They clearly recognized melodic contour and applied their understanding of songs and recorded music when they moved their bodies high and low to the sounds they heard. When the teacher played the piano, the children moved their bodies from bottom to top and vice versa, following the teacher's music. Especially when they sang traditional Korean songs, they were able to describe that "the sounds are going down or up," but verbalized this understanding by saying that "the balls went up and down" when they listened to Western classical music (even though there was no ball present). The music seemed to inspire the children to imagine the rise and fall of a bouncing ball. This implies that they respond to music and movement as a whole, not as separate entities, and they identified the shared, integrated arts concepts with their bodies. This finding matches the Korean indigenous arts notion of Ki-ak-mu.

Children repeated the same movements with each listening of a musical selection with no movement variation. They expressed well in their bodily movement the musical ideas of repetition and contrast. Sometimes the repetitive song texts and the repetitive melodic patterns seemed to help children's movement. Moreover, they moved and sang freely and creatively with the song texts directed through words such as "stop," "hop," and "as you wish" (meaning to move by free choice). Children voluntarily controlled the power of the tension of their movement and distance when music sounded loudly. Children naturally changed directions in their movement in various ways when musical phrases changed. They made big circles with their hands moving from down-up to top-down, or they sang from loud to soft or from high to low sounds. In many other ways, they demonstrated that they understood the shared concepts of the integrated arts.

Children in this study connected tempo with movement speed. They were able to sing loudly and perform strong corresponding movement to the music they heard or sang. Even prior to the teacher's request, they played and combined loudness with movement, based on song texts. For example, in the song titled *Talpiaengi chipul chipsida* (Let's make a snail house), children changed singing volume and movement strength as the song directed them. Children recognized the tempo change heard in two different unfamiliar musical pieces and applied them to their movement and art activities. This finding was similar to that of S. Lee's (2003) study of traditional Korean music and movement integration. Differing from the younger children, 4- and 5-year-old children responded well to the expressive concepts of staccato and legato during their music and movement classes. Children were able to switch from tapping to fingering clay freely according to these two expressive elements. Children showed more interest in staccato qualities than in legato, verbally and nonverbally, and in the use of ribbons, balls, tips, and toes of their bodies. However, children confused melodic changes with tempo and loudness. When they integrated music and movement during the activity named "animal walking," they pretended to be a bear in low tones while they became like mice or ants in high tones. Also, they walked faster to high melodies and slower for low melodies. This was also the typical response from younger children.

In conclusion, the 4- and 5-year-old children in this study showed high levels of interest and understanding of the shared concepts of integrated music and movement, and they seemed to utilize their knowledge of integration intellectually in integrated activities. They willingly used terms such as "personal space" or "public space" in their music and movement classes. Differing from the younger children, the 4- and 5-year-old children understood concepts comparatively more. This means that the appropriate and positive usage and application of a concept-based arts integration curriculum may enhance the scope and speed of development of children's artistic knowledge and skills, so that arts education could fit the educational goal of the development of children's holistic and sensitive selves. Also it could be interpreted that the Korean concept of Ki-ak-mu fits to the children's music and movement integrated classes. This research is limited to one specific group of children in Korea, so the research findings should not be generalized to populations at large; however, Ki-ak-mu may have implications for children's music classes in other countries, for music and movement integration is not solely for Korean children. There seem to be philosophical similarities between Ki-ak-mu and Dalcroze's Eurhythmic teaching method. Ki-ak-mu reflects music and movement as a whole while Dalcroze's Eurhythmic teaching method focuses on movement during the process of music teaching. So in future research, there is a need to consider various other locations and ages.

RESEARCHER'S REFLECTION

This study traced the shared concepts of music and movement in an integrated arts curriculum for young children. The findings might help to guide preschool teachers in ways of understanding concept-based integrated arts curricula. Recently, some music education scholars (Campbell, 2004) have been increasingly coming to view music as social action and to examine even more closely teaching and learning embedded in social and cultural values. Following this notion, this study also aimed to understand music in the context of children's behavior. Therefore a naturalistic approach was chosen as the research methodology for this study. In order to gather valid data in the natural setting of the preschool classroom, the researcher selected participant observation for the music classes and non-participant observation and video-recording for movement and visual arts classes. Keeping a reflective journal was also an important part of the chosen methodology. Brief informal interviews with the mothers and teachers were also conducted. These were not only to survey how mother and teachers felt about their experiences, but also to obtain information that the researcher was not able to gather via direct observations in the field, capture multiple realities or perceptions of a range of situations, which was vital to the interpretation of what was happening. This methodology allowed me to find that despite initial intention, integration of music and movement was more common than integration of music, movement, and art. This may be interpreted as a natural and instinctive cohesiveness of music and movement existing within Ki-ak-mu (music and dance always together), bringing out the essence of arts integration passed down from the old days of Korean history.

NOTES

1. Concept-based integration denotes a teacher's selection of a certain concept (i.e., space, power, rhythm, etc.) as the starting point in the process of curriculum design. For example, if space is selected by the teacher, the concept of space is used within music, movement, and visual arts activities at the same time.

REFERENCES

Ahn, J. (1998). *Early childhood music education*. Seoul: Kyoyuk hwahaksa.
Andress, B. (1989), *Promising practices: prekindergarten music education*. Reston, VA: MENC.
Bresler, L., & R. E. Stake (2006) Qualitative research methodology in music education. In R. Colwell (Ed.), *MENC handbook of research methologies* (pp. 75–89) Oxford, England: Oxford University Press.
Bruner, J. S. (1995). *Culture of education*. New York: Schirmer Books.
Campbell, P. S. (2004). *Teaching music globally: Experiencing music, expressing culture*. New York: Oxford University Press.
Campbell, P. S., & Scott-Kassner, C. (2006). *Music in childhood* (3rd ed.). New York: Schirmer Books.
Choksy, L., Abramson, R. Gillespie, A., & Wood, D. (1986). *Teaching music in the twentieth century*. Englewood Cliffs, NJ: Prentice-Hall.
Chosunilbosa. (1995). *Chipan Koguryo Pyokhwa* [Mural paintings in *Chipan* of *Kogury*]. Seoul: Daily Chosun.
Dalcroze, J. (1921). Music and child. In *Rhythm, music and education* (H. Rubinstein, Trans.). New York: Knicherbroder Press.
Doosan Ch'ulp'ansa. (2007). *Doosan encyclopedia*. Seoul: Doosan.
Feldman, R. (2006). *Development across the life span*. Upper Saddle River, NJ: Prentice Hall.

Gordon, E. (1990). *A music learning theory for new born and young children*. New York: GIA.

Haines, B., & Gerber, L. (1992). *Leading young children to music* (4th ed.). Hillsdale, NJ: Merrill.

Han, H. (2000). *Haniguk ui umak sasang* [Philosophy of music in Korea]. Seoul: Minsogwon.

Holt, D. (1988). *Reading, movement education and music: An integrated approach.* (ERIC Document Reproduction Service ED 309853)

Im, E. (2001). Development of the integrated music program for children. *Journal of Early Childhood Education Research, 21*(1), 51-70.

Jang, E. (2007). *Music education model for early childhood teacher training.* Unpublished doctoral dissertation, Ewha Women's University, Korea.

Kim, E. (2004). *Theory and practice of child's movement education.* Seoul: Ch'angjisa.

Kim, M. (2007). *Effect of music listening based on movement on children's musical aptitude and creativity.* Unpublished master's thesis, Chonnam University, Korea

Kim, S. (2008). *Early childhood music education curriculum models.* Unpublished doctoral dissertation, Seoul Women's University, Korea.

Kim, S. (1995). *The relationship between the use of body expression and musicality development.* Unpublished master's thesis, Yonsei University, Korea.

Kim, Y. H. (1982). *Study on the child's fundamental musical ability development.* Unpublished master's thesis, Ewha Women's University, Korea.

Kim, Y. O. (2008). Task and meaning of integration in early childhood educational curriculum. *Proceedings of the Annual Conference of Korean Early Childhood Education*, pp. 28-51.

Kim, Y. Y. (2002). *Early childhood music education* (2nd ed.). Seoul: Hakjisa.

Korean Ministry of Education and Human Resources Development. (2007). *Revised the 7th National preschool curriculum.* Seoul: Author.

Korean Ministry of Education, Science and Technology. (2008). *Teacher's guide of preschool curriculum I, II, III.* Seoul: Author.

Laban, R. (1948). *Modern educational dance.* London: Macdonald and Evans.

Laban, R. (1963). *Modern educational dance* (2nd ed.). London: Macdonald and Evans.

Lee, E., & Lee, S. (1997). *Teacher's guide to children's musical activity.* Seoul: Kyomunsa.

Lee, H. (1981). *Essays on Korean traditional music* (R. Provine, Trans.). Seoul: Seoul Computer Press.

Lee, H. (2002). *Music education for feeling and intuition.* Seoul: Sekwang umak ch'ulp'ansa.

Lee, M. (2001). Understanding of child's musical activity and teacher's role from observation. *Journal of Research of Educational Theory and Practice, 11*(2), 273-282.

Lee. M. (2002). A phenomelogical study of the meaning of child musical activity. *Journal of Research on Anthropological Education, 5*(2), 55-82.

Lee, S. (2007). *Music movement integration for three year old children.* Unpublished master's thesis, Silla University, Korea.

Lee, S. (2003). *Research on effect of the integrated movement with Korean music.* Unpublished doctoral dissertation, Songshin Women's University, Korea.

Lee, Y. (2004). *Creative movement education for children*. Seoul: Kyomunsa.

Marsh, K. (2008). *The musical playground*. London: Cambridge University Press.

McDonald, D., & Ramsey, J. (1992). Awakening the artist: Music for young children. In B. Andress & M. Walker (Eds.), *Readings in early childhood music education* (pp. 89-96). Reston, VA: Music Educators National Conference.

Metz, E. (1989). Music and movement environments in preschool settings. In B. Andress (Ed.), *Promising practices in prekindergarten music* (pp. 89-96). Reston, VA: MENC.

Moog, H. (1976). *The musical experience of the pre-school child*. London: Schott Music.

Moorhead, G., & Pond, D. (1951). *Music of young children*. Vancouver, BC, Canada: Pillsbury Foundation.

Nye, V. (1975). *Music for young children*. Dubuque, IA: Wm. C. Brown.

Paek, S. (2005). *A study of the program development for movement education for children based on movement elements*. Unpublished master's thesis, Pusan National University, Korea.

Park, E. (2004). *Effect of movement expression with music listening on emotional quotient*. Unpublished master's thesis, Sungsin Women's University, Korea.

Pica, R. (1995). *Experiences in movement with music, activities, and theory*. New York: Palmer.

Shin, Y. (2005). *Effect of music listening combined by body expression on children's creativity development*. Unpublished master's thesis, Duksung Women's University, Korea.

Yang, O. (2008). *Early childhood curriculum*. Seoul: Hakjisa.

Yu. S. (2001). *Yuís Dalcroze class I*. Seoul: T'aerim ch'ulp'ansa.

CHAPTER 6

WHERE EVERY CHILD IS SMART

Nurturing Musical Intelligence Through Traditional Musics in Early Childhood Education in a Multiple Intelligences International School, Manila, Philippines

Pamela Costes-Onishi

When the Harvard cognitive psychologist Howard Gardner (1983/2004) published *Frames of Mind*, it was intended for psychologists to rethink the notion of intelligence and the functioning of human cognition. The multiple intelligences (MI) theory put forward in the book, however, garnered unprecedented interest among educators, and various schools based on MI theory were successfully established across the United States and later on around the world.

The multiple intelligences theory offers an alternate educational style that pays attention to the pluralistic view of the individual mind on the premise that "people have different cognitive strengths and contrasting cognitive styles" (Gardner, 2006b, p. 5). Addressing the eight intelligences identified by Gardner, "MI schools" try to create a learning environment wherein a concept is taught through the development of intelligences

Musical Childhoods of Asia and the Pacific, pp. 101–131

such as musical, bodily-kinesthetic, logical-mathematical, linguistic, spatial, interpersonal, intrapersonal, and naturalist.

In the Philippines, the first MI school was founded in 1996 by Joy Abaquin,[1] a psychologist educated in both the Philippines and the United States with a genuine interest in improving early childhood education in the country.[2] MI International School, Manila is a privately funded, progressive school that started with Child's Place, a preschool that caters to the needs of toddlers up to 5 years old. Howard Gardner remarked upon his visit to the school, "Of the many "MI schools" that I have visited over the years, the Manila-based school stands out in terms of the care with which the program has been conceptualized and carried through" (Multiple Intelligence International School, 2008). The school was also mentioned in his book, *Multiple Intelligences: New Horizons*, published in 2006 as one of the impressive MI schools outside of the United States and was featured in the 2009 book *Multiple Intelligences Around the World* (Chen, Moran & Gardner, 2009), of which Gardner is one of the editors.

In this study, the definitions of *multiple intelligences* and *musical intelligence* are mainly based on Howard Gardner, with discussions of Bamberger (1991) and the school directress' opinions to provide more insight on the applicability of the theories. In some cases, my own interpretations of Gardner's MI theories influenced by my primary training as an ethnomusicologist contributed to my assessment and evaluation of the data.

This chapter assesses the differences of the MI International School's overall approach to music education as compared to the standards of the Department of Education, Philippines. It seeks to find out the relevance of rooting musical studies in local cultural traditions, an approach different from the general music education in the Philippines and central to the director's vision of the school's overall education system, and how such rooting accomplishes the goals of musical intelligence within the MI framework in a child's education. This study focuses more on the merits of the MI International School's approach to music learning and assesses whether through it, the goal of musical understanding is achieved. Education for understanding is a shared goal by MI theory and music educators such as Susan Mills (2001), Cathy Kassell (1998), and Richard Colwell and Lyle Davidson (1996), who evaluated the ways in which the theory has been applied to music. In this study, I seek to define "music understanding" from the perspectives of the MI International School and available scholarship in music education.

Given the many concerns in the implementation of MI theory in a child's education and, most importantly for our concern, its implications on a child's musical growth, a case study such as this is imperative. The more we look into the methodologies of schools adapting MI theory, the more music education can best assess the merits of MI to the actual understanding of music. Since this particular MI-based school is highly lauded by Howard Gardner himself, it renders itself as a good case study for the evaluation of the concept of musical intelligence. Important to this study's inquiry is the delineation between using musical intelligence as one means to achieve understanding of a more theme-focused goal of this particular MI curriculum and viewing musical intelligence as a manifestation of growth and development in the understanding of the music itself.

The sample student population in this study is preparatory to second grade, ages 6–8. The field research was conducted in October–December 2008 and April 2009. This is limited to the third quarter of the school year and the only opportunity I can do actual field research from the time my project proposal was accepted to the deadline given to submit the findings. The research had been conducted primarily for this special book project and was personally funded. I was an independent scholar during the time of this research and in no way connected to the MI International School or the Philippine Public Education System. All materials used in this research, including photos and brochures, obtained proper permission from the directress, teachers, and students of the MI International School.

Prior to and in between the actual field observations and interviews, correspondences were done through telephone and e-mail. During the 3 months of field research in late 2008, the learning processes and the quality of musical activities used to stimulate musical intelligence leading to one "portfolio" assessment period were documented. Music lessons were evaluated as to how they fall within the multiple intelligences objectives: whether they are designed simply as entry points to understand concepts or if there is a clear curriculum that hones musical growth. Videos of past portfolio performances were reviewed and questionnaires addressing teaching styles, understanding of music's relevance to the child's education, and perception of MI theory had been distributed to teachers of all domains, parents, and students. Interviews were also conducted with representative students, the music teacher, and the school's director. The April visit in the Philippines was to the Department of Education where I interviewed the Program Specialist in the Curriculum Development at the elementary level and the Music Specialist of Secondary Schools. The goal was to learn the current state and direction of music education in the Philippines so as to evaluate better the claimed new approach being implemented at the MI International School.

The incorporation of traditional Philippine instruments was likewise examined in terms of its productiveness to musical understanding and as to whether a broader link to the community and Philippine culture is established through its introduction. The research, therefore, seeks to reveal the end goals of the MI International School, Manila with respect to music education in the Philippines and the community, and to find out how musical intelligence, through incorporating Philippine traditional musics, becomes an effective route in accomplishing these goals.

NOTES ON THE FIELD RESEARCH

My entry into the school in order to conduct the research was made possible by my connections in the music sector of the Philippines. I had been away from my country for 12 years and I would admit that it was not all that easy to gain back the confidence of my former colleagues. However, everyone I contacted was very helpful and it was the department chair of the Music Research department of my former college, the University of the Philippines, who recommended the school to me. It so happened that the music teachers were my former schoolmates, which made it easier for me to receive consent to observe the classes, although efficient communication was a problem and most of the time I received either none or very late responses to my questions and the materials I requested. But the directress was quite accommodating and I received timely replies to my inquiries.

With regards to my way of approaching children, I did an informal group interview for three reasons: (1) the student's lunch break was the only time I could talk to them; (2) I found that children of this age open up more when part of a group; and (3) I did not have time to conduct individual interviews because of the tight schedules of the students. During the interviews, I positioned myself at the front of the room and explained my intentions to the children. My questions were prepared but the actual interview tended to take its own direction. I was given 30 minutes by the section advisers for each class but after just 10 minutes the children became restless as expected and seemed to want to be in the video and so most moved closer to me. The second graders ended their interview session with a song and dance number that they had been practicing in their music class.

I had a chance to get into a class where students not yet picked up by their parents remained. This was a small group and, as expected, students were a little reluctant to give answers. The presence of the adviser made them relax and more sharing took place after a while. What I observed was that the MI children were generally very outspoken. They were more comfortable speaking in English too, a sign that they came from affluent families. The MI education of emphasizing individual "smarts" definitely boosted the confidence of these children in a good way. It was easier for me to get responses. The children also remembered me well and they would unfailingly greet me as "Teacher Pam" in the school corridors and even during their final performance at the outdoor mall. Given more time, I would have established more rapport with the children that eventually could open doors to more specific experiments on music learning.

I had wanted to observe the Child's Place children as well but for some reason I was not allowed to. I went to the classroom and spoke to the teacher about coming in to observe but this plan did not materialize. I assume this must have been caused by the tender ages of the children in these classes. The directress mentioned concerns about videotaping the lessons and the children and told me that I would need to obtain permission first from each parent. It could take a longer time to consider including in this case study. Besides, I wanted a more focused research project and the Child's Place scenario would deserve separate observations. The teacher was also not a music specialist unlike the one in the MI International, which operates somewhat differently even under the same administrator. Other than this, the school has supported my research and allowed me to publish the pictures I have taken of the preparatory to second-grade level music classes.

The visit to the Department of Education proved fruitful. Dr. Lilian Luna, the Secondary Schools Music Specialist, was more than accommodating. I was referred to her once again by former schoolmates who are now with the department of music education at the University of the Philippines, Diliman. One amusing experience I had in visiting the Department of Education was that people thought I was Singaporean. This is another setback I often have when going back to my own country: my countrymen often would not recognize me as being one of them. This played to both my advantage and disadvantage. Some would think foreign connection would be good, whereas others would be very wary to share information. I also felt that my colleagues in the academe were sizing up my knowledge of my own culture as if they doubted whether I still knew what I was talking about. The distrust could be felt and I had to assure them through my actions that I still hold a genuine concern for the country. In this particular case, being mistaken as a foreigner worked well to my advantage and even more so when they later learned I was also Filipino.

BRIEF BACKGROUND OF THE PHILIPPINE SCHOOL SYSTEM

The Department of Education (DepED) in the Philippines had been changed to its current name in 2001. The free and compulsory education system in the Philippines was established earlier on through the Malolos Constitution during the American Occupation and a public school system was in place since 1901. The primary educators during that time were mainly Americans known as the Thomasites. Filipinization of the school system began in 1916 and for some time had been run by the Japanese during World War II (1942–1944).[3]

Children in the Philippines start school at age 4 to attend nursery and kindergarten. These are the preschool levels. The Preparatory Level is already part of the overall compulsory school education and at age 6 or 7 students are already attending first grade. Elementary education lasts for 6 years then students attend 4 years of high school. By the age of 16–17 students are already at the college or university level. The first 2 years of university education is spent on pre-major preparatory courses equivalent to a junior high or junior college in other Asian countries. Thus, time spent in the university can last between 4 and 6 years depending on the number of loads per semester a student can handle. The school year in the Philippines is from June to March, with summer breaks in April and May. There is a 2-week break for Christmas.

While public schools outnumber private schools, in terms of quality of education, more affluent Filipinos would prefer to send their children to a private institution. In a private school such as the MI International School, students are believed to be given more individualized attention and alternative, more effective approaches to learning are available. In private schools, class size ranges from 15 to 25 students, while in public schools it is common to find 40–45 students. There usually are longer hours in private schools even for the elementary level, which could average 8–10 hours in a day as compared to 4–5 hours in the public schools.

THE CURRENT STATE AND DIRECTION OF MUSIC EDUCATION IN THE PHILIPPINES

Prominent music educators in the Philippines appear to acknowledge that there are two ways of transmission of musical knowledge in the country (Borromeo, 2008; del Valle, 2008; Maramba, 2008): (1) informal as seen among the indigenous groups and (2) formal as practiced in institutions dating back during the Spanish colonial period in the 16th century. The division between informal and formal ways of learning is not exclusive and simply means that in traditional societies, formal ways associated with education such as writing and notation are absent but a structured system of transmission could be well in place.[4]

Music has always been central to the lives of the Filipinos. When the Spaniards came to colonize and Catholicize the Philippines, they found that music permeates much of the native culture. Spanish Chroniclers during the sixteenth century, for example, noted the pervasiveness of suspended bronze gong instruments wherever they went (Scott, 1994). This centrality of music in every aspect of culture such as marriage, birth, rituals, and entertainment can still be observed even at present. Ethnomusicological studies stand as testimonies to the richness of indigenous musical cultures in the Philippines.[5]

The Spanish missionaries did not waste time in cultivating this perceived inherent musical talent among the Filipino natives, and as a result music schools were established as early as the 1600s to train young boys in singing, musical instruments, and formal theory lessons such as solfeggio and composition (Bañas, 1969). Since then, blending local and foreign sensibilities, Filipinos produced operas, composed orchestral and chamber music, organized marching bands, created their own brand of arias called *kundiman*, string ensemble that is the *rondalla*, and an indigenized brass band consisting of bamboos shaped after their brass counterparts known as *musikong bumbong*.[6]

At present, music colleges continued the tradition of formal music education in training potential musicians, composers, and singers to hopefully carry on the musical excellence exhibited by their predecessors during the Spanish times. Notable higher-level music colleges are the University of the Philippines College of Music, University of Santo Tomas, and the Philippine Women's University College of Music and Fine Arts.[7]

The incorporation of music at the elementary level came hand in hand with the establishment of public schools during the American occupation from the early to mid 1900s. The music curriculum during that time was based on the Progressive Music Series, "a graded foreign collection of songs and a Philippine edition of the same series by Norberto Romualdez" (del Valle, 2008).

In the 1950s and 1960s, several memoranda regarding music education in the primary and secondary levels were released by the Department of Education Culture and Sports (DECS), including the first Legislative Act 4723, dubbed the Music Law. These memoranda stressed the importance of art, music, and physical education to a child's education advocating a definite period of time for music alone; the memo also stipulated that music should be taught only by a qualified teacher.[8]

In my conversation and interview with Rogelio O. Doñes, Education Program Specialist of the Curriculum Development Division, Bureau of Elementary Education, he stated that music, at present, is an integrated subject in any learning area in the preparatory to second-grade level. It is only in the third to sixth grades that music is taught as a separate subject. Mr. Doñes expressed that the music integration in the preparatory to second grade means songs such as "Twinkle, Twinkle Little Star." He said that as much as possible the teachers try to teach songs that would be related to the subject being taught. When asked why the Bureau thinks music education should only start in the third grade, he explains the following:

[In the] lower grade, the attention span of children is short. If they stay longer [in school] they will be bored. We give them the "musts" to learn; like,
for example, Language, Math, [and] Values Education. Music is not necessarily a must in a child at the lower grade ... because music is a skill; a God-
given talent that not all of us are gifted. (personal communication, April 20,
2009)

In the third to sixth grades, music education is made to share its time
with the arts and physical education in what they refer to as MSEP
(Musika, Sining, at Edukasyong Pangkatawan or Music, Arts, and Physical
Education). Each school implements one of these schemes: (1) alternate
music, art, and physical education for the 40 minutes allotted three times
a week or (2) divide the 40-minute allotment between the three components. In either scheme, music lessons will total to about 40 minutes or
even less each week out of the 25 hours spent weekly in school, which is
only a maximum 2.6% of the total contact hours per week. In reality,
music will receive very little or no time at all as it shares with the arts and
physical education. This will be even less now that the latest DepED
Order No. 90, s.2009 states further curriculum integration of subjects
with MSEP sharing its 40 minutes three times a week with geography, history, and social studies.[9]

With this approach to music education, the Department of Education
in the Philippines is setting a nationwide standard of regarding music
simply as a means to expose and bring out the talents of those naturally
gifted. Music for the preparatory to second grade simply means singing
and for the third to sixth grades, a very minimal instruction on the basic
elements. Indeed, Dr. Lilian Luna, Music Specialist in the Secondary Education, lamented the fact that by their first year in high school, students
still need to be taught the foundations of music and so teachers at this
level are having a difficult time advancing the students' musical aptitude.
Dr. Luna mentioned how the members of the Philippine Society for Music
Education (PSME)[10] are constantly pushing for an early start in a child's
training in music in order to nurture musical talent better.

Looking back at the long history of music education in the Philippines, it seems improbable that it will decline this much in quality at
present. When asked what could be the reason for this, both Mr. Doñes
and Dr. Luna pointed to the dearth supply of qualified music teachers in
the country as compared to the "old days." Mr. Rogelio O. Doñes said,
nowadays, it is really difficult to find a music teacher who can even read
notes. This could be due to the Filipinos' inclination to learn music by
ear and, in his opinion, the advent of technology such as karaoke
wherein people think musical talent could be enhanced even without a
formal music education.

Likewise, Dr. Luna explained how most teachers at the elementary level are generalists and therefore not really music educators. She said at the high school level they still get qualified teachers but it is also becoming more difficult to find one. To rectify the problem, the Bureau of Secondary Schools provides summer training for their teachers and gives out scholarships to encourage the teachers to minor in music.

Another problem why music education is not emphasized in the schools is the general priority of the Department of Education, which places more importance to English, math, and science. The curriculum is thus affected by the budget and so even special co-curricular programs, where students could possibly learn instruments such as the *rondalla*, guitar, or even recorder, suffer through the lack of ability to hire teachers and purchase instruments for student use. As Mr. Doñes puts it, "If the budget is depleted, instruction ceases."

Although the curriculum representative admits that since he is not a music specialist, he does not fully understand why music is not included in the early years of the child's education or why it is needed for that matter, he quips that music will stay in the curriculum because he believes that music will always be central to the lives of Filipinos, as evident in the way they excel in it even without the proper education.

THE MULTIPLE INTELLIGENCES ALTERNATIVE TO MUSIC EDUCATION IN THE PHILIPPINES

The MI International School's approach to education espouses the multiple intelligences framework that recognizes that students possess different "smarts" and therefore have different learning styles. The classes are individual/child-centered as compared to the traditional curriculum-centered school. The colorful brochures (Appendix A) and magazine clippings[11] written about the school parallels Gardner's view on individual learning and classroom instruction: The emphasis on regarding each child as possessing unique "smarts"; focus on learning for understanding; doing away with traditional paper-and-pencil testing and conducting assessments through projects, exhibitions, and portfolios; and making sure that students learn in order to apply their skills to address the needs of their communities and society at large (Gardner, 1991, 1999, 2006b; see Appendix B). In the words of the directress Joy Abaquin:

> His [Gardner's] theories of cognition inspired our educational framework in terms of believing in children as intelligent in many ways versus just an institution that focuses on academic excellence. So we've tried to develop the whole child from preschool. Throughout all the programs there is an

emphasis on using MI as a framework to think about children, a framework for curriculum instruction, a framework for assessment, and as well as a framework that inspires children to apply themselves into the world. So meaning, one of the emphases in our school is to use their intelligence to make a difference. Because they have different intelligences the application to the world may be in different forms. (personal communication, December 2, 2008)[13]

Musical intelligence is one of the eight intelligences recognized in multiple intelligences theory. It is considered independent of other intelligences. Following the research of musician-psychologist Jeanne Bamberger (1991), MI contends that there are two contrasting ways of processing music: *figural* (intuitive, right hemisphere) and *formal* (learned, left hemisphere). Musical processing is believed to involve different brain faculties than those of logical-mathematical and linguistic thinking (Gardner, 2004). Studies among individuals with brain damage and prodigies also prove the independence of musical thought processing (Gardner, 2004). MI also believes that music can be experienced by individuals through a variety of means and not exclusive to listening (e.g., rhythmic organization), acknowledging the differences in what individuals can do and the degree and type of encounters with music. What is important is the proof that "music is represented *with some localization*" and that when other brain faculties break down (speech, for example), musical ability remains intact (Gardner, 2004).

Music educators Campbell and Scott-Kassner (2006, p. 6) stated that "music is basic because it is a critical component of international societies as well as a repository of historical traditions and contemporary ideas." While this statement is very true, MI theory forwarded a biologically grounded argument that could help in the advocacy of the imperativeness of music in education. Nurturing musical intelligence, being equal to the other intelligences, should be given much care and thought in a child's education regardless of whether the child will turn out to be gifted in it or not. Music then should not be just in the form of passive education (such as singing some songs in the class) and co-curricular activity. It should be regarded equal to what general education considers as "musts" in a child's education.

Multiple intelligences theory stresses the importance of nurturing musical intelligence for the reason that external factors remain a source for its stimulation. Gardner (2004) explained how musical precocity could be developed either undergoing formal music education training or simply growing up in an environment where music is a central activity. Musical aptitude can also be a product of natural or nurtured talent and thus it is important to create opportunities to develop and exhibit this talent.

Multiple intelligences theory provided an alternative strategy in nurturing a holistic child in the classroom and beyond. It is an approach that seeks to create a global mind that is prepared to meet the challenges of the twenty-first century. MI realizes the potential of the so-called disadvantaged child that the "uniform view" in traditional schools often creates.

In the Philippines, as my experience would attest, most schools, be it private or public, follow the traditional way of teaching and testing, holding a narrow view of the intelligent child. A child, who excels in reading, writing, and math, typically would belong to the top 10% of the class and will be identified as "smart." Other children who do not perform well in the standardized exams are simply regarded as weak students. There is very little measure being used to help out these weak students aside from summer or remedial classes. Students therefore are made to reach the standards of the uniform schooling and to fit in the accepted category of an intelligent child.

Progressive schools like the Child's Place and MI International School seek to address the problems inherent in this type of educational learning by creating alternative approaches that aim to focus on the individual needs of students, often by keeping the classes small. Joy Abaquin recognizes that the Philippines, as a developing country, needs to prepare a new generation of thinkers that are able to face the demands of the twenty-first century: children who can think out of the box, who are able to problem solve, and who are creative.

Compared to the currently practiced method in music education in the Philippines, there are definitely significant differences in the way music is taught in the MI International School: (1) the way music is prioritized in a child's education and (2) the emphasis on rooting music education in Philippine traditional cultural values. In the previous section, we discussed how in the Bureau of Elementary Education the presence of music in the curriculum is simply for exposure; truly learning and understanding what music is proves to be secondary.

The education program specialist views that music is a natural gift to the few and that no amount of intervention would be possible to develop the musicality of those who were not gifted. Indeed, he said there used to be a Secretary in the Department of Education who contends that it is possible to nurture a holistic child even if the child is not exposed to components of music, arts, and physical education. This Secretary believes that these components should be offered as electives and have the child choose what she or he thinks will be interesting.

Music educators and ethnomusicologists generally believe that every child is musical (Blacking, 1973; Keil & Feld, 1994; Small, 1998). Campbell and Scott-Kassner (2006) commented that children are inherently musical and already have the ability to hear sounds and therefore should be led to listen intelligently as to how sounds are organized as music. And since children have this inherent potential musical ability, "musical training should not be reserved for the hypothetical talented few" (p. 9).

In the MI International School, the directress purposefully seeks teachers who are not only knowledgeable about music in the Western view but someone who practices and advocates Philippine music. The reason is very simple, "Because we're Filipinos!" exclaimed Joy Abaquin. The directress explained that being a pioneering school they wanted to make sure that they introduce a different approach to music education and to set an example in advocating our own cultural traditions. As much as possible Philippine instruments are included in the music performances, regardless of whether they are played traditionally or in combination with other non-Filipino instruments. The themes surrounding each quarter also address Philippine values, connecting history with current events. Indeed, the students of MI International School, even at an early age, are very much aware of their musical heritage, which is quite rare compared to other children in most schools.[13] Through the pervasiveness of Philippine traditional instruments in their music education, the children are able to cultivate a deeply rooted admiration and pride for their culture.

THE MI INTERNATIONAL SCHOOL'S APPROACH TO MUSIC EDUCATION

Stimulation of Intelligences on a Daily Basis

In an MI school, the founding principle is that each child should have multiple intelligences stimulated each day. Each child participates regularly in activities in computing, music, and bodily-kinesthetics. They also master theme-centered curricula (Gardner, 2006). In the MI International School, stimulation of musical intelligences outside of the regular music classes takes the form of entry points to the subject matter a non-music specialist will teach. According to the interviews with the music teacher and second-grade adviser, they try to look for songs, for example, that teach the skeletal system in science and relate addition and subtraction to meter and note values in mathematics.[14]

In the MI International School, music is not simply regarded as supplementary to other subjects but as an area of intelligence that is equal to the other intelligences. Music is already a separate subject from preparatory unlike in the general public school systems in the Philippines. But still, all grade levels receive music instruction only twice a week: 30 minutes each meeting for preparatory to second grade and 40 minutes each lesson for third to sixth grades. This constitutes 5% of the total 20 school contact hours for the preparatory to second grades and 3.3% of the 40 hours for third to sixth grades. Daily stimulation as MI theory would recommend still has yet to happen. However, these twice a week lessons are supplemented by external mentors once a week or "pods" where students can participate and share with others what they have learned outside the class time.

Theme-Based Curricula

According to Music Instructor Malou Matute, music is considered an independent subject but is also used to enhance the designated themes for the school each quarter (3 months for each of the four quarters). As an example, during the field research for this chapter, the musical activities for the third quarter were focused on the general school "Kids Can" movement where the students are taught that they can have leadership to influence others such as indigent children and their communities. The music teachers prepared a module on the theme of *Harana* (serenade),[15] in which the MI children expressed their love and affection to the disadvantaged. The event also featured a Kid's Bazaar, which is produced and operated by MI students for the benefit of other children. Three things are targeted here: (1) demonstration of understanding of classroom theories through concrete projects, (2) extension of the classroom to the actual community to which the students are a part of, and (3) devotion to country through an increase in national and heritage awareness. Through this nonuniform approach to the curriculum, each quarter can be shaped according to what is most relevant not only in the academics but also in the Philippine society. The students then learn not only theoretical concepts, but what is more important, to connect and apply readily these concepts to their everyday lives.

Performances of Understanding

"It is clear that understandings can be apprehended and appreciated only if they are *performed* by a student" (Gardner, 2006, p. 127). One of the foremost differences of an MI approach to education from that of traditional schooling is that students are taught only what would be relevant to practical situations that students are encountering or might encounter. Past, present, and future incidents are connected within a subject matter and what is more important is not to teach everything but only the "core knowledge" that would enable the student to generate ideas about music at any given situation, thus the "less is more" principle (Gardner, 2006b). As explained by instructor Malou Matute and directress Joy Abaquin, the end goal in their music subject is performance and not music theory, the latter being taught only in as much as it deemed useful to the former.

> Theory is not the end goal. The end goal is that children understand the music, appreciate it, know where it's coming from, and at the same time use what they know to perform. Kids learn music theory as a function of performance. (personal communication, December 2, 2008)

Sensitivity to Class Needs and Compositions

The classes I personally witnessed differ in the content of performances for the *Harana* nights. The preparatory students and second graders did dance or movement, while the first graders played musical bells and sang. The repertoire for this performance is mostly Western Christmas songs even for the upper grades. Thus, only the concept of *harana* is tied to the Filipino tradition. It was explained by the instructors and directress that the reasons for this are (1) they just finished doing an all-Filipino repertoire during the past two quarters, especially during the *Linggo ng Wika* (Filipino Language Week); (2) they try to vary the type of music activities each quarter, incorporating not just playing of instruments but other ways of learning music such as singing and dancing; and (3) they have to consider logistical aspects of the performance, which will be outdoors in the mall this time and so the soft-sounding traditional musical instruments would not be very effective.

The difference between what each class prepares for the end of each quarter performances is determined based on the general strengths of the class musically. Thus, if a class has strong singers they will most likely do a song number with dance or instruments. Dance and movement is considered music because, as explained previously, MI acknowledges that music can be experienced and expressed through many channels and one of them is rhythm. This view is backed up by music educators as well. Campbell and Scott-Kassner (2006) explained how movement can determine how children perceive rhythm, melodic contours, and patterns in music, translating active listening into dance movements.

I have observed that children with special needs such as those who have ADHD (attention-deficit/hyperactivity disorder) were given different activities during the performance. For instance, the first graders sang and played musical bells following a notation of pitch names while students who are unable to follow this method were taught simple gestures in time to the rhythm. Likewise, for the preparatory performance, those who have problems following the movements were lined in the back with a teacher guiding them; one boy had been separated and given a drum to play since he could follow the music more effectively that way.

Strong Connection to Philippine Culture

The themes are revisited throughout the school education of the students in order to reinforce the core knowledge or generative ideas. An example of this is the different ways traditional Philippine music would be introduced under different topics relating to nationalism, heritage, and culture. I viewed past performances of the students and saw how Philippine instruments such as stomping tubes (*tongatong*), bamboo buzzers (*bungkaka*), percussion tubes (*patang-uk*), shakers (*angklung*),[16] and suspended knobbed metal chimes (*saronay*) are used in different contexts. Malou said that depending on the skills of the students, the instruments can be used in the traditional interlocking way or in combination with other Western instruments or singing.

For the *Linggo ng Wika*, the featured traditions were lowland and Spanish-influenced and so folk songs were taught and the *angklung* was used. During the "Portfolio Nights" where students explored the concept of Philippine heroes and how they can be heroes themselves to society, the students combined drama with songs and some instruments. In their year-end presentation called *Pamana* (Heritage), students were given a chance to perform with top neo-ethnic performers in the Philippines like Joey Ayala and Grace Nono. Here, the gong chimes (*kulintang*) and metal chimes (*saronay*) were played by selected students.

Opportunities such as this are constantly engaged for the education of the students as MI treats the community, including parents, as an extension of the school and educational resources. This is to encourage the students to look beyond the classroom and to constantly learn from a multiple of sources, especially things they encounter in their everyday lives. The concept of apprenticeship is espoused greatly in multiple intelligences-based education. This is the notion that children learn more by observing actual practitioners of a particular intelligence. It enables students to glimpse how a particular knowledge is applied in actual living. I already mentioned how in the "pods" students bring what they learn from external sources to their peers. Mentorship then can also come from a student to another student.

Teachers as Specialists

In the multiple intelligences approach to education, teachers should be specialists and practitioners in their subject matters. The whole apprenticeship concept should manifest inside the classroom where the students will receive most of their interactions with the mentor. A qualified teacher is therefore very important.

The music instructors, Malou Matute and Grace Bugayong, at the MI International School are both graduates of Asian Music at the University of the Philippines. They are, however, not music education majors but received excellent training in music theory, history, and Philippine instruments. Malou is a competent pianist as well and an active performer with recording artists in neo-ethnic Philippine music. Grace is a qualified singer and also has an active performing career as a musician in Philippine instruments. Both have taught in various schools before they were hired at MI International School. According to the directress Joy Abaquin, "We wanted somebody who will be good with kids but at the same time really have their own personal advocacies; they have personal vision."

In the classroom, Malou and Grace teach by doing and demonstrating. They dance and sing with the students. Whenever necessary, they would use hand gestures to simulate the rise and fall of the melodic contours, sing the melody to the students, and demonstrate dance movements slowly. Actually, even the non–music specialists who are the advisers of the classes learn the movements and songs to help out in the demonstration. The result is a fun class where students and teachers all enjoy in learning the performances.

Classrooms as Museums

Setting up a classroom appropriately is important in teaching music. With the multiple intelligences approach, classrooms should be spaces that do not threaten learning but be familiar enough to encourage students to explore. They should be surrounded with engaging materials that will help stimulate their intelligences (Gardner, 1991). This does not mean that each classroom should be turned into a museum, but rather just have a similar atmosphere.

In the music room of the MI International School, there are no chairs but only a large space in the middle. A wall-to-wall mirror is situated on one side and the instruments were placed around the classroom where students can see them every day. Some are behind glass cabinets but are readily accessible when needed. The piano occupies the centre of the room. All classrooms at the MI International School and Child's Place are air conditioned. (Please see Appendix C.)

Philippine instruments dominate the instruments displayed and used in the classroom. Indigenous bamboos, gongs, and drums become normal staples in music learning for the students from preparatory. The children embrace these traditions as equal to Western music.

Social Relevance and Responsibility

Important to the cultivation of the multiple intelligences is to create minds that are prepared for the global world and the future. Howard Gardner (2006a) outlined the five minds that MI theory is hoping to cultivate: (1) disciplined mind, (2) synthesizing mind, (3) creating mind, (4) respectful mind, and (5) ethical mind. With these minds in balance we will be able to raise individuals who possess not only the discipline and creativity needed but also socially responsible thinkers that take into account how their works and intelligences could impact their society and world at large.

The kinds of performances that the MI International School aims for are precisely to teach their students how to connect the knowledge they gather in the classroom to the community in positive ways. At a young age, music as performance does not only mean learning melody, rhythm, and harmony but also seeing how Philippine music can be used for serving the indigent and raising funds to help alleviate their living conditions. Music is also a way to raise awareness of the students as Filipinos. They learn how music can be used to help their countrymen in reconceptualizing Philippine history in order to revive cultural esteem and respect.

EVALUATION AND ASSESSMENT

Music educators have evaluated the merits of multiple intelligences theory, specifically musical intelligences, as applied to classroom instruction. The primary concern is the methodology used by teachers or schools claiming to be applying MI theory as their instructional framework. As observed by Mills (2001), Kassell (1998), and Colwell and Davidson (1996), the ways in which musical intelligence has been applied in schools either failed to demonstrate what Howard Gardner puts forward in his theory, or *musical growth is sacrificed over exposure and performance.*

In this section, I reflect on the methodologies that were applied to the music classes at the MI International School, Philippines. As discussed in the previous section, by far the MI International School has already introduced alternative ways to the traditional teaching methods of music as stipulated by the Bureau of Elementary Education. Although the Bureau claimed to be applying MI theory in its school systems, the few hours and "integrated" approach they devote to music deserves a lot more scrutiny in terms of effectiveness. Since this research is constrained by time, I was not able to observe firsthand what's going on inside the classrooms in the public schools. The person I was able to interview from curriculum development did not mention any other specific methodologies being used in the classroom. The alternative methodologies of the MI International School prove to follow closely Howard Gardner's MI theory, specifically with the goal of teaching music for understanding and performance. However, three important things are still not addressed in the current curriculum: (1) the forms of assessments that would enable a gauge of individual musical growth, something that would indicate an actual understanding of the systems of music; (2) the lack of emphasis in a specific time devoted to some form of music instruction, placing overemphasis on performance instead; and (3) a limited view of what performances of understanding music should be.

Lack of Individual Assessments

I was told that grades like A, B, C, or D are given to the students. To be fair, there is a form of assessment but this is not fixed and will be based, again, in the final performance of the student every quarter. The instructor said that they follow a checklist and note down improvements;[17] grading is group based. It has not been clarified whether the actual end of the quarter performance is the sole basis for grading or if students are given any additional individual evaluations during the quarter.

During the months that I witnessed, there was no separate time for assessments and any indication if students were actually evaluated for the final *Harana* nights. Class times were devoted mostly to rehearsals of the musical numbers that will be performed. There was no indication as well that the essential music theory that students should learn as a function of performance was ever emphasized. Herein lies the problem with the approach as Mills (2001) stated: "Without assessment of musical intelligence, or some aspect of musical growth, there is no way of knowing whether music activities are helpful, harmful or ineffective for musical growth in MI schools."

Another pitfall is grading based on ensemble performance. To quote Colwell and Davidson (1996), "In such an instructional mode, many students are able to avoid developing their musical intelligence as they participate in a rote fashion, dependent on teachers and/or peers" (p. 60). If understanding is to be achieved, there should be some form of measure in order to assess individuals outside of ensemble participation. There should be clear goals regarding what students are expected to achieve in their music classes. In this way, students would be guided to understand how music functions as part of their intelligences and lives.

In my interview with the students, they seem to be unable to explain why dance is an integral part of their music learning. Most students at this age expressed they like their music classes because they find it fun and they love to dance. When asked what they suppose is the connection of music to dance, out of 40 students, only two responses actually addressed the question: "Music sounds boring without dance," "I can follow the beat easily." Others simply say, "I like to play the instruments," "I like what we are singing," "I like singing because you're exercising your throat."

It is important to note that musical understanding, even if focused only on the essential ones that are needed for a specific purpose, involves the ability of the student to read, perform, create, or analyze music.[18] One of the grave misunderstandings is in the way music theory seemed to be equated with Western music theory. When the directress and instructor adamantly denied that music theory is not the end-means, they were referring precisely to that type of theory (note reading, staff writing, etc.).

In Bamberger's (1991) excellent experiments on the workings of the mind behind musical perceptions, musical intelligence was measured by means of theory in the way a child hears the music.[19] In the end, the essential aspects of the elements of rhythm and melody are understood in the healthy exchange between musical ideas as expressed by both *figural* and *formal* perceivers of music. There has to be some form of expression besides a group performance where students can actively engage in the workings of musical sounds using their individual "smarts." Children should be made aware of how their varying perceptions are means to understanding the music, even as simple as "twinkle, twinkle," for example. Only in this manner can a music instruction and activities be said to be effectively honing musical intelligence as a function of multiple intelligences.

Overemphasis on Ensemble Performance

The emphasis on ensemble reflects the goal every quarter to perform what the students understand about music. The instructor expressed that the students are engaged in the decision-making process of what activities they should do for each quarter in connection to a given theme. It is clear from student responses that they understood even at this young age the connections of music to culture and historical context; for example, the importance of learning Filipino repertoire and instruments. However, when it comes to musical understanding based on the music itself, it is hard to tell whether this has been accomplished through the performances. So while students would be able to clearly state the importance of learning indigenous Philippine instruments, or even familiarity with them, it does not necessarily follow, in terms of the assessments used to measure musical ability, that they indeed come to the "understanding of the music," that is, that they understood the function of music theory in their actual performance. The intent is clear and in alignment with the goal of MI theory but there is still much to do in the actual application.

As mentioned earlier, a child becomes dependent on their peers and teachers because of the rote learning. The lack of individual assessment makes it harder to evaluate musical understanding.[20] If Philippine musical traditions will be emphasized, ensemble participation will be an effective measure of understanding as independent parts usually create musical lines. However, instructional time is not devoted to playing the instruments in their musical context; rather, most of the time these instruments are used as supplements to the music they are learning. The reason given is the difficulties of having very young children learn the complicated traditional rhythms. Perhaps a more simplified version that will be suitable for this age group should be created as part of the instructional process. Indeed, a more structured process that would target musical goals beyond public performance is imperative. Using the different musical system of traditional instruments can be an effective route to genuine musical understanding, but the way they will be utilized in class instruction should go beyond asserting the students' Filipinoness. They should be used first and foremost to open the ears of students to the Filipino musical systems, targeting at the same time the goal of achieving genuine musical understandings.[21]

Some form of theory instruction should be incorporated in order to develop musical intelligence. After all, Gardner (2004) himself stated that musical understanding involves not only performance but also creation and intelligent listening in which a listener should be able to comment on the aspects of music heard. Gardner is actually referring to *performances* of understanding, which can be in many forms aside from actual ensemble performance. In the MI International School, at least based on what I actually observed and gathered from the interviews, *performances* in this age group have been narrowed down to ensemble public performance.

Limited View of Performance

An indication of musical growth or development is the ability to demonstrate understanding beyond performance in a group. Eventually, the sophistication of musical comprehension should be evident, whether instruction would be in Western notation systems or not. Students should be able to articulate their musical understandings in a variety of means. Colwell and Davidson (1996) commented, "Research shows that musical intelligence does not develop without broad-based instruction that extends beyond performance opportunities.... Some form of concentrated engagement beyond performance is necessary to raise musical intelligence beyond that level" (p. 57).

This form of instructional engagement should begin in the preparatory level, otherwise the MI music curriculum will not be any different from other traditional approaches, which focuses only on having the students learn songs or movements. Perhaps the important differences would be that they have more "class rehearsals," they formally perform by the end of the quarter, and they realize the relevance of music to nation building. But in terms of musical growth, if careful forms of individual assessment and other evidences of performances of understanding will not be given emphasis, the new methodology offered by MI International School will not accomplish the goals of offering an alternative approach to the understanding of music and honing musical intelligence as a function of multiple intelligences.

At this point in the discussion, I think it is important to understand that "individual growth" does not necessarily mean highlighting individual learning as in the American education system. Individual growth simply means demonstrating understanding of music even without simply following others. There has to be some form of clear assessments in determining if musical growth has indeed been achieved even at the early stages of music learning. This is perfectly congruent to the Philippine way of thinking about music. *In Philippine music ensembles, the resulting sound is communal but the contribution is individual.* In the way the players would interact with each other in an ensemble setting, it is clear that each player knows how their part fits within the structure, enabling each of them to be creative in their improvisations that would enhance the resulting sound as a whole. The good thing about MI theory is precisely the fact that it is not bounded and dominated by any cultural paradigm but that it could be adjusted to any culture's or community's needs and standards.

CONCLUSIONS AND REFLECTION ON
THE RESEARCH METHODOLOGY

The primary methodology to any research that I use as an ethnomusicologist is ethnography and its practice of fieldwork. I particularly espouse the type of ethnography that bears the influences of cultural studies, which views ethnography as an institutionally, historically, and politically situated writing genre (James, Hockey, & Dawson, 1997). In this regard, I view this study more as my personal story of the implementation of MI theory by the MI International School's music program, although grounded by empirical facts. Inasmuch as possible, I tried to balance my own opinions in music learning and understanding of Gardner's MI theory with that of the directress, music instructor, and the students. My evaluation, therefore, is a position that is influenced by my own academic and musical backgrounds. What I hope to have achieved is to raise more questions about the ways in which MI theory is used in the understanding of music in a child's education.

In my assessments, it is evident that I am following the voices of music educators regarding the tendency of MI applications to music studies, which often overlook the need for individual growth measurements and for actual emphasis on music instruction. Since I am primarily an ethnomusicologist, I also find that there is a need to develop a curriculum that highlights the essential musical elements of indigenous instruments even though they are used as supplements to another musical system. Context is important but understanding a musical system means knowing not only the extra-musical aspects but the musical ones as well. Music should be viewed as an activity that involves not only planning and choosing a repertoire for a certain cause but also music-making with an awareness of the various dialogues that can be created among different perceivers of the musical elements.

This study is limited in a way that it fails to contextualize the music learning in the early grades within the framework of the school's overall music curriculum development. Ideally, I would not limit myself to observing only my main concern, which in this case is preparatory to second grade music education. In order to complete the picture, I would observe the upper levels as well to better assess musical growth. I would also spend at least a full year to observe all the classes each quarter and include observations in nonmusic classes. What would be helpful is to follow specific individuals as they move to other grade levels or simply observe their development within an academic year. All of these can be accomplished in an ideal research situation where time is not a constraint. However, when I responded to this project, the school was already toward the end of the year and thus some of the instructional processes that I hoped to have observed were already completed. I relied on videotapes of the past final quarter performances but did not actually have the opportunity to see the process except for the third quarter that I used as the basis for my observations. Nonetheless, the interviews, actual classroom observation for a quarter, videos, and hours of readings on the subject matter provided me with tools to get an overall view of how music is taught in this MI school and used for its evaluation. I want this study to contribute to future researches on musical intelligence and MI theory as applied in the classrooms. Specifically, I hope that this study would open up opportunities for a reassessment of the music curriculum in the Philippines, particularly those that affect early childhood education.

The current undertaking enabled me to see how I can be of better use to my own country when it comes to the development of music curriculum. This study pushed me to think further about MI theory and its applicability in the effective honing of musical intelligence. It is my intent to continue this study and hopefully to engage the collaboration of the MI International School and the Bureau of Music Education in the Philippines to rethink approaches to music learning and design an MI theory-based curriculum that is sensitive to the important perspectives offered by music educators regarding its application. This study convinced me of the useful ways MI theory can be put into practice in the development of forward thinkers and future leaders of my country, which is what we need the most in order to compete in this global age. I would like to be part of this unique nation-building advocacy as a music scholar. In the MI sense, I too would like to make a difference in the larger community through my intelligences.

APPENDIX A1: MI INTERNATIONAL SCHOOL BROCHURE— INSIDE FRONT COVER

APPENDIX A2: MI INTERNATIONAL
SCHOOL BROCHURE—BACK PAGE

Dr. Gardner with the M.I. Kids 2005

" *The school we envision commits itself to fostering students' deep understanding in several core disiplines. It encourages students' use of that knowledge to solve problems and complete the tasks that they may confront in the wider community. At the same time, the school seeks to encourage the unique blend of intelligences in each of its students, assessing their development regularly in intelligence-fair ways*"

Howard Gardner (1983)

Http:\\www.mi-childsplace.com.ph

Preschool and Grade School
4 Escaler st., Loyola Heights, Q.C.
Tel: 4334948 4334949 9280143

High School
3rd Floor Elizabeth Hall, Katipunan, Q.C

APPENDIX B: TRADITIONAL VERSUS MI CLASSROOMS

DIFFERENCES BETWEEN TRADITIONAL AND MI CLASSROOMS

In a traditional classroom	In an MI classroom
The kids with strong scholastic intelligences are smart and the other kids are not.	Everyone has a different profile of intelligences; we are all smart in different ways.
Teachers create a hierarchy of intellect.	Teachers use all students' intelligences to help them learn.
The classroom is curriculum-centered.	The classroom is child centered.
Teachers help students acquire information and facts.	Teachers help students create meaning in a constructivist way.
The focus is on the scholastic intelligences, the 3 R's.	The personal Intelligences are valued: Who you are is more important than what you know.
Teachers work from texts.	Teachers create curriculum-lessons, units, themes.
Teachers assess students by paper and pencil "objective" measures.	Teachers create assessment tools - Projects, Exhibitions, Portfolios (PEPs) - which incorporate MI.
Teachers close the door and work in isolation.	Teachers work with colleagues in using MI, developing collegiality.

APPENDIX C1: MUSIC CLASSROOM AND ACTIVITIES

APPENDIX C2

APPENDIX C3

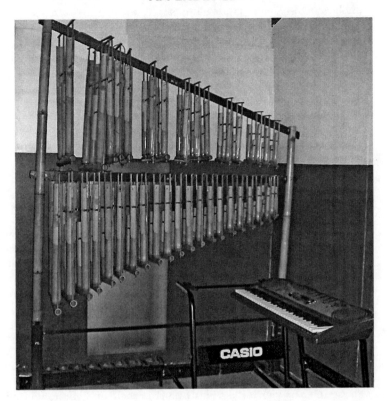

NOTES

1. Ms. Abaquin is a magna cum laude Psychology and Education major from the University of the Philippines and a summa cum laude Master's degree holder in Early Childhood Education from Boston University. She also holds a certification from Harvard Graduate School of Education Programs in Professional Education where she personally met Howard Gardner.

2. My interview with the representative of the elementary Curriculum Development Division claims that the multiple intelligences theory has been incorporated into the general education system in the Philippines ever since its introduction by Gardner. He does not necessarily attribute the implementation of MI theory in the public schools to the MI International School of Abaquin. However, during the course of this research, it is evident that Philippine general education remains to be mainstream and centers heavily on IQ testing and paper-and-pencil-based examinations, which are biased toward logical-mathematical and linguistic intelligences.

3. The Department of Education provides more information on the history of public school systems in the Philippines. Please refer to www.deped.gov.ph.

4. The apprenticeship system is common in the music learning of the gong ensemble kulintang and vocal music among the Maranaos (Cadar, 1971, 1980). This involves certain formalities in education, including teacher–student relationship, and progressive accumulation of patterns and vocabulary in order to unleash creativity in the student.

5. See, for example, Maceda's (1963) pioneering study on the music of the Magindanao in the Philippines; Trimillos's study on the vocal music of the Tausug of Sulu (1972); and important studies on the kulintang written by culture bearers such as that of Cadar (1971) and Kalanduyan (1984), just to name a few.

6. As early as 1886 there was already an opera company in the Philippines founded by Ladislao Bonus, who also composed the first Filipino opera, Sandugong Panaginip (Dreamed Alliance) in 1902. The 1800s also witnessed the flowering of classical music in the country, exposing Filipinos very early on to European singers, musicians, composers, and a wealth of repertoire. Orchestras with native instrumentalists abounded, including an all-woman orchestra. These orchestras were conducted by Filipinos as well. The 1800s also saw Filipino talents internationally with some receiving training in Europe like violinist Manuel Luna; this period also showcased local pianists, flutists, organists, and singers to the European world (Dioquino, 1998).

7. Other colleges that offer music degrees are Centro Escolar University, Santa Isabel College, St. Scholastica's College, and St. Paul College. These institutions are concentrated in the National Capital Region and mostly in Metro Manila.

8. Please refer to Violetta Hornilla's (2008) article on "Music Education in Philippine Primary and Secondary Schools" for a detailed discussion of each memorandum and legislative act released.

9. The DepED Order No.90, s. 2009, released on August 25, 2009, stipulated more integration of class hours (4–5 hours only) on the elementary level as a response to the lack of classroom facilities in relation to the population size of students. In this scheme, not only music would be affected but the overall learning time in the elementary level as classes such as English and Filipino are integrated as well with other subjects.

10. The PSME is a nonprofit organization founded in 1971 for music educators all over the country. Membership includes distinguished music educators in the Philippines. According to Hornilla (2008), "Its primary intent was to improve music education in all its areas, to share knowledge and ideas on music and music education." The founding president is Dr. Lucrecia Kasilag, Philippine National Artist.

11. The school's website provides useful links to articles about the school published in newspapers and magazines. For reference, please visit www.mi-childsplace.com.ph.

12. Also see Canon-Abaquin (2009) for the school director's own article on the visions and goals of the MI International School, Manila, Philippines.

13. My personal experience would attest to this in that only the lowland Christian traditional dances were made familiar to us through co-curricular activities. I only learned of the beautiful indigenous traditions of my country when I entered as an undergraduate piano major student at the University of the Philippines, Diliman, where a strong program on Philippine and Asian musics is being offered.

14. Detailed observations on this integration had not been feasible during the time the field research was conducted.

15. Harana is a Philippine tradition normally associated with traditional courtship where the man sings songs of love and affection to the woman of his liking.

16. Angklung came from Indonesia but is now widely used in the schools in the Philippines.

17. I requested to see the forms of assessments or checklists but I unfortunately did not receive a response from the instructor until the time the deadline for this chapter was due.

18. This does not necessarily mean patterned after Western classical music learning. In multiple intelligences theory, these forms of understandings can be in a variety of means.

19. In the form of mere scribbles, dots, and even tracing their hands to represent a simple rhythmic clapping pattern for children ages 4–5. As the children mature in their perceptions, not necessarily musical, the representations change, with some using lines, spaces, and circles. The same kind of musical understanding can be elicited and observed among children who are considered "slow learners" in math and language, as evident in a case study included in the research.

20. By individual assessment, I mean not just a one-on-one evaluation with a child but a method wherein a child's understanding could be observed even as he or she interacts within a group setting. For example, in Bamberger's (1991) research, students were asked to work on a piece of music heard in class and discuss first what they perceive to be the major boundaries they can hear (in this example of Hindemith's Kleine Kammermusik, the class deduced a tension between CHORUS and SOLO sections). They were then asked to render these perceptions on paper as a group and design their "class piece." During the process, different perceptions of rhythms were put on paper and children discussed these differences, with the teacher guiding them to hear each other's renderings.

21. As an ethnomusicologist, I believe that as much as possible these traditional instruments should be used in the way they should be musically rendered. The musical elements should be taught without compromising the way the instruments should be played. This is far from the purist claims of not using traditional instruments in other ways, but rather, for musical understanding of Philippine cultures and traditions to take place, these instruments should function in the ensemble the way they would originally function, regardless if combined with foreign instruments and contexts. For example, the northern bamboo instruments should be played in an interlocking or alternate manner, even when patterns are simplified but

not in unison to simply keep time (suspended metal/gongs should be played as melodies, etc.).

REFERENCES

Bamberger, J. (1991). *The mind behind the musical ear: How children develop musical intelligence.* Cambridge, MA: Harvard University Press.

Bañas, R. (1969). *Filipino music and theatre.* Quezon City: Manlapaz.

Blacking, J. (1985). *How musical is man?* Seattle: University of Washington Press.

Borromeo, M. (2008). *Philippine music education.* Retrieved from www.ncca.gov.ph.

Cadar, U. (1971). *The Maranao Kolintang music: An analysis of the instruments, musical organizations, etymologies, and historical documents.* Unpublished master's thesis, University of Washington, Seattle.

Cadar, U. (1980). *Context and Style in the Vocal Music of the Maranao in Mindanao, Philippines.* Unpublished doctoral dissertation, University of Washington, Seattle.

Campbell, P. S., & Scott-Kassner, C. (2006). *Music in childhood: From preschool through the elementary grades* (3rd ed.). New York: Thomson Schirmer.

Canon-Abaquin, M. J. (2009). Multiple Intelligences Make a Difference. In: J-Q. Chen, S. Moran, & H. Gardner (Eds.), *Multiple intelligences around the world* (pp. 111–120). San Francisco: Jossey-Bass.

Chen, J. -Q., Moran, S., & Gardner, H. (Eds.). (2009). *Multiple intelligences around the world.* San Francisco: Jossey-Bass.

Colwell, R., & Davidson, L. (1996). Musical intelligence and the benefits of music education [Electronic version]. *NASSP Bulletin, 80,* 55–64.

del Valle, L. (2008). *History of music education in the Philippines.* Retrieved from www.ncca.gov.ph.

Dioquino, C. (1998). The Lowland Christian Philippines. In T. Miller & S. Williams (Eds.), *The Garland encyclopedia of world music: Vol. 4. Southeast Asia* (pp. 839–867). New York: Garland.

Gardner, H. (1991). *The unschooled mind: How children think and how schools should teach.* New York: Basic Books.

Gardner, H. (1999). *Intelligence reframed: Multiple intelligences for the 21st century.* New York: Basic Books.

Gardner, H. (2004). *Frames of mind: The theory of multiple intelligences* (Rev. ed.). New York: Basic Books. (Original work published 1983)

Gardner, H. (2006a). *Five minds for the future.* Boston: Harvard Business School Press.

Gardner, H. (2006b). *Multiple intelligences: New horizon.* New York: Basic Books.

Hornilla, V. (2008). *Music education in Philippines primary and secondary cchools.* Retrieved from www.ncca.gov.ph

James, A., Hockey, J., & Dawson, A. (1997). *After writing culture: Epistemology and praxis in contemporary anthropology.* London: Routledge.

Kalanduyan, D. (1984). *The performance of the Maguindanaon Kulintang music of the southern Philippines.* Unpublished master's thesis, University of Washington, Seattle.

Kassell, C. (1998). Music and the theory of multiple intelligences [Electronic version]. *Music Educator's Journal, 84*(5), 29–32, 60.

Keil, C., & Feld, S. (1994). *Music grooves*. Chicago: University of Chicago Press.

Maceda, J. (1963). *The Music of the Magindanao in the Philippines*. Unpublished doctoral dissertation, University of California at Los Angeles.

Maramba, M. P. (2008). *Tertiary level music teaching*. Retrieved from www.ncca.gov.ph

Mills, S. (2001). The role of musical intelligence in a multiple intelligences focused elementary school. *International Journal of Education and the Arts, 2*(4). Retrieved September 30, 2008, from http://www.ijea.org/v2n4/

Multiple Intelligence International School. (2008). *A message from Dr Howard Gardner*. Retrieved September 30, 2008, from www.mi-childsplace.com.ph

Scott, W. H. (1994). *Barangay: Sixteenth-century Philippine culture and society*. Manila: Ateneo de Manila University Press.

Small, C. (1998). *Musicking*. Hanover, NH: Wesleyan University Press.

Trimillos, R. (1972). *Tradition and repertoire in the cultivated music of the Tausug of Sulu, Philippines*. Unpublished doctoral dissertation, University of Hawaii, Manoa.

CHAPTER 7

INCORPORATING FORMAL LESSON MATERIALS INTO SPONTANEOUS MUSICAL PLAY

A Window for How Young Children Learn Music

Mayumi Adachi

One of the ideal music learning environments for preschool children is free play, or nonconstrained adult-guided situations, in which they can discover new things and explore their own interests (e.g., Adachi, 1994; Campbell, 1998; Littleton, 1998; Marsh & Young, 2006; Morin, 2001; Niland, 2009; Whiteman, 2001; Young, 2003, 2005). However well this may be known by experts, many preschool-age or even younger children are engaged in formal music instruction. Nowhere is this truer than in Japan: Teachers at enthusiastic preschools instruct children to play tunes on the keyboard by rote. These young children invest great energy in playing a few keys for one particular tune with no knowledge of other ele-

Musical Childhoods of Asia and the Pacific, pp. 133–160

ments such as the quality of their sound. For many, such experiences provide little but painful memories. At the other end of the spectrum, the main musical activities in the majority of preschools are merely casual singing of many different songs, lacking creative challenge (Adachi, in press). There should exist a happy medium of *planned* teaching and learning, establishing a foundation for a life-long love of active engagement with music.

In this chapter, I demonstrate a possibility of achieving such a happy medium by letting preschoolers integrate what they learn in planned instruction with what they do spontaneously during their own playtime at home. To do so, I share the findings of three case studies: first with an American 4-year-old girl, second with four Japanese 2- to 4-year-olds, and finally with seven Japanese 5-year-olds. A portion of the first case study has been reported in Adachi (1994), in which I followed how material introduced in an adult-guided interaction was reviewed *spontaneously* by a preschooler named "Mary" at home. In this chapter, I describe the types of lesson material Mary spontaneously practiced while reviewing social and private contexts of her spontaneous practice, the detail of which has not been reported elsewhere. The goal of the two Japanese case studies was to examine the replicability of Mary's findings with a 4-year-old (the same age as Mary) and younger as well as older children in Japan. Even though Mary was not Japanese, she had something in common with Japanese children in these case studies: She was taking *Music for Moppets*, an introductory music program for young children within the Pace Method, a system of piano instruction developed by Robert Pace. For this reason, the "preschoolers" portrayed in this chapter do not represent preschoolers in general, but they represent a particular population, learning music through one particular system. A musical childhood illustrated in this chapter could not be regarded as a Japanese musical childhood per se, but as that of children wherever they are and, possibly, that of those who are taking similar music programs under similar circumstances (i.e., a middle-class family of parents with college [or higher] degrees who are interested in their children's musical development).

SPIRAL LEARNING FOR PRESCHOOLERS

Before detailing the case studies, I first overview the Pace Method, perhaps lesser known than other music programs (such as those based on the work of Dalcroze, Kodaly, Orff, or Suzuki), in order to illustrate the kind of musical culture to which children of my case studies were exposed. The Pace Method is a robust adaptation of Bruner's spiral learning curriculum that extends into formal piano instruction. Bruner's (1996) spiral learning theory addresses the importance of age- and skill-appropriate learning through a carefully organized long-term instructional program. The content of this method is constructed on backward task analyses carefully conducted from what is required in the highest level of musicality, that is, level VI of the Pace Method, targeted at an expert piano student pursuing an advanced degree in music.

At the professional level, musicians interpret music by analyzing the score and express absolute or referential meanings of a piece in their performance. They need to monitor constantly what they produce while performing, not only for the accuracy of notes but also for artistic delivery. Professional musicians also improvise and compose a piece as they wish. By setting up this ultimate level of musicianship as the goal, good music instruction should cover all the elements in each level, such that learning in one level is linked conceptually to that in the next level, forming a system of spiral learning in music. The introductory level, therefore, should build a foundation of "comprehensive musicianship," including music-reading skills, improvisation, attentive listening, referential meanings of music, and theoretical concepts through activities that are accessible to preschool children (Pace, 1982, 1999a, 1999b). It is this comprehensive musicianship that attracted hundreds of piano teachers in Japan when this system was introduced in the early 1980s. They were attracted to a methodology that could seemingly help their students to achieve a truer musicianship than they were capable of reaching themselves.

According to Bruner (1966), material can be learned in three different ways: by doing ("enactive"), by using visual image or simple visual aids ("iconic"), and by using symbols unique to a particular field of study ("symbolic"). The notion of enactive and iconic ways of learning in Bruner's theory has been adapted in music education. Early childhood specialists emphasize young children's enactive music learning (e.g., moving/clapping to music, singing/making up songs, improvising on simple instruments), and often suggest the use of arm-signs and graphic icons to help children focus on a particular element of music such as contour, pitch, and rhythm (Campbell & Scott-Kasner, 1995). Although these strategies are discussed often as introductory learning aids for further musical understanding, rarely demonstrated is how they can be transformed into a more sophisticated, or *symbolic*, level of musical functioning in an actual practice.

The primary means of learning in *Music for Moppets* also relies on enactive and iconic activities, with clear and specific goals that relate to a symbolic level of functioning. For example, on the first page of the *Music for Moppets* student book, children will find a picture of hand spreading five fingers surrounded by playful characters (Figure 7.1). This page, titled *Where is Thumbkin?*, allows children to become aware of the individuality of fingers through an action song allowing them to identify five fingers with character names (e.g., Thumbkin, Pointer, Tall Man, Ring Man, Pinky). Awareness of individual fingers is a prerequisite for learning "fingering," a symbolic system for the motor component in musical performance. Children will absorb the identity of fingers by means of similar action songs throughout the program so that they will be able to use their individual fingers on the command of fingering when they become physically and cognitively ready.

On the second page, *Clouds,* children find an image of two clouds floating in the blue sky. While listening to the teacher's improvised music on the high range of the piano, children will talk about properties of clouds such as soft, light, white, and fluffy. Experientially they touch clouds made of cotton or cloth, move as floating clouds, place cloud icons on the board, and make the gentle cluster sound on the black twins in the high range of the piano (see also Katsuyama, 2001). Children are guided through metaphoric experiences surrounded by various musical styles using pentatonic scale, whole-tone scale, diatonic scale, chromatic scale,

Figure 7.1.   The first textbook material in *Music for Moppets: Where is Thumbkin?* (Copyright @ 1971 by Lee Roberts Music Publications, Inc. Reprinted with permission.)

12-tone, blues scale, and church modes, to name a few. Given such an experience these children will soon develop awareness that music for Clouds should be different from that for *Elephants*, the characters representing contrasting images from clouds, such as heavy and grand. On the *Elephants* page, adult and baby elephants are depicted; children may differentiate the walking paces between them. When children experience *Scuba*, there are different motifs for different scenes, such as diving into the ocean (e.g., descending cluster sounds); swimming in deep, mysterious water (e.g., whole-tone motif); and encountering various fish, seashells, and seaweeds (e.g., motifs with different tempo, meter, and styles). When a shark appears (e.g., chromatic scales in thirds with dramatic expressions), children hide behind rocks until it swims away. Finally, children swim up to the surface (e.g., ascending cluster sounds).

Metaphors associating particular music with movement and pictorial icons develop awareness in children that tonal, or auditory, events can be represented in a visual form. This is the first step for guiding children into the world of musical symbols (notation). Moreover, participating in a part of musical metaphors (e.g., playing the gentle cluster for icons of *Clouds*) provides an opportunity for children to transfer a visual symbol (notation) into the sound, which is a rudiment of music reading. The enactive activities such as moving to particular motifs depicting characters, scenes, and images, along with pictorial notation, introduce a referential meaning of music to children. Once children become familiar with the idea of expressing a story with various sounds, they can create their own "story without words" (Pace, 1999b, p. 4). These creative activities are the rudiment of improvisation (Pace, 1999b).

At the same time, children are introduced to three-tone notation (Figure 7.2) that represents a structural unit of a melody, the first step for understanding an absolute meaning of music. Typically, children are presented with two contrasting three-tone patterns, such as one with stepwise motion (Figure 7.2a) and the other with a skip-and-staying-the-same motion (Figure 7.2b). These three tones represent the first three notes of a major scale. Children sing these patterns as "low, middle, high" and "low, high, high," respectively, while showing the shape of the pattern in the air. While playing a listening game in which they pick one of the two cards based on what they hear, children experience the first step toward melodic dictation. When children play these patterns on chime bars, they learn the concepts of "steps" (i.e., playing chime bars next to each other) and "skips" (i.e., playing every other chime bar) as well. While children are being familiarized with these three-tone patterns and how to play the steps and the skips, they are also introduced to the concepts of lines and spaces, but not with the standard stave yet. By introducing just one line and two spaces (Figure 7.2c), the three-tone notation can become contextualized into pseudo-Western music notation. When children become familiar with this system, they are introduced to two lines and three spaces (Figures 7.2d and 7.2e). With this two-line system, children can practice larger intervals such as "a skip and a step" (i.e., a fourth) and "two skips" (i.e., a fifth).

Rhythmic concepts are introduced, first, separately from melodic concepts, with mnemonics such as "long" (a half note), "short" (a quarter note), and "short-er" (two eighth notes) along with line notation (e.g., two short horizontal lines followed by one longer horizontal line for "short, short, long"). In line notation, "short" and "short-er" notes are often depicted in black, and "long" in white. Children clap simple rhythmic patterns shown in line notation while chanting the mnemonics. They also

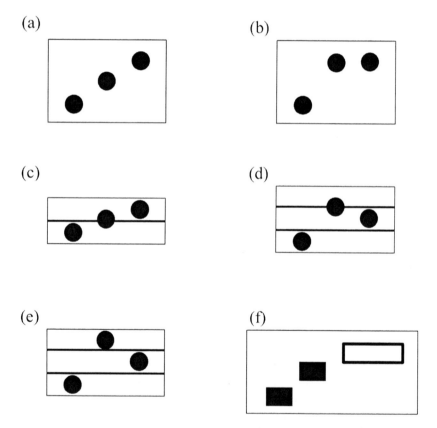

Figure 7.2.   Three-tone patterns: (a) step-wise, "Low-Middle-High," (b) skip-and-stay, "Low-High-High," (c) "Low-Middle-High" on a pseudo-stave, (d) a pattern with a fourth, (e) a pattern with a fifth, and (f) "Low-Middle-High" with rhythmic information.

pick appropriate cards for rhythms they hear and make rhythm patterns by combining such cards. After the children become familiar with the three-tone melodic patterns and the simple rhythmic patterns, the melodic and the rhythmic concepts are combined (Figure 7.2f).

Thus, the children are carefully guided into the Western symbol system. The focus of learning is not mastering specific songs, tunes, or activities but understanding concepts introduced through them (Pace, 1982). The description above illustrates how the enactive and the iconic activities can be related to more sophisticated learning through a real score that children may encounter in the future, the mechanism called transfer of knowledge and skills (Bruner, 1966), an efficient way of learning. This transfer of knowledge, indeed, occurred in my earlier study (Adachi, 1992), where 4- to 5-year-old children managed to read unfamiliar melodic patterns after 12 weeks of similar instruction.

HOW TO ACHIEVE INDEPENDENT FUNCTIONING: THE ROLE OF SPONTANEOUS MUSICAL PLAY

When preschoolers manage to interpret unfamiliar melodic patterns by transferring what they learn through music lessons, it means that they perform without any adult guidance. This is the developmental path predicted by Vygotsky (1978): Children first become able to function in an *interpsychological* plane, in which a child and an adult work together to achieve a particular goal, and later to function in an *intrapsychological* plane, in which the child works alone. There is time lag between the child's interpsychological functioning and his or her intrapsychological (or independent) functioning. What would actually be happening between the original episode of an adult-guided learning situation and a preschooler's independent achievement?

To answer to this question, I conducted an ethnographic study with a preschool child named "Mary," one of the children who demonstrated successful independent functioning in Adachi (1992), by living in her house in Seattle as a housemate (see Adachi, 1994). As previously reported, while living together, I played three different roles for Mary: as a housemate who joined dinner, as a playmate who shared 30-minute music time with her on a weekday morning, and as a music teacher who taught a weekly lesson. I audiotaped sessions of music time and music lessons, and kept a journal about Mary's episodes related to music either that I observed or that her parent or nanny reported to me.

During the 3 months of that study, I discovered Mary's spontaneous musical play was serving as an informal practice of what she learned during her formal lesson, in music time, or at her preschool (see also Adachi,

1994). Such practice appeared to occur primarily through interaction with her family or friends, and occasionally during her own private time, first, by reconstructing an original episode through an interaction while switching roles, and then, by extracting a particular element of her interest or concern from its original episode either in a social or in a private context. For example, when Mary sang *Where is Thumbkin?* to her mother for the first time, she also warned her which finger would be hard to pop up, just like I did in my music lesson; she was playing the music teacher's role in this episode.[1] A few weeks later, when her mother entered her room to wake her up, Mary was already awake practicing how to pop up a ring finger, the difficult one, to make an appropriate action for *Where is Thumbkin?* Mary's private practice followed her social practice with her mother, in line with Vygotsky's (1978) theory.

Mary's spontaneous practice during her play reminds us that children's play represents what they enjoy or care about in their lives (Marsh & Young, 2006; Whiteman, 2001; Young, 2005). In this sense, musical activities observed in Mary's play represent what she enjoyed and cared about musically. Mary incorporated the following types of material she learned in music lessons, during music time, or at her preschool into her spontaneous musical play.

Characters/Images. This can be regarded as musical make-believe or a musical pretend play. In Mary's example, the "music and dance" activity (Adachi, 1994) involved a "musician" and a "dancer"; two parties in this activity pretended to play these roles. In the *Rain Drops, Thunder, and Rainbow* episode (Adachi, 1994), primitive cluster sounds were played with different tempos and dynamics in different ranges on the piano such that each sound would depict a particular scene in the improvised story.

Marching. Marching to a particular tune (see Appendix A) or marching while singing a song can develop a sense of beat. Mary took the initiative to share this activity with her family. On one afternoon, for example, Mary was leading her mother and me by making a flute-like sound while marching around a table. Then Mary, playing the role of her preschool teacher, brought rhythm instruments for us to play and reinitiated our march to her chanting (Figure 7.3).

Action Song. Singing an action song can develop awareness for the body part involved in the action. In addition to the aforementioned episodes of sharing *Where is Thumbkin?*, Mary often taught me what she had learned at her preschool, including the timing of a jump at the end of *Frog Song*.

Notation. Enactive and iconic forms of notation express limited concepts of tones in a system similar to, but simpler than, Western notation. Mary shared the first three pitches of a major scale with her father in the "low–middle–high" dinner episode (Adachi, 1994), and one month later, she demonstrated "low–middle–high" and "low–middle–middle" to her

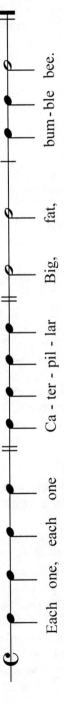

Figure 7.3. Patterns of Mary's chanting while leading a march at home.

Each one, each one   Ca - ter - pil - lar   Big,   fat,   bum - ble bee.

mother. The contour and the intervallic relation of the three tones were depicted in her hand shape, an enactive representation of this melodic pattern. Moreover, Mary was placing buttons vertically between stripes of the tablecloth by herself, and said to her mother, "[This is] going up." In this episode, Mary reviewed the concepts of lines and spaces, as well as how to represent a going-up pattern by placing buttons on lines and spaces. Through these spontaneous practices, Mary familiarized herself with the concept of music notation, which perhaps allowed her to play a melodic pattern on the G staff even without officially learning how to play such notes (Adachi, 1992).

Playing an Instrument. This is probably the most typical form of "practice" in music. Mary played musical instruments as part of a reconstructed episode (e.g., "music and dancing," "rain drops"; see Adachi, 1994) and as a social practice (e.g., playing "low–middle–high" and "steps and skips" on fake chime bars such as wooden blocks while asking me to watch her).

Question and Answer. This is a melodic improvisation using a call–response structure. Its simplest form can consist of a three-tone "question" and its reversed pattern as an "answer" (e.g., Adachi & Chino, 2004). Mary sang and played both question and answer portions on fake chime bars: "Stepping up, stepping down (i.e., low–middle–high, high–middle–low)" and "Skipping up, skipping down (i.e., low–high–high, high–high–low)."

These six types of material were covered in each lesson of *Music for Moppets* in which Mary was enrolled. The material covered must have stimulated her interest and curiosity, important factors of facilitating intrinsic motivation in learning (Marsh & Young, 2006).

A FOLLOW-UP CASE STUDY WITH JAPANESE PRESCHOOLERS (1): 2- TO 4-YEAR-OLDS

In Mary's case, spontaneous musical play was observed almost every day, which may have been a result of her weekday "music time" with me (Adachi, 1994). Unlike her music lesson, music time was where Mary took the initiative for activities that she was engaged in. For this reason, music time often turned into nonmusic time, such as drawing pictures and fantasy play with stuffed animals. Even so, Mary identified her morning playtime with me as music time; having a regular "music" time in her daily schedule may have enhanced her spontaneous engagement with music, including reviewing of material from music lessons. Preschool children in general do not have daily music time with a musically experienced adult.

How often would a preschooler be engaged in spontaneous musical play? What would be the proportion of spontaneous practice of music lessons incorporated in their musical play? Would there be any differences in the type of material practiced at home based on age? Could a role-switching phenomenon observed in Mary's spontaneous practice be replicated by other children? Would younger children be prone to review material through interactions more than older children? To answer these questions, I conducted two case studies with Japanese preschoolers who were enrolled in *Music for Moppets*. The first study focused on four 2- to 4-year-olds, and the second study on seven 5-year-olds.

My first study was conducted in Kofu, located in Honshu Island, where music education majors taught *the program* to four children 2–4 years of age—three boys (Hiro, Sho, and Ryu) and one girl (Emi)—under my supervision. The study set up two instructional periods (Spring and Fall 2001), each consisting of 10 weekly lessons. Three boys participated in both Spring and Fall sessions, and one girl only in the Fall session. These children lived in the same neighborhood, playing together regularly.

The mothers of these children filled out daily journals during these instructional periods, which served as records for children's spontaneous musical behaviors at home. To ensure the mother's records of her child's musical behaviors to be "spontaneous," parents of the participating families made an agreement with me (see *Researcher's Reflections*), including instructions that parents would not interfere with their child's musical engagement but they were allowed to participate in his or her musical play when they were invited by their child.

Each form of the daily journal was printed double-sided on A4-sized paper (Figure 7.4). On the front side, the mother provided the date, circled "Yes" if she saw her child engaged in some kind of musical behavior, indicated the type of musical behaviors she observed by selecting the appropriate one from the boxed list, circled the approximate time(s) of the day when that behavior occurred, and circled the appropriate person(s) with or to whom the child was showing that behavior. On the backside, the mother described the detail of each behavior, with the numbered references corresponding to what was indicated on the front side. Even though the target behavior for the study was "(g) talking/doing what the child did in music lessons," I included an exhaustive list of musical behaviors (see Table 7.1), so that I could reveal the weight of "spontaneous practice" in a preschool child's musical life, which may change as the child grows older.

Table 7.1 shows the summary of spontaneous musical behaviors observed in each child. Overall, these children's spontaneous musical behaviors were observed at home by mothers during 55–97% of days, that is, at least every other day. For Hiro, a 2-year-old boy with advanced

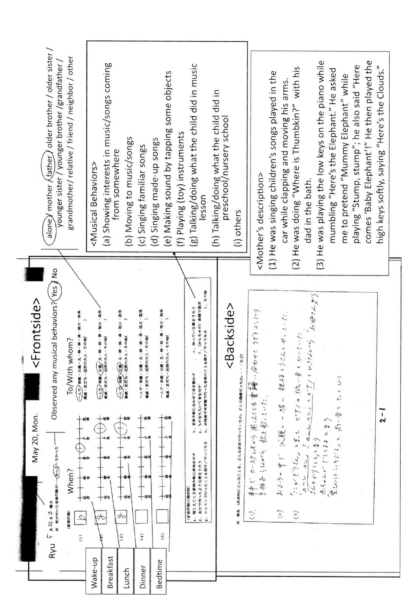

Figure 7.4. An example of a mother's journal record.

144

language skills, approximately 80% of his musical episodes consisted of showing interest in or moving to music and songs coming from somewhere, as well as singing songs (especially made-up songs); for him, music appeared to be something attractive and enactive. Very little time was spent in reviewing material from music lessons (see Type (g) in Table 7.1). For Emi, 3 years of age, over 80% of her musical episodes was similar to Hiro's, but she was engaged less in made-up songs and more interested in moving to music and playing (or pretending to play) instruments than Hiro. Emi did not spend much time reviewing lessons either, but did so more than Hiro. For Sho, late 3 years of age, approximately 60% of his musical episodes was moving to music, singing familiar songs, and making up songs. Over 20% of Sho's episodes was reviewing of material either from music lessons or from preschool. For Ryu, 4 years of age, approximately 60% of his musical episodes were those identified with other children as well, but over 30% was reviewing material either from music lessons or from preschool. Especially during Spring session, Ryu reviewed material taken from *weekly* music lessons as often as those taken from *daily* preschool activities; music lessons must have contributed something special to him. Once Ryu got to know the basics of music in the Fall session, the proportion of lesson-related episodes decreased to the same level as that observed in Emi and Sho. These children voluntarily reviewed lesson material at home, although the frequency of such engagement was scarce compared with moving to music or singing familiar and made-up songs, typically observed musical behaviors during preschoolers' free play (Custodero, 2006; Littleton, 1998; Marsh & Young, 2006; Niland, 2009; Whiteman, 2001; Young, 2002).

Table 7.2 summarizes the list of lesson material reviewed at home and the social context of each reviewing episode. (A brief description of lesson material is presented in Appendix A.) The entries in each cell indicate episodes recorded in the mother's journal. Hiro, a 2-year-old boy, reviewed *all types* of material except for *March/Beat*. Emi and Sho, both 3-year-olds, reviewed *Notation with a song or a chant*; in addition, Emi reviewed *Question and Answer*, and Sho reviewed *Action Song*. Ryu, a 4-year-old boy who was the same age as Mary, reviewed *all types* at home, just as Mary did.

Of the four children studied, Hiro and Emi, the younger children, reviewed lesson material with others, in particular, with their mothers. Sho and Ryu, the older children, reviewed not only with their family members but also by themselves. This illustrates the interpsychological nature of young children's learning and its shift toward an intrapsychological operation as they grow older.

Setting aside the aforementioned individual differences that can be related to the age of each child, let us examine an overall tendency of the

Table 7.1. Summary of Spontaneous Musical Behaviors Observed at Home By Japanese Preschoolers' Mothers

Musical Behavior	Hiro Spring (2:5–2:7)[2] No. of Episodes (%)[3]	Hiro Fall (2:9–2:11) No. of Episodes (%)[3]	Emi Spring[1] No. of Episodes (%)	Emi Fall (3:5–3:7) No. of Episodes (%)	Sho Spring (3:5–3:7) No. of Episodes (%)	Sho Fall (3:9–3:11) No. of Episodes (%)	Ryu Spring (4:1–4:3) No. of Episodes (%)	Ryu Fall (4:5–4:7) No. of Episodes (%)
Showing interest in music/songs	73 (15.9)	79 (22.9)	–	12 (10.2)	0 (0.0)	0 (0.0)	6 (5.1)	0 (0.0)
Moving to (and singing along with) music/songs	107 (23.3)	93 (27.0)	–	49 (41.5)	12 (15.0)	12 (23.5)	29 (21.8)	18 (17.5)
Singing familiar songs with or without modifying lyrics (while moving body)	41 (8.5)	42 (12.1)	–	17 (14.5)	39 (48.8)	13 (25.5)	31 (23.3)	21 (20.4)
Singing made-up songs	176 (38.3)	88 (25.5)	–	1 (0.9)	8 (10.0)	6 (11.8)	6 (4.5)	3 (2.9)
Making sound by tapping/rubbing/blowing into some objects	12 (2.6)	12 (3.5)	–	8 (6.8)	3 (3.8)	1 (2.0)	4 (3.0)	5 (4.9)
Playing/pretending to play (toy) instruments (while singing/moving)	27 (5.9)	24 (7.0)	–	21 (17.8)	1 (1.3)	3 (5.9)	14 (10.5)	14 (13.6)
Talking/doing what the child did in music lesson	14 (3.0)	4 (1.2)	–	7 (5.9)	5 (6.3)	3 (5.9)	19 (14.3)	6 (5.8)
Talking/doing what the child did in preschool/nursery school/daycare	1 (0.2)	2 (0.6)	–	0 (0)	11 (13.8)	13 (25.5)	21 (15.8)	35 (34.0)
Other	8 (1.7)	1 (0.3)	–	3 (2.5)	1 (1.3)	0 (0.0)	3 (2.3)	1 (1.0)
Total no. of episodes	459	345	–	118	80	51	133	103

Notes:
[1] Emi participated only in the second half of the study.
[2] Children's ages presented in years:months.
[3] Percentage of total episodes per child

146

four children's reviewing of music lessons at home. There were 23 materials (including songs, tunes, and activities) introduced during two sets of 10 weekly instruction sessions, 11 of which were presented as a song or a chant (i.e., those indicated with double quotation marks in Table 7.2) and the rest as an imaginary story with musical themes or a simple game. Nine out of the 11 "song" materials were reviewed at least once, whereas only five out of 12 "nonsong" materials were reviewed. The children appeared to incorporate "song" materials more than "nonsong" materials into their spontaneous play. Moreover, of 11 "song" materials, six songs portraying some characters or visual images were all reviewed, but only three of those without characters were reviewed.

These findings indicate that the children are more likely to review lesson materials presented as songs than those presented otherwise, and that they are inclined to review songs with characters than those without. Nonsong materials such as *Characters/Images* and *Marching/Beat* also appear to contribute to their spontaneous musical practice. Of five nonsong materials reviewed at least once, four were reviewed in a context where a child reconstructed a lesson by playing the role of a teacher, that is, replication of a role-switching phenomenon (Adachi, 1994), whereas this was observed only in two out of nine song materials. In other words, song materials and nonsong materials appeared to elicit different forms of interactions in the children's spontaneous musical play: doing (or singing) together or leading family members. These differences, however, may reflect how the children could perceive their roles while being engaged in these types of materials in music lessons. In song materials, both the teacher and children were singing together, whereas in nonsong materials, the teacher was playing thematic tunes of particular characters/images or those for marching activities as she guided children to move appropriately. The distinction of roles between the teacher and children was clearer during nonsong than song materials. It is possible, then, that children may have been pretending to be a teacher in their own minds even though they seemed to be singing a song from music lessons simply with their family members.

A FOLLOW-UP CASE STUDY WITH JAPANESE PRESCHOOLERS (2): 5-YEAR-OLDS

Based on these findings with four 2- to 4-year-olds, I conducted another study, primarily to investigate whether the proportion of spontaneous practice of music lesson materials would increase as children grow older, secondly to investigate whether the role-switching phenomenon would occur in older preschoolers, and finally to examine whether older pre-

Table 7.2. The Content and The Context of Spontaneous Practice of Music Lesson Materials (2-4 Years Old)

Child	Hiro	Emi[1]	Sho	Ryu
Sex	Boy	Girl	boy	Boy
Age (years:months)	(2:5–2:11)	(3:5–3:7)	(3:5–3:11)	(4:1–4:7)
Type				
Characters/Images				
Clouds				[M/F]
<Animal World>[4]				
Elephants	M[2]			[*M/F*], A, OC
Glider				M
Scuba	*M*[3]			
<All Gathering>				
<Leaf-Falling>				
Fog Horn				
<Rowing Boat>				
March/ Beat				
<Marching>				*YB*, A, YB, YB, F, A
<"Good-Bye Song">[5]				
Action Song (Hands/Fingers/Keyboard)				
"Where is Thumbkin"	M, M, M, M, M, GM, GM, M		A, A, A, A	A, *F*, F, [M/YB]
<"RH and LH">				
<"Twins and Triplets">	M			
<"Finger Song">				YB

148

Activity				
Notation (w/song or chant)				
"The Farmer in the Dell"	M, M			F, A
"Autum Leaves"	M		[M/OB/YS], <u>YS</u>	A
<"Steppie/Skippie">				A, A
<"Three Dots">			A, [M]	F
<"Long/Short">	M			
Notation (other)				
<Moppet Cards>				
<Acorn Game>				
Q & A				
<"Question and Answer">	[M/F], *M*	M		[F/YB], [F/M/YB]
Others				
Pretending to play the piano	M			
Talking about lesson	M, [M/F], [M/F]	E, M, M		[M/F]

149

Notes:

1 Emi participated only in the second half of the study. Materials taught only during the first half of the study were shown in cells with a diagonal line.

2 The letter(s) in each cell indicates the context of the activity. A: alone; M: with mother; F:with father; O with older brother; OS: with older sister; YB with younger brother; YS with younger sister; OC with older cousin; GM with grandmother; [M/F] with mother and father

3 Bold and italicized letter indicates that the child switched the roles in this activity. Single underlined entries indicate that the child played an instrument other than a piano/keyboard. Double underlined ones indicate the child played the piano/keyboard.

4 Bracketed materials <X> are supplementary materials; others are from the textbook.

5 Materials with quotation marks are songs.

schoolers' spontaneous practice would occur more privately than younger children's. This study was a collaboration with an experienced Pace Method teacher who had two different weekly group lessons using *Music for Moppets* for eight children whose ages ranged from 4 years, 7 months to 6 years, 5 months at the beginning of the study. In Mary's and the aforementioned Kofu studies, I organized their lessons; studying children taught by a different teacher allowed me to examine my hypotheses in a more general context.

The group lessons were conducted at Kurume and Fukuoka on Kyushu Island, Japan, with four boys (Jiro, Ray, Dai, and Taka) and four girls (Nao, Ai, Lisa, and Kimi). Data for children's spontaneous musical behaviors at home were collected with mothers' journals in the same way as the Kofu study. The period of data collection in the present study also fell into two sessions, each of which consisted of 3–4 months. According to her mother's diary, Kimi did not review any formal lesson material at home, and was later identified with a learning disability. Consequently, the following discussion pertains to the other seven children only.

The proportions of spontaneous practice of music lessons against all the spontaneous musical behaviors per child ranged from 5 to 27% ($M = 15.71$, $SD = 8.36$; Table 7.3), which was greater than for the 2- to 4-year-olds ($M = 6.22$, $SD = 3.42$). For the majority of the 5-year-olds, the proportion of spontaneous practice during their spontaneous musical play appears to be doubled, or even quadrupled, from that observed in their younger counterparts.

Role switching was observed in two boys (Jiro, Ray) and two girls (Ai, Lisa) while reviewing *Characters/Images* (e.g., *Elephants* with a younger sister, *Glider* with a mother), *Finger Exercises* (with an older sister or with parents), *Notation* (with a younger sister), and *Playing the piano* with the mother or a friend (see Table 7.3). When children did not switch roles, they simply reviewed together with their family members, relatives, and/ or friends. In one of Lisa's episodes, she requested her mother to "Please hide my fingers [with a textbook], so that I cannot see them [while playing the piano]." This was a replication of an exercise introduced in a regular lesson; the mother was playing the role of Lisa's peer (or teacher) in the lesson. The majority of spontaneous practice in 5-year-olds was observed in social contexts in which their mothers were actively involved as cooperative practice partners. Five out of seven children were privately engaged in spontaneous practice (see "A" in cells in Table 7.3), a greater proportion than two out of four 2- to 4-year-olds in the Kofu study.

Table 7.3 outlines the types of lesson material reviewed at home. *Characters/Images* were reviewed by two boys (Jiro and Taka) and one girl (Ai). *Question and Answer* was reviewed by one girl (Nao). Reviewing of these materials was the same as the younger children in the Kofu study. Another

Table 7.3. The Content and the Context of Spontaneous Practice of Music Lesson Materials (5 Years Old)

Child	Kurume					Fukuoka	
	Jiro	Ray	Dai	Taka	Nao	Ai	Lisa
Age (years:months)	(4:8–5:4)	(4:8–5:4)	(5:1–5:9)	(4:7–5:3)	(4:11–5:7)	(5:3–5:8)	(5:3–5:8)
Family Members	M, F, YS	M, F, OS	M, F, YB	M, F	M, F	M, F, YB	M, F
Spontaneous Practice (%)[1]	22.05	11.21	4.76	21.53	7.14	16.36	26.83
Characters/images	*YS*[3]			A, A, A[2]		M	
Marching/beat							
Action Song (hands/fingers/keyboard)							
Finger Exercise (on the piano)		*OS*, [OS/F/M]		M		M, [*M/F*]	M, M, *M*, A, M; M, M, M, M
Notation (w/song or chant)	YS	A, A, A		A, A, A, M	[M/F/GM], [M/Fr], M		M, M, M, M
Notation (other)							M
Question and Answer					[M/Fr]		
Playing the Piano/Keyboard	*M*, M, M, M, M, M, M, M, M, M, M, YS, A, A, [M/YS], M, M, [M/YS], A, [M/YS], M, M, A	A, OS, A, OS, *M*, OS, M	M, M; M	A, A, M, M, GM, C, C		*M, Fr*, M, A; M	M
Pretending to play the piano							
Talking about "lesson"					M, [M/Fr]	[M/F]	M, M

Notes: [1] Proportion of spontaneous practice of lesson materials of all the musical behaviors observed by each child's mother. [2] The letter(s) in each cell indicates the context of the activity. A alone; M with mother; F with father; OB with older brother; YB with younger brother; YS with younger sister; OS with older sister; O)C with (older) cousin; GM with grandmother; Fr with a friend; [M/F] with mother and father. [3] Bold and italicized letter indicates that the child switched the roles in this activity. Single underlined entries indicate that the child played an instrument other than a piano/keyboard. Double underlined ones indicate the child played the piano/keyboard.

151

tendency similar to the younger children was the use of songs. Most of the textbook material reviewed by 5-year-olds was presented as songs or chants in their lessons; if not, children generated their own songs. Three boys (Jiro, Ray, and Taka) and two girls (Nao and Lisa) reviewed *Notation with song or chant* (i.e., material regarding notation presented with songs or chants during lessons). One girl (Lisa) generated ascending and descending stepwise melodies to her chanting of "line, space, line, space," even though the concept of "line and space" was not presented with a particular melody during a lesson (i.e., *Notation (other)* in Table 7.3). Taka generated his own song for *Glider* (i.e., *Characters/Images*). The tendency to review materials with songs or chants was observed in 5-year-olds as well.

No record of reviewing *Marching/Beat* or *Action Song* was found in the older preschoolers' spontaneous practice. Instead, *Finger Exercise* (i.e., playing short repeated patterns with designated fingers) was practiced by two boys (Ray and Taka) and two girls (Ai and Lisa) and *Playing the Piano/ Keyboard* was practiced by all but Nao. Because these children were old enough to play the piano with individual fingers, their lessons covered playing the textbook materials on the piano much more than the aforementioned lessons for the younger group, who used a gently closed hand rather than individual fingers in playing the piano. *Finger Exercise* and *Playing the Piano/Keyboard* require children to identify their fingers and to keep the beat, the elements also covered in the activities of *Action Song* and *Marching/Beat*. In this sense, 5-year-olds were practicing these elements not through bodily activities but through the actual piano playing.

The nature of *Pretending to Play the Piano* observed in a 5-year-old girl (Lisa) was also different from that observed in a 3-year-old girl (Emi). Lisa was actually practicing designated fingering by moving the actual fingers on the surface of the bathwater, whereas Emi was reviewing only the "image" of piano playing by moving fingers randomly on a keyboard. This may be evidence of a shift in the focus of the children's spontaneous practice from an overall image of music to a specific element of music learning.

CONCLUSIONS

The majority of early childhood music programs try involving parents (usually mothers) in their children's music learning, often expecting them to be instructional assistants who can monitor their children's practice at home and provide appropriate advice to them (McPherson & Davidson, 2006; Stupay, Galvagno, Rosi, & Ceri, 2009). The case study findings described in this chapter corroborate those of previous studies reporting that the majority of preschoolers' spontaneous practice occurs in social contexts at home, involving, especially, parents. However, in these case studies, parents did not play the role of home teachers (as usually assumed by early childhood music programs) but that of practice partners, who respect children's own interests and thought processes while participating in their spontaneous musical play only upon *invitation* (Adachi, 1994).

The nature of young children is to assimilate reality into their own terms until they feel comfortable accepting how the world actually works. It is this assimilative or *generative* mode of thinking that allowed preschoolers to interpret unfamiliar musical symbols in their own way (Adachi, 1992), to create one's own song to an episode introduced in the textbook, and to play finger exercises on an invisible keyboard in the bathwater.

Reconstruction of a lesson episode and practice of a particular skill or music introduced at the lesson are based on an *iterative* mode of thinking, an internalized guidance for children to become functional within a musical system (Adachi, 1992). The present chapter indicates that even a child under age 3 can operate iteratively in his or her spontaneous musical play, without explicit parental guidance at home, demonstrating his or her potential to become an independent learner. Producing an independent learner is the ultimate goal of the Pace Method (Pace, 1982), and the hope that every teacher holds for his or her student.

A *transferential* mode of thinking, which allowed preschoolers to read musical symbols without explicit instruction by applying what they learned at music lessons (Adachi, 1992), was also observable in preschoolers' spontaneous musical play. For example, Sho (a 3-year-old boy in the Kofu study) created a crocodile song while opening up his arms as if they were the crocodile jaws and pretending to attack his mother, a clear application of a shark episode in the *Scuba* lesson. This type of play episode was not counted as spontaneous practice presented in this chapter because this is qualitatively different from reviewing lesson materials directly and should be treated separately. The proportion of practice behaviors related to music lessons in preschoolers' musical play, therefore, would be higher than what was presented in this chapter.

Integration of movement, listening, and visual images into one cohesive learning episode in each lesson helps children practice "how to think in motion" and develop "the eye that hears and ear that sees" (Pace, 1999a, p. 4), necessary skills to achieve a full appreciation of music as a "time art" (Pace, 1982, p. 1). Preschoolers' music reading skills (Adachi, 1992), along with the superior sight-reading and memorization abilities of the intermediate students taught by the Pace Method (Sampei, 2001), support the validity of an integrated approach where instruction for music literacy is coupled with music by ear (Lehmann, Sloboda, & Woody, 2007; McPherson & Gabrielsson, 2002).

In sum, "the tradition [of formal learning] is didactic and non-constructivist in nature" (Campbell, 1998, p. 179). This may be true for the majority of music lessons; however, there are ways to incorporate young children's interest, their current level of musical achievement, and instructional goals into multifaceted, yet cohesive, instruction. The series of case studies reported in this chapter demonstrate such an instructional possibility, proposing various ideas that children can take home and assimilate into their own spontaneous play.

Findings presented in this chapter demonstrate how formal learning can be integrated with preschool children's spontaneous musical development through musical play at home, facilitating the development of their musical understanding and skills without tears. Whether preschool children in other introductory music programs review their music lessons in a similar manner awaits further investigation. A role-switching phenomenon in preschool children's spontaneous music learning has been reported in their spontaneous song play in a daycare center as well (Whiteman, 2001). The replicability of this phenomenon may, at least, ensure that young children need to play the role of teacher outside of formal instruction, which, in turn, implies no need of another teacher at home.

RESEARCHER'S REFLECTION:
INVOLVING PRIMARY CAREGIVERS IN DATA COLLECTION

In this chapter, I described findings from three case studies about the nature of preschoolers' music learning through formal instruction. In developmental research, over-time interviews/observations are often used as a record of *achievement* at a particular point in a child's development. Once a research question begins addressing *how* each child achieves a particular level, the over-time research design is not good enough; one needs access to the child's musical behaviors outside of the music lesson or interview. For one particular child (such as Mary), an ethnographic study would be the best. If one wants to observe multiple children's everyday musical lives at home during the same period of time, however, this presents some logistical challenges. This is why I decided to involve mothers in data collection, as reported in the two case studies in Japan.

There were three things to consider in the mother's data collection. First, I needed to create a recording system that would be easy enough for the mothers to follow (see Figure 7.4 and the main text for detail). Second, I needed diligent reporting by mothers. So, at each music lesson of the Kofu study, the mothers were given a set of journal forms to be filled out everyday. They brought back the completed forms on the following lesson, and took home the new set of journal forms for the upcoming week. By doing so, the mothers did not lose their forms, and kept being reminded of their roles as observers. This was not possible in the second study due to the circumstances surrounding participation, which are addressed below. Finally, I needed to ensure that children's musical behaviors to be observed at home would be all *spontaneous* rather than something intentionally generated by parents. To achieve this, I made the following agreement with the participating families.

1. Parents would not mention the word "practice" to their child.
2. Parents were not to force anything related to music lessons.
3. Parents may ask what the child did in music lessons, but they must let the child decide whether he or she would tell.
4. Parents could participate with whatever the child invites them to do musically.
5. Parents would not correct mistakes the child makes regarding music lessons.
6. Parents would fill out the *daily journal* everyday during each instructional period.
7. Parents may come to see music lessons, but they would not interfere with the child unnecessarily (e.g., parents could not scold even when a child did not cooperate with the teacher).
8. Parents would have their child participate in interviews.
9. Parents would contact me if they had any questions.
10. Music lessons and supplementary materials were free of charge, but each child was required to have his or her own textbook.

This system worked very well for the Kofu study, in which the mothers were taking records in exchange for free music lessons, and the student teachers prepared each set of recording forms every week as part of their research project. However, in the second study, in which both the mothers and the teacher were collecting data solely as volunteers, I could not keep the system as strictly as the Kofu study. For example, I gave 3 months' worth of forms to fill out and collected them after each instructional period rather than doing so weekly, so that I could minimize the teacher's involvement in data collection. Without a weekly reminder with a new set of forms, some of the mothers in the second study tended to forget to fill out the forms. For this reason, the accuracy of the mothers' records may not be as high as those in the Kofu study. My analyses of data from the second Japanese study were based on the assumption that for each child, the observational records were generally consistent over time.

One must be aware of possible disadvantages of collecting data through children's own mothers. For example, mothers may exaggerate what really happened to present their children favorably (although the low percentage of practicing lesson material at home implies that this was not the case in my studies). On the contrary, mothers may miss a very interesting spontaneous practice of lesson material occurring on the street corner while talking to their peer mothers (which I actually happened to observe). The structured observation sheet may disturb mothers' own ways of describing their children, resulting in the loss of potentially valuable information.

At the end of data collection mothers expressed their appreciation for the opportunity to witness the focused musical development of their children that would otherwise have been overlooked without the journal keeping. All stated that the positive experience far outweighed the obligation or the time burden. One mother in the Kofu study confessed that she broke the agreement of "no intentional practice of instructed items at home": "Just once I tried to check my son's understanding of black 'twins and triplets' on the keyboard, but he rejected me by saying 'no'." In an observation sheet of the same mother, she successfully stimulated her son's interest and active engagement in *Where is Thumbkin?* by modifying lyrics. Through her son's positive/negative feedback and his musical growth even without forceful practice, the mother soon realized her role as a "facilitator" who could integrate the child's structured learning with his favorite mode of musical play. Having such a coordinator at home can result in an ideal marriage of early childhood formal instruction and children's spontaneous musical play. Supporting parents in their role as musical facilitator using tools and circumstances such as those reported in these studies may prove helpful in children's ongoing musical development.

ACKNOWLEDGMENTS

I express my sincere appreciation to the student teachers of the Kofu study (Michiko Nakajima, Mariko Nakai, and Anna Irizuki), the teacher for the Kurume/Fukuoka study (Mitsuko Nakajima), all the mothers who dedicated their time and efforts in recording their children's musical behaviors at home, and the research assistants (Akio Akasaka, Izumi Kida, and Takeshi Okamoto) who generated the database and conducted descriptive statistics for the journal records. I also thank two anonymous reviewers and the series editors for their valuable comments for the draft of this chapter, Gary Vasseur for his proofreading, and Peter Whiteman and Chee Hoo Lum for their patience and support for my writing.

Appendix: Summary of Activities for Each Learning Material Conducted at Music Lessons in the Kofu Study

Textbook Materials	Activities
"Where Is Thumbkin?" (SF)	Action song identifying 5 fingers with names; *Father, Mother, Brother, Sister, & Baby* in Japanese.
Cloud (S)	Moving to music (pentatonic) on the high range. High, Soft, and Fluffy. After moving, children put Clouds (made of cotton) in blue sky on a magnet board, Children played black Twins on the high range of piano with a gently closed hand pretending to be a cloud.
Elephant (S)	Moving to music (atonal) on the low range. Low and Heavy. Slightly different music for Daddy, Mummy, and Baby elephants. Children discriminate differences by ear and moved differently, putting different-ent sized icons on the magnet board. Children held small bean bags looking like elephant foots and played black Twins on the low range.
Gliders (S)	Moving to music (whole-tone) on middle-high range while holding paper gliders. Moving Up and Down, & Floating. Children moved from left to right as music going up and vice versa on silent keyboards. Children played black Triplets on the piano.
Scuba (S)	Children played black Triplets of middle-low range while going down to the ocean. Moving Down and Up. Many characters and their theme music (tremolo-like chromatic; dominant-tonic; etc) were introduced. Children discriminated character music by ear, and moved accordingly.
"The Famer In the Dell" (SF)	The rhythmic structure AABA was emphasized with a special action in B, visualized with pictures. Children put four pictures from left to right while singing. Children also played a simple ostinato (holding a key per phrase, presented in line score) while singing.
"Autum Leaves" (F)	Children sang the song while shaping the contour with a hand. The rhythmic and melodic motifs were visualized with line score. Children played two pentatonic phrases (going up and going down) on the chime while singing.
Fog Horn (F)	Children played tritone either with both hands or from one hand to another while shifting weight as if they were rowing.

Supplementary Materials

Q & A (SF)	Name-calling game. The teacher called a child's name with three tones ("Low, Middle, High" in Spring, "Low, Low, High" in Fall) while playing the chime, and the child responds in contrary motion (first singing and clapping only, then on the chime).
"Three Dots" (SF)	Three filled circles laid out on a card. Three pitch levels represents pitch names; Low, Middle, & High. The child sang the pattern while shaping with a hand. The child also identified the card while listening to the teacher. In Fall, the card consisted of one line (and two spaces).
Animal World (S)	Discriminating character music and moving to each theme.
"RH & LH" (S)	Action song identifying right and left hands.

(Appendix continues on next page)

Appendix: Continued

Textbook Materials	Activities
Marching (SF)	Marching to music in which either low or high cluster tone was inserted at a phrase boundary. Children bent down for the low and jumped up for the high tone, and learned to anticipate the phrase boundary.
"Good-Bye Song" (SF)	A simple song serving as an ending theme for each lesson. Its melody consisted of the first half of Frere Jacques, the same tune as "Where Is Thumbkin." Children clapped while singing, feeling the beat.
"Twins & Triplets" (SF)	A song to enhance the location of black Twins and Triplets on the keyboard.
"Long/Short" (SF)	Clapping simple rhythm while singing the rhythm of line scores as Short (quarter), Long (half), Short-er (eighths).
All Gathering (S)	Moving to all the character music covered in Spring session.
Leaf-Falling (F)	Introductory activity for "Autumn Leaves." Someone moved as wind while others held paper leaves as trees that let leaves go.
"Finger Song" (F)	An original action song identifying 5 fingers; *Father, Mother, Brother, Sister, & Baby*. The tune consists of three tones (Low, Middle, High).
Moppet Cards (F)	Each card contains a theoretical concept with a picture (line, space, note on a line, note in a space, step up, step down, skip up, skip down).
Acorn Game (F)	Activity that connects original "three dot" cards (without line) to new cards with line. Children simply put the felt acorns as shown.
"Steppie/Skippie" (F)	A character song to emphasize the difference between steps (2nds) and skips (3rds) (Adachi,1992). Children moved characters Steppie and Skippie on a staff-like paperboard while singing the song.
Rowing Boat (F)	Introductory activity to "Fog Horn." The child and the teacher sat on the floor while taking each others' hands, and rocked to music.

Notes: Textbook materials are from *Music for Moppets* (Robert Pace Piano Series, Lee Roberts).

Materials sung as a "song" are indicated with quotation marks. (S) and (F) stand for the material taught in Spring session and in Fall session, respectively.

NOTE

1.   Mary's episodes described in this chapter have not been published elsewhere, unless specified otherwise.

REFERENCES

Adachi, M. (1992). Development of young children's music reading via instruction. *Proceedings of the Fifth Early Childhood Music Education Seminar* (pp. 83–107). Tokyo: Kunitachi College of Music.

Adachi, M. (1994). The role of the adult in the child's early musical socialization: A Vygotskian perspective. *Quarterly Journal of Music Teaching and Learning, V*(3), 26–35.

Adachi, M. (in press). Musically rich but creatively poor: A cautionary tale of music nurturing in Japanese preschool. In P. S. Campbell & T. Wiggins (Eds.), *The Oxford handbook of children's musical cultures*. New York: Oxford University Press.

Adachi, M., & Chino, Y. (2004). Inspiring creativity through music. In S. Lau, A. N. N. Hui, & G. Y. C. Ng (Eds.), *Creativity: When east meets west* (pp. 305–340). Singapore: World Scientific.

Bruner, J. S. (1966). *Toward a theory of instruction*. Cambridge, MA: Harvard University Press.

Campbell, P. S. (1998). *Songs in their heads: Music and its meaning in children's lives*. New York: Oxford University Press.

Campbell, P. S., & Scott-Kassner, C. (1995). *Music in childhood: From preschool through the elementary grades*. New York: Shirmer Books.

Custodero, L. A. (2006). Singing practices in 10 families with young children. *Journal of Research in Music Education, 54*(1), 37–56.

Katsuyama, H. (2001). Case report: A boy who is recovering from suspected MELAS through weekly music instruction. In Y. Minami & M. Shinzanoh (Eds.), *Proceedings of the Third Asia-Pacific Symposium on Music Education Research, Vol. II* (pp. 61–66). Nagoya, Japan: Aichi University of Education.

Lehmann, A. C., Sloboda, J. A., & Woody, R. H. (2007). *Psychology for musicians: Understanding and acquiring the skills*. New York: Oxford University Press.

Littleton, D. (1998). Music learning and child's play. *General Music Today, 12,* 8–15.

Marsh, K., & Young, S. (2006). Musical play. In G. E. McPherson (Ed.), *The child as musician: A handbook of musical development* (pp. 289–310). New York: Oxford University Press.

McPherson, G. E., & Davidson, J. W. (2006). Playing an instrument. In G. E. McPherson (Ed.), *The child as musician: A handbook of musical development* (pp. 331–351). New York: Oxford University Press.

McPherson, G. E., & Gabrielsson, A. (2002). From sound to sign. In R. Parncutt & G. E. McPherson (Eds.), *The science and psychology of music performance* (pp. 99–115). New York: Oxford University Press.

Morin, F. L. (2001). Cultivating music play: The need for changed teaching practice. *General Music Today, 14,* 24–29.

Niland, A. (2009). The power of musical play: The value of play-based, child-centered curriculum in early childhood music education. *General Music Today, 23,* 17–21.

Pace, R. (1982, October). *Position paper*. Paper presented at the National Conference on Piano Pedagogy, Madison, WI.

Pace, R. (1999a). *The essentials of keyboard pedagogy: I. Sight-reading and musical literacy*. Chatham, NY: Lee Roberts Music Publications.

Pace, R. (1999b). *The essentials of keyboard pedagogy: II. Improvisation and creative problem-solving*. Chatham, NY: Lee Roberts Music Publications.

Sampei, S. (2001). Effects of spiral learning on intermediate piano students' sight-reading and memorization processes. In Y. Minami & M. Shinzanoh (Eds.), *Proceedings of the Third Asia-Pacific Symposium on Music Education Research, Vol. II* (pp. 10–13). Nagoya, Japan: Aichi University of Education.

Stupay, A., Galvagno, E., Rosi, F., & Ceri, V. (2009). The Suzuki method: Music as a magnifying glass for viewing the world. In A. R. Addessi & S. Young (Eds.), *MERYC2009: Proceedings of the Fourth Conference of the European Network of Music Educators and Researchers of Young Children* (pp. 81–88). Bologna, Italy: Bononia University Press.

Vygotsky, L. S. (1978). *Mind in society: The development of higher psychological processes*. Cambridge, MA: Harvard University Press.

Whiteman, P. J. (2001). *How the bananas got their pyjamas: A study of the metamorphosis of preschoolers' spontaneous singing as viewed through Vygotsky's Zone of Proximal Development*. Unpublished doctoral dissertation, University of New South Wales, Australia.

Young, S. (2002). Young children's spontaneous vocalizations in free-play: Observations of two- to three-year-olds in a day-care setting. *Bulletin of the Council for Research in Music Education, 152*, 43–53.

Young, S. (2003). Time-space structuring in spontaneous play on educational percussion instruments among three- and four-year-olds. *British Journal of Music Education, 20*(1), 45–59.

Young, S. (2005). Musical communication between adults and young children. In E. Miell, R. McDonald, & D. J. Hargreaves (Eds.), *Musical communication* (pp. 281–299). New York: Oxford University Press.

CHAPTER 8

PICTURE IT!

Young Children Conceptualizing Music

Peter Whiteman and Patricia Shehan Campbell

MUSIC IN HUMAN LIFE

Music is a constant in human life. Over time and across cultures, music's presence is confirmed in daily life, even as it is also a meaningful component of extraordinary life events. Music is both mediated and live, and people of every age know music as meaningful and useful to them, and as both a personal and a collective cultural experience (Wade, 2004). As a powerful human resource, music serves many purposes—ranging from its uses in social interactions (as in romancing lovers), joyous celebrations (such as birthdays, weddings, graduations) and other emotionally charged moments (such as funerals), to the inspiration of political movements (as in peace rallies and election campaigns) and the sustenance of friendships (in jam sessions, sing-a-longs, and Saturday night dance clubs). Musical experiences are valuable for "the process of personal and social integration that make us whole" (Turino, 2008, p. 1).

Music matters to young children, too. It figures in lullabies and resting times; in the mediated amusements of their favorite TV shows, movies, video games, and child-friendly Internet sites; and in the singing games and spontaneous songs they sing while at play with toy cars and

Musical Childhoods of Asia and the Pacific, pp. 161–189
Copyright © 2012 by Information Age Publishing
All rights of reproduction in any form reserved.

action figures. Children do not typically define and describe music, but their world is blanketed in the music that they make and listen to (Campbell, 1998). Far from a formal music or music-educational experience, music is there "in the air" they breathe, weaving through their day in school and far on the outside (Lum & Campbell, 2007). For young children, music just *is*, and the songs and sounds of their environment brings them joy, solace, safety, and a sense of identity. Music for them is an experience beyond words, where words may simply not suffice to explain its meaning.

Multiple Perspectives, Multiple Musics

Humans have made music for a very long time and the breadth of perspectives taken in defining music is as wide as this history in humanity is long. Over time, scholars have conceptualized music as organized sound, a byproduct, adaptive behavior, a harmonizing influence, an act, and a symbol system.

As organized sound. Possibly one of the most palpable positions from which definitions have been drawn is the sonic perspective. After all, few would argue that music is devoid of sound. A keen pusher of boundaries, Edgar Varese was of the opinion that music is a collaboration between science and art and it is science that allows music to evolve (Weng-Chung, 1967). He considered music to be "organized sound" (p. 207) and, as a composer, he viewed music as the organizer of the plethora of sonic elements that constitute this. John Cage concurred (Schafer, 1969), taking the inclusive position that music is all sounds within a temporal framework, whether in or out of the formal music-making environs of the Western tonal tradition. Cage notably widened this perception to include the absence of sound in his composition *4' 33"* (Davies, 1997), partly in order to stimulate listening attention to the spectrum of ambient sound even in the absence of intentional structures of composed music. While devoid of sounds emanating from the piano, this composition still has possibilities for the extraneous sounds that occur in its performance (e.g., feet rustling in the concert hall, traffic noise outside).

As a byproduct. Although humans like order and function, some things exist purely for pleasure or decoration. Examples of such phenomena can be found in domains such as architecture and biology. In architecture, bridges and buildings are rife with spandrels. These are the approximately triangular areas created in the space between two arches or an arch and the straight line of a rectangular area (Harris, 2006). These areas have no structural significance, but provide opportunities for elaborate decoration that have been taken up in the design and construction buildings and bridges since Medieval times. Similar byproducts can be found in evolutionary biology where the notion of spandrel has been used to signify "presently useful characteristics [that] did not arise as adaptations ... but owe their origin to side consequences of other features" (Gould, 1991, p. 53). Of note is the peacock's magnificent tail. Whether architectural or biological, spandrels did not come about because of a need to decorate, but rather as a byproduct of creating something else.

Some scholars (e.g., Pinker, 1997) have likewise conceived of music as nonadaptive, pleasure-seeking behavior. Pinker posited (1997) that music serves no purpose other than that of "auditory cheesecake" and in fact is nothing more than a byproduct of the adaptation of language, which had a clear evolutionary basis. He maintained that just as humans evolved a liking for the elements that constitute a cheesecake (e.g., fat and sugar) rather than the cheesecake itself, language was the activity important for survival of the species and music just "comes along for the ride" (Levitin, 2006).

As adaptive behavior. Conversely, a not uncommon viewpoint has been that of music as adaptive behavior. From this perspective, music has been linked to the development of complex behaviors such as language (Levitin, 2006, 2008; Miller, 2000). Such perspectives present music at its most functional. Music is positioned as an imperative factor in human evolution "that appears to play a significant role in the achievement or enhancement of cognitive flexibility as well as being efficacious in the rehearsal (and hence the acquisition) of competencies in managing social relationships" (Cross, 2005, p. 39)

As a harmonizing influence. Aside from function as a means of defining music, there is also Murray Schafer's (1969) more metaphysical notion of music as a harmonizing influence, a neo-Pythagorean conception of music representing the order of the universe. Drawing on Ancient Greek myths, Schafer reduces the origins of all theories of music to two. The first locates the essence of music within the realm of emotion, in response to the cries of Medusa's sisters. The second places importance on the manner in which the universe is bound by the harmonies produced by its components. We are told how Pythagoras believed that different musical modes evoked different responses from listeners and that people could be aroused or sedated, for example, by listening to music in a specific mode, with specific types of rhythm.

As an act and a symbol system. Following this functional vein, Small (1977, 1998) defined music as a human act rather than a thing, and a process of human engagement. Keil and Feld (1994) and Turino (2008) similarly underscore the potential of music as a social act and a communal art. Not only is the sound itself significant, but equally important are the facets of who is making it, where it is being made, and for whom. From this perspective, music becomes a verb rather than a noun. Small's classification of music as a verb goes far beyond composers making music for performers or performers making music for listeners. "Musicking," according to Small, does not delineate between these roles. In fact, the notion of music as an act encompasses all roles equally. Whether singing, playing, moving, or listening, we are all in it together, for a purpose. This functional approach was advanced earlier by Gardner and Wolf (1979) in their landmark study of early symbolization, with music seen as a semiotic system with which people (in this case children) make meaning.

From this review of the literature, it is reasonable to assert that "music" is a contested domain, with definitions often devised according to the purpose at hand. One thing that appears to be common to all explanations, however, is that they originate from the judgment and reason of adults. Within this plethora of available meanings, none emanate from the deliberations of children. In these times of renewed child-centered approaches to education (e.g., Wood, 2007), the central importance of child agency (Woodrow, 1999), and calls for bottom-up approaches to early childhood pedagogy (e.g., Lambert & Clyde, 2000), this is unacceptable. To begin redressing this state of affairs, we turned to children themselves in an effort to start understanding what music means from their perspectives.

METHOD

Setting and Participants

This study was undertaken in an Australian childcare center (hereafter referred to as "the center"). Operating Monday to Friday from 7:00 A.M. to 6:00 P.M., 50 weeks per year, the center caters to up to 50 children per day. Children are generally grouped in one of three rooms according to age: birth–2 years, 2–3 years, or 3–5 years. Rather than labeled according to children's age, these groups are known by names drawn from Australian flora and fauna. The center is staffed by early childhood teachers, trained childcare workers, and untrained assistants. Additional staff include visiting experts such as special education teachers on an as-needed basis and administrative and kitchen staff. Participants were 20 4- to 5-year-old children, all of whom were entering their first year of formal school the following year.

Data Collection

Each child was issued a digital camera. The cameras were the same model that was in regular use by staff as part of everyday life in the center.

The children have seen cameras used to document their learning, but this was most often an activity undertaken by staff. After checking operational procedures, the children were asked to "take photos of music" over the ensuing week. Researchers were mindful of not requesting photographs of "people making music" or something similar, so as to minimize any bias toward any one of the above-mentioned positions on the nature of "music." Parents were also asked to allow children to make decisions about what to photograph and were reminded about this during the week. The children kept the camera with them at the center, at home and in the community. One week later, they viewed their photographs on a computer and discussed them in small groups of two or three with a researcher. Small groups were favored over individual interviews, as this approach is known to spark more animated and eager discussion on the part of the children (Parkinson, 2001). The discussions were framed with questions such as "Tell me about your picture," "What kind of music is that?", "Why did you take that picture?", and "What else would you like to tell me about the music in the picture?". The discussions were recorded on video and transcribed verbatim for coding and analysis.

Coding and Analysis

Data were manually coded by two researchers in a recursive manner that mirrored Morse and Richards (2002) and Richards (2005). Themes were derived from the data themselves rather than from an a priori coding frame in an effort to minimize researcher bias and to allow the children's views on what music is to be heard as fully as possible. Patterns became apparent from repeated readings of the data with discrepancies between researchers resolved by negotiation.

FINDINGS

The camera work of young children in the field of their own childcare center, and their family and neighborhood surroundings, offered clear testimony of the experiences they deemed and described as music. Although yet early on in the full development of their expressive language, and certainly without the full complement of technical language common to those with music-educational experience, the 4- to 5-year-old children in this project had plenty to say about the photographs they themselves had made. Were they to have had the beginnings of music-related language, of which they are developmentally capable at an early age, their explanations might have been more clear-cut. Some children struggled to talk about a song, or a timbral quality, or a rhythm, which raised the question of teachers teaching and tracking basic (music) vocabulary usage at the ages of 3 and 4 years. Still, as one image after another lit up in high resolution on the computer screen, children spontaneously described their "pictures" with the words they had at hand, and responded to questions objectively delivered to them to clarify or extend an understanding of their meanings.

Children's conceptualizations of music fell into two broad categories: sound and function. While these were mutually exclusive at times, in other contexts they were aggregated by the children in various combinations. Photographs of instruments and their players were captured in various contexts and for various functions, including a birthday party, a church service, a family gathering, and a wedding. Furthermore, the two broad categories can be subdivided, as children referred to sound in terms of human musical practice, sonic hardware, and natural sound sources, and as their descriptions of music as celebration and as ritual fit within the category of function. The range of photographic images the children produced was impressive, and yet patterns emerged in visual depictions, which, amplified by children's own verbal descriptions, clarified the sonic and functional meanings of these images.

Sound

Children identified music for its sonic objects and practices. As evidenced in their collection, they seemed to be searching for sources of sound—be they originating from human behavior, solid objects intended to produce or communicate sound (or not intended, but which were in fact sonic sources), or things or forces of nature, including animals and insects. As human musical practice, they captured their friends, family members, and sometimes total strangers in various musicking activities—singing, playing musical instruments, dancing, clapping, stamping, and engaging in actions and gestures corresponding to a song or listening selection. The photographs portrayed individuals or groups of people, while other times just their singing heads were featured, or their hands playing on drums, guitars, keyboards, and other instruments.

Among the photographs associated with sound as *human musical practice*, singing was a consistent depiction. The images captured by children were evidence of mothers singing favorite songs with and without the accompaniment of CDs, radios, and other playback devices. Fathers appeared only rarely among the photographs, yet one father was depicted and described as singing to the rhythm of his tapping of a fork and knife at the kitchen table. Groups of children were captured singing together, especially familiar songs learned at preschool, such as *Iddy Biddy Baby, Twinkle, Twinkle, Little Star,* and The *Wheels on the Bus.* One child excitedly described an image he had captured: "...It's Casha and Kate, and it's the bus. The wheels on the bus go round and round. Oh and that's Emily and that's Jordan and that's Georgia and they're singing." In another image of children gathered together, one child's response to the question "How do you know that's music?" was a description of a musical game, much loved by the group, underscored with conviction: "Because they go around in a circle because it's duck duck goose and you sing it along." Occasionally, children sang the songs they remembered hearing in the photographs they took, rather than taking the longer verbal route of explaining the photograph. Furthermore, singing seemed to spontaneously happen, in the form of "la-la's," which could be heard as an expression of pleasure or even mild excitement at the appearance of the photographic image of a musical sound source.

Movement, including dancing and action songs, figured prominently in children's photographs. In fact, the frequent descriptions by children of movement to music triggered thoughts of *ngoma,* the pro-Bantu concept referring to the widespread weave across sub-Saharan African cultures of music with dance, drama, poetry, and the visual arts (Keil & Campbell, 2006). As one girl told it, "Dancing is part of music ... because you sing and wiggle ... you wiggle your hips and go." Another child observed that "in wiggly music, wiggle your hips.... We can do whatever we want—for crazy." As a photograph appeared of herself with her arms raised high in the air, the girl explained that "I'm making a star, and going 'a diamond and a star'." Another boy identified his own photograph with certainty: "It's Twinkle, Twinkle, because all the hands [are] up." Still another boy clarified the importance of movement to the preschool song, *Iddy Biddy Baby:* "We lie there on the tummy in the blanket and then we crawl over ... then you put your head up on the ... and you crawl around. And then down onto my feet. And then we walk." He appeared to know the sequence of the words and melody by showing and telling of the movements that coincided with the song. Dance, actions to underscore song texts, and various gestures to indicate sound qualities appeared in the photographs as well as in the discussions by children of the various images.

Other examples of human musical practice were evident in the children's "eye-view" for music. There were photographs, and explanations, of people playing instruments ("That's mum playing piano ... it's again, it's again, it's again"). Clapping and tapping arose as examples of music that children could easily make ("Dane's going clap, clap ... Flynn is going tap, tap, tap"). As well, stamping images appeared, as in the case of Teila, a child who was caught stamping her foot on the side of the sandbox ("And she's going knock, knock, knock"). One girl's photograph of a floor below her was her intent to show that this was a surface on which stamping transpired ("It goes … [she stamps her feet]"). When asked whether she could stamp on the carpet, she responded that "that makes it softer."

In their identification of sonic hardware as music, children ran wild with images of musical instruments within their homes, at their preschools, or in music shops. They depicted household items too, and their own toys, as hardware sources of musical sound. Their photographs included musical (and video-with-music) playback devices, sound storage items, and technical means for amplifying and recording sound. There were also several surprise images, when children's sensitivity and invention brought out the aural potential of everyday objects.

A musical instrument qualified as sonic hardware when it stood alone in a photograph, without a player's fingers, hands, head, or body present and active in the process of performance. Children captured string and wind instruments, and a handful of percussion instruments. Several children were attuned to guitars, and related instruments, both in image and description. One boy told of the guitars of his brother, Rowan ("He's got two and he doesn't let me [play]"), and of his Uncle Dean's three guitars. Another child described a pink-colored guitar he had photographed at a music shop. Jordan's artistic photograph of a "red guitar" (Figure 8.1) was actually a ukelele, whose sound he described as follows: "It went ching, ching, ching, ching." A photograph of a double bass brought these enthusiastic remarks on its size from another boy: "A guitar? It's so more bigger. He's standing up (like a) big giant."

A number of children found wind instruments worthy of a photograph. One boy leaped through topics that began with "instruments in the baby's room" to a description of his Spiderman "jamies" (pajamas), returning to "drums that go boom, boom," and then on to mention a toy fire engine with a whistle. He noted that "Whistles make music" and that "I just pretend (to play) mine." In a lengthy conversation, one child eventually determined that a photograph she had taken of her cousin Shane featured him on his flute turning from a first impression that "He's eating something" to "He's blowing something. He might be playing music from himself."

Keira happily described a photograph of trumpets (Figure 8.2) that were displayed in a music shop: "Trumpets. They play music. That one's sitting in the box." She continued with certainty to clarify the manner of sound production on a trumpet: "You press the buttons. And [you] get it near your mouth. [You] Blow it."

Drums, tambourines, maracas, and castanets appeared in children's photographs. One child was fascinated with the drumsticks, calling them "the things for his drum." He observed that "you only hit it with the

Figure 8.1. It went ching, ching, ching, ching.

Figure 8.2. Trumpets.

drumstick," and that "when you bump it, it makes music." Another child described her photograph of a "tambourine drum," and that its sound emanates from "this silver stuff ... they shake it." Plastic maracas, played by a toy monkey, appeared in a photograph, along with castanets played by a toy lion. Several photographs of a piano (without someone playing) surfaced too, with one of the children clarifying the instrument's harmonic function: "It's called chords ... and you do it like this...."

Children continued the stream of sonic hardware with their descriptions of the presence of radios, televisions, CDs and DVDs (and their players), microphones, and iPods in their lives. The all-purpose "boom-box" emerged in conversation as a sound source found in various rooms of the family home (Figure 8.3), which was observed by children to contain multiple sources of musical sound: radio, CD, and tape playback systems; speakers from which speech, song, and instrumental music originated; and even microphones with which children could amplify and record their talking and singing. One girl explained a photograph of her own audio equipment: "It's mine and it went in my room. You sing in that thing and the switch is to turn it off and on." She described the outcome of turning the knob to the microphone: "It makes your voice go louder." Another child responded to the image she had captured: "That's my radio singing music." She went on to explain the function of the microphone: "You sing in that thing and the switch is to turn it off and on."

An image of a car radio provoked this description: "Mum got one of them for her birthday. It's in her work car. We put kids' music on there." TVs were viewed by children as musical sources, and one child enthusiastically described the family's "wild and big" TV, "a music TV" on which penguins appeared on screen and "ice music" sounded from its speakers. Other children told of DVDs "with music," played on TV and computer screens, as standard family practice. A photograph of a large CD collection stimulated a discussion by one child of her "heaps of favorite CDs at home, like *Aladdin, Aladdin*," along with the statement that "I really, really do like to sing." One image of an iPod brought a discussion of locations on the screen to be "pressed" so that music selections could be accessed. This intrigue was a common one, where questions of how to access music, to play an instrument or electronic device, to draw sound out of an object often captivated children who struggled with words to express what they would otherwise explore and manipulate in real time.

Beyond musical instruments and playback (and recording) equipment, sonic hardware captured by children in photographic images included household items, toys, and items that would not typically surface in an adult-conceived compilation of musical sound sources. Cookware, dishes, and dining utensils were mentioned for their capacity to "ding," "DONG," "jingle," "ching," and "boom." One child enthusiastically explained one

Figure 8.3.   The all-purpose boom-box.

afternoon's musical entertainment: "I played with the pots and pans and I got the spoon and then I jumped with them, pretending they were drumming." Toy animals—a lion with plastic maracas, a monkey that clacks together castanets—prompted another child to capture their images and describe the sounds of their instruments. Kira, a girl enamoured of feminine things, was pleased with her photograph of a pink jewelry box, her "love heart box," with a winged fairy that pops up as the box opens. She listed with delight and little-girl pride the contents of the box, including ribbons, jewelry, hair bands, badges, bracelets, a ring, and a necklace, and spoke of the fairy that "spins around" to the music that plays (Figure 8.4).

Several children set their sites on capturing images of "musical books." Stories of composers or performers were not so much their focal interest as were songbooks, where actual music notation appeared on the book pages. One young boy identified his songbook, whose purpose he described thus: "So we can play whatever kind of music." He identified the song as *Hot Cross Buns,* and then proceeded to describe how he "reads" it to play music: "Because I look at the words and you do "Hot Cross Buns" three times. You do the words three times and go one-a-penny, two-a-penny, hot cross buns." He continued to explain that the song words "help you to do the playing, absolutely." That children viewed

Figure 8.4.   The fairy that spins around.

music book notation as sonic hardware—sources of sound—was a surprising revelation, in that it tracked children's perception of iconic symbols as stimulation for the making of musical sounds by players and singers. To them, the notation both inspired and represented music.

A wide array of *natural sound sources* were identified by children as music, many of whom were clearly entranced with the potential of nature's forces and living creatures to produce differentiated timbres, pitches, and rhythms. Some children went so far as to suggest that the sounds of nature were capable of expressive features, including articulation and dynamics. Their photographs depicted trees, animals, insects, shells, and various perspectives of water and wind.

Brian's photograph of a dense forest of deep green fir trees was his evidence of the natural sounds he defined as music, produced when the wind whistled through the leaves and the pine needles. Several children attempted to imitate the sound of wind through trees, vocalizing with "shoosh," "siss," and "whoosh" sounds. There were several references to "the waving wind" by children as they vocalized their tree sounds. One child offered his imagined sound of "whoo whoo" for "plants (that were) a little bit like trees." Kade produced a child's-eye view of a wind chime: four metal disks hanging from thin cord high above him, swaying gently, chiming their resonant pitches as they bounced into one another (Figure

8.5). He noted that "when the wind's going, the wind is blowing, it goes like that."

Water figured prominently among the natural sources of musical sound captured by children in their photographs. One child offered the standard "pitter-patter" onomatapoeic sound of rain as plausible "water music." There were the musical "waves and waves and waves" of brown river water, as depicted in one boy's photograph, and another boy's depiction of the sound of water "whooshing" along in the wake of a line of ducks (Figure 8.6). The sound of "wind" in a seashell was music to Jordan, who explained that "when you put it in your ear, [it] makes music" and that you hear the waves "whooshing" (Figure 8.7). Children perceived the flow of water from faucets and spouts as sounding musical to them. Kade's photograph of a water faucet, or tap, provoked a stream of ideas from him (Figure 8.8). He explained: "It's a tap. And if you put the water on, it's music. I was taking (a photograph of) the music because it was dripping, and then I thought it was music and I take the picture. Like this—click." He added, "If you tap on the end [of the faucet], it makes music." Zach defended his photograph of a watering can (Figure 8.9) as music, claiming that there was sound "because the water's coming … and I'm stepping on the flowers" (as if this action could also produce musical sound).

Figure 8.5.   The wind is blowing.

Children were convinced of the sound potential of animals, and called their sounds music. According to one girl, "snakes make music when they put their tongue" to produce "ssss." Another girl described the rhythmic sounds of a bird's flapping wings. One child photographed his puppy (Figure 8.10), and described his bark: "Dogs go ruff-ruff," as compared to the cat's "meow." Another child described his cat, a healthy Chartreux with a thick beige coat (Figure 8.11), as capable of "making music by scratching." Marlon was eager to show and tell of his photograph of silk worms "munching" (Figure 8.12). Zach's photograph of goldfish was the launch to his soliloquy on their sound, describing it as "music in the water, because they're going blob, blob, blob" (Figure 8.13). He observed that the goldfish move quickly, and in patterns. He explained that their movement sounded like "clap, clap, clap. And it's more than a minute [of sound] and then zero [silence]."

Function

Children's photographs showed an assortment of situations and settings in which music played a role in performing a social function. Children explained these photos in no uncertain terms as events in which

Figure 8.6.   Water whooshing.

Figure 8.7.   When you put it in your ear [it] makes music.

Figure 8.8.   It's a tap.

Figure 8.9.   The water's coming.

Figure 8.10.   Dogs go roof-roof.

Figure 8.11.   Making music by scratching.

Figure 8.12.   Silkworms munching.

Figure 8.13.   They're going blob, blob, blob.

music sounded, from go-to-bed lullabies, to music as celebration and as ritual. While sonic aspects may have been present to some extent, images and discussions categorized as function were identified as such because children's explanations clearly prioritized the use and/or context of the music.

Children perceived music as prominent in certain social celebration events in which they have participated. They are well aware of music at birthdays and at weddings, and their discussion of music sometimes encompasses people at play and party mode. One child propped up his well-used and weary stuffed teddy bear, hunched over the edge of a plate on which were placed two candles, a cake, and streamers (Figure 8.14). This young boy explained the occasion that prompted the photograph: "It's Teddy's birthday night and I have to take a picture because it was his birthday." He recalled the standard song for the family's gathering: "Yeah, and we were.... We sang happy birthday to you." In a description of another photograph, one girl explained that it was music because of the wedding she had captured. She clarified that in her wedding photograph, "They're singing. Because weddings sing." She also observed that violin music was a typical component of a wedding ceremony.

Children described and depicted music as ritual. One boy's image of a CD brought him into a conversation about the music he listened to at

Figure 8.14.   It's Teddy's birthday night.

bedtime—"go-to-sleep" music that was standard procedure every eve-
ning, the CD music functioning as a lullaby to soothe and settle the child
to slumber. Several children were able to capture the music of religious
ritual, taking their cameras to church to produce photographic images of
a piano or organ that played alone and as accompaniment to hymns.
Brian's church piano was an electronic keyboard on a steel-legged stand,
complete with a stand on which a songbook was positioned, with a gold
chair pulled up for the player's use (Figure 8.15). He explained his photograph: "That one is from church. They play when it's starting [and] big
people are allowed to play and sing. They're allowed to do it [make music]
at church." As one of music's many functions, most of ritual music for
children not yet in school appears to transpire in church. Once they enter
school, other types of ritual music may well emerge in their lives.

REALIZING THE CHILDREN'S CONCEPTIONS

Clearly, for these young children, music cannot be situated fully in the
sonic realm, nor entirely in the functional. For them, music could take
either of these poles or any combination in between. Most certainly, their

Figure 8.15.   That one is from Church.

descriptive language was not so developed, either, for them to be able to wax eloquently about music. Indeed without their photographs as prompts, details about music would likely have been scant, at best. The most salient domain in which we find implications for this thinking is that of early childhood curriculum and the decisions that are made as part of its construction. In order to explore these fully, it is necessary to examine the notion of curriculum. For us, the notion of curriculum as a document or set of documents that prescribe content and/or the pedagogical approach that should be taken in its delivery is limiting in the extreme. When we refer to curriculum, we are referring to a lived entity; or "all the provisions professionals make for the whole of the child's experience in the service" (Stonehouse, 2001, p. 19). We see the term "curriculum" as operating as a verb, rather than as a noun, in that it pertains to processes that are evolving and dynamic, rather than static and fixed. This inclusive designation not only includes what teachers do, but the understandings that underpin it, the space in which they do it, and the resources with which they do it. A range of theoretical frameworks can be used to swathe this idea of curriculum, each of which is bound by different underlying philosophical perspectives of learning and teaching, and pedagogical approaches. These positions are outlined below.

Approaches to Curriculum

Developmentalist approaches to curriculum are steeped in the Piagetian tradition. Children are thought to develop and learn by engaging with concrete materials from their environment. In general, reaching a developmental milestone means that a child is ready for learning something. That is, development precedes learning and does so in a stage-like fashion (Siegler, Deloache, & Eisenberg, 2006). Developmental curricula often focus on the individual and how far that individual is from a predetermined end-state. This often leads to a deficit model in practice, where teachers look for what is missing in a child's development and learning and proceed to teach to that particular aspect. In this sense, many developmentalist approaches are end-state focused. A developmental music curriculum might be characterized by teachers carefully observing the children, and planning according to what they see and what they know about children's musical milestones. They will ensure a musically rich environment, carefully planned according to the children's known and expected development. Musical development will rarely be seen beyond the individual child.

Behaviorist approaches to curriculum are built around a predetermined body of knowledge that is thought to be necessary for children to learn. While these approaches share with the developmentalists, the notion of learning occurring through direct interaction with the environment, behaviorist approaches position this learning as developing and adapting links between stimuli and responses (Ormrod, 2006). A chief point of difference between this and more developmental approaches is that children are seen to need guidance and extrinsic motivation to learn. Early childhood music curriculum built on behaviorist principles may involve rewarding children for displaying discrete musical skills and demonstrating musical knowledge. Rewards might be given for remembering a song deemed to be important, singing in tune or in time, or remembering musical facts.

Sociocultural approaches to curriculum involve viewing learning as socially located, collective action. Often bound by Vygotskian principles, with relationships deemed of paramount importance, this approach positions children as capable and resourceful. In contrast to the more developmental approaches, learning precedes development (Lambert & Clyde, 2000) with children still seen as relatively capable, but carefully guided by a knowledgeable other. An early childhood music curriculum built on sociocultural tenets would be characterized by children and adults musicking together, engaged in songs and the like that are deemed to be important to the culture that is being constructed by the musick-ers. Children would be afforded the opportunity to learn new musical skills and knowledge by naturally participating with others and learning would be underpinned by scaffolding from adults or peers. This scaffolding would be naturally lessened over time until there was no further need for it and that particular piece of musical knowledge or musical skill could be independently applied in a range of novel circumstances by the children.

Postmodern, poststructural, and critical approaches to curriculum also give value to children's social worlds. Developing an identity in a complex, many-sided world, gender, race, and class all exert powerful influences on children's development (Arthur, Beecher, Death, Dockett, & Farmer, 2008). Acknowledging these ideas and that of multiple truths in early childhood music curriculum may result in music itself (as conceptualized by the children or others) being eschewed in favor of social justice, power, control, and the like. A child's use of a musical instrument, the development of their musical understandings, and positive musical dispositions may be overshadowed by concerns about why that particular child and not another used that particular instrument.

A Generative Approach

We propose that while many of the above approaches to curriculum have a lot to offer, there is room for a more generative approach to early childhood music education. Our concern is that children's true voices are otherwise not well heard. Using the two primary dimensions of sound and function as described by the children's conceptualization of music in this study, a model for situating early childhood music curriculum and the decisions that teachers make in enacting it is shown in Figure 8.16.

By opposing sound and function in this way, musical engagements can be divided into four categories. The sf (low sound, low function) category is characterized by passive musical consumption on the part of the children. Commonplace in these types of environments is recorded music playing in the background while children play but with no active musicking. The Sf (high sound, low function) category is characterized by excessive focus on musical skill and knowledge development. These environments are those where teachers are too concerned with children singing in tune, moving in time, and so on, often to the detriment of using music to do things like communicate. The sF (low sound, high function) category describes environments where music is used as a means to achieve something else. These types of classrooms are those where music is used primarily to sing *Happy Birthday* to children, assist in transitions from one physical area to another, and manage routines such as queuing to wash hands in the bathroom. The final category, SF (high sound, high function) depicts environments where there is optimal active engagement in the two dimensions as appropriate.

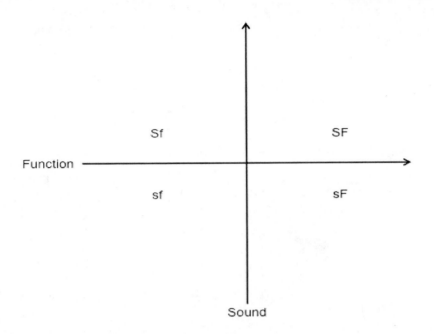

Figure 8.16.   A generative approach to curriculum.

These classrooms of children are engaged in singing and playing "instru-ments" during play, making up songs to communicate, spontaneously improvising and producing standard songs from their cultures. Teachers in these rooms know their charges well and plan accordingly. At times, there is evidence of intentional teaching and use of musical metalanguage. This means that children are critical musickers, able to explain what they are doing and why. At times, teachers use music to achieve a particular purpose (such as wishing someone "Happy Birthday") and at times teachers take a sensitive back seat, affording children opportunity to musick as they see fit.

As with all curricula, monitoring the quality and goodness of ecological fit is an important activity. We propose that this could by achieved by gauging the "curricular temperature." Figure 8.17 demonstrates how this can be achieved by overlaying the model with a continuum from inert (cold) to sublime (hot).

This schematic allows the curriculum temperature or quality to be gauged by plotting it in one of three areas. We have designated the cool zone (sf) as "inert" or of low quality. In this zone, children take a particu-larly passive role, with music often just used as background filler. This has been designated as a cool zone because there are no real curriculum deci-sions being made. Children are not actively musicking and teachers do

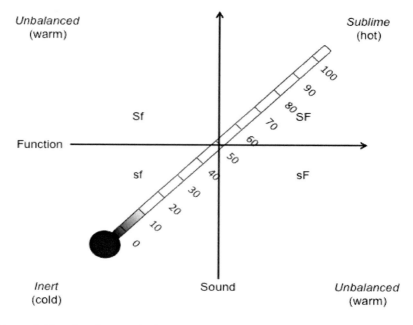

Figure 8.17.   Gauging curricular temperature.

not intervene and facilitate active involvement. Moving to the middle of the thermometer describes a warmer (Sf, sF) yet unbalanced zone. While there is some increase in quality here, curricula in this zone do not take consideration of the dual dimensions in which children conceptualize "music." In this unbalanced zone, teachers might be making curriculum decisions based on a relatively exclusive philosophy. Those for whom musical skill development is most important will focus on the children's musical development, to the exclusion of the many functional aspects ascribed to music by the children. Conversely, and equally problematic, are those teachers who forsake children's musical skill and knowledge development and focus mainly (or solely) on the functional features of music. In this warm zone, children may have limited opportunity to participate in decisions, but hardly at a level that challenges them or demonstrates a commitment to their agency. The sublime zone (SF) is the area we have designated as hot, and is the zone in which high-quality early childhood music education curriculum is enacted. In this zone, optimal active musicking is evident as is equal consideration of the dual dimensions as appropriate. Children's agency is respected and where possible, children are actively involved in making decisions about the place of music in the curriculum and the manner in which this is realized. It is the sublime zone in which children's conceptualizations of music inform the everyday musical practices that are undertaken by children and adults alike. It is within this zone that the development of a shared musical metalanguage is vital in order that the children become musically aware and critical and have the tools with which to engage in reflection and discussion about their musics and music-making.

THE NEXT STEP

This research project draws on a range of emerging notions in the field. Children actively gathered data and unpacked these with an adult researcher, and as these discussions proceeded, the idea of power was always consciously present. We do not claim that the model and the gauge of quality will necessarily hold true for children beyond the current sample. Yet this was a useful and necessary exercise in testing a methodological approach and sharpening teachers' awareness of their own practices in light of the beliefs and understandings of young children. More research is needed in order to begin to assess the viability of applying the model and the temperature gauge to wider contexts. To this end, it is our intent to explore a range of early childhood modes of expression in projects that are yet ahead of us.

RESEARCHERS' REFLECTION

In the logical-positivist past, research in early childhood, like that in other educational domains, was characterized by the search for a single truth. As observational studies became more commonplace, a range of areas for investigation gained prominence. Aubrey, David, Godfrey, and Thompson (2000) identify these as context variables, which are best described as the children's environments (e.g., the playroom or classroom); presage variables, which are those such as learner or teacher characteristics that predate the learning under examination; process variables, which describe behavior or interactions in the classroom or playroom; and product variables, which relate to learning outcomes, knowledge acquisition, and the like. Research techniques have continued to move further away from a focus on the end-state, but in our quest to interrogate children's conceptualization of music, we were keen to capture and preserve in analysis the complexities of contemporary childhood: we wanted to acknowledge all the above-mentioned variables and then some. To that end, we adopted a participatory technique, based on current pedagogical approaches and leading research tools in early childhood. Children taking photographs as research is not new (see, e.g., *Early Child Development and Care, 175*(6), an issue devoted entirely to matters related to young children's involvement in research), but there are few music education studies that have taken this line of inquiry. We believe that the best informers on children's perspectives are children themselves, so we set about maximizing children's opportunities to furnish rich data about their conceptualization of music. This was a main impetus for utilizing photography. Restricting data gathering to a verbal protocol may have limited some children's ability to do this due to the minimal extent of their expressive language facility at this early age or, more specifically, the development of a musical metalanguage with which to have the discussion (Makin & Whiteman, 2006, provide an example of children's development of shared metalanguages in literacy and music).

The children quickly mastered the use of the camera and in some instances took in excess of 100 photographs of music in one week. It became apparent during the interviews that some system of filtering the photographs was necessary due to the enthusiasm with which children photographed events and experiences that did not relate to music. From early on, the children themselves were adept at identifying these photographs and discarding them as "practice" or "other" shots, which then did not form part of the discussion. Interestingly, some children were forthcoming with a surprising richness of information about music and their photographs. In some cases, they replaced technical terms with nonspecialist, colloquial words—and with no disruption to the conversation. At the other extreme were the rare instances of children using a range of avoidance tactics such as total disregard of questions around music in an image, apparently offering a response to a question that they would rather have answered, or presenting information apparently unrelated to the image under discussion. At all times, the researcher speaking with the children was wary of the delicacy with which the discussions were facilitated, probing where necessary and minimizing prompts in an effort to maximize the authenticity of the data. Establishing rapport and knowing the children well was of prime importance.

As with any research project, consideration of analytical techniques formed an important component of the design phase. With initial excitement about the visual data we imagined would be generated, the search for an analytical tool became captivating. Contemporary constructions of multiliteracies (e.g., New London Group, 1996) accorded us with robust approaches to the analysis and understanding of the visual (Kress & van Leeuwen, 2006; Schirato & Webb, 2004). However, it quickly became apparent that imposing such frameworks on the children's photographs would relegate the children to a position of relative powerlessness and render the findings of the study questionable at best. Consequently, the photographs were used as an aid for the children to "revisit" with the researcher, with the transcriptions of these discussions assuming primary importance in the investigation, after the photographs themselves. Drawing on practices such as revisiting (Forman, 1999; Rinaldi, 2005) and listening (Clark, 2005; Clark & Moss, 2001) allowed further insight into the children's intended meanings exemplified in their photographs. While mindful of sometimes needing to have materials for young interviewees to engage with props such as toys during interviews (Doverborg & Pramling Samuelsson, 2003, cited in Einarsdottir, 2005), it was decided that such supports would be unnecessary in this case as the children already had their photographs to look at, talk about, and point to. Previous experience with interviewing young children indicated that undertaking interviews in pairs or small groups (Graue & Walsh, 1998) was indeed the most likely scenario to realize rich and absorbing data. We were not disappointed! The aforementioned awkwardness with technical terms notwithstanding, discussion around meaning and intent of the children's photos and the music they depicted was often animated and lively. At all times, the children were eager to share their thoughts and did so with an air of authority.

As we move forward in early childhood music education research, refining methods and challenging conventions, it is perhaps worthwhile to keep foremost in our minds the democratic notion of participation. To this end, we remind early childhood researchers and educators of Article 12 of the Convention on the Rights of the Child (United Nations, 1989): "When adults are making decisions that affect children, children have the right to say what they think should happen and have their opinions taken into account." We believe that this project opens the door for young children to "say" through photographs and discussion what they believe does and should happen in their musical childhoods.

REFERENCES

Arthur, L., Beecher, B., Death, E., Dockett, S., & Farmer, S. (2008). *Programming and planning in early childhood settings* (4th ed.). Melbourne, Australia: Thomson.

Aubrey, C., David, T., Godfrey, R., & Thompson, L. (2000). *Early childhood educational research: Issues in methodology and ethics.* London: Routledge Falmer.

Campbell, P. S. (1998). *Songs in their heads: Music and its meaning in children's lives.* New York: Oxford University Press.

Clark, A. (2005). Listening to and involving young children: A review of research and practice. *Early Child Development and Care, 175*(6), 489–505.

Clark, A., & Moss, P. (2001). *Listening to young children: The mosaic approach.* London: National Children's Bureau.

Cross, I. (2005). Music and meaning, ambiguity, and evolution. In D. Miell, R. MacDonald, & D. J. Hargreaves (Eds.), *Musical communication* (pp. 27–43). Oxford, UK: Oxford University Press.

Davies, S. (1997). John Cage's 4'33": Is it music? *Australasian Journal of Philosophy, 75(4)*, 448–462.

Einarsdottir, J. (2005). Playschool in pictures: children's photographs as a research method. *Early Child Development and Care, 175*(6), 523–541.

Forman, G. (1999). Instant video revisiting: The video camera as a "tool of the mind" for young children. *Early Childhood Research and Practice, 1*(2). Retrieved from http://ecrp.uiuc.edu/v1n2/forman.html

Gardner, H., & Wolf, D. (Eds.). (1979). *Early symbolization*. San Francisco: Jossey-Bass.

Gould, S. J. (1991). Exaptation: A crucila tool for evolutionary psychology. *Journal of Social Issues, 47*, 43–65.

Graue, M. E., & Walsh, D. J. (1998). *Studying children in context: Theories, methods and ethics*. Thousand Oaks, CA: SAGE.

Harris, C. M. (Ed.). (2006). *Dictionary of architecture and construction*. New York: McGraw-Hill.

Keil, C., & Campbell, P. S. (2006). *Ngoma*. Retrieved January 20, 2010, from www.borntogroove.org

Keil, C., & Feld, S. (1994). *Music grooves: Essays and dialogues*. Chicago: University of Chicago Press.

Kress, G., & van Leeuwen, T. (2006). *Reading images: The grammar of visual design* (2nd ed.). London: Routledge.

Lambert, E. B., & Clyde, M. (2000). *Rethinking early childhood theory and practice*. Katoomba, NSW, Australia: Social Science Press.

Levitin, D. J. (2006). *This is your brain on music*. New York: Dutton.

Levitin, D. J. (2008). *The world in six songs*. New York: Dutton.

Lum, C. H., & Campbell, P. S. (2007). The sonic surrounds of an elementary school. *Journal of Research in Music Education, 55*(1), 31–47.

Makin, L., & Whiteman, P. (2006). Young children as active participants in the investigation of early literacy. *European Early Childhood Education Research Journal, 14*(1), 33–42.

Miller, G. (2000). Evolution of human music through sexual selection. In N. Wallin, B. Merker, & S. Brown (Eds.), *The origins of music* (pp. 329–360). Cambridge, MA: MIT Press.

Morse, J. M., & Richards, L. (2002). *Readmefirst for a user's guide to qualitative methods*. Thousand Oaks, CA: SAGE.

New London Group. (1996). A pedagogy of multi-literacies: Designing social futures. *Harvard Educational Review, 66*, 60–92.

Ormrod, J. E. (2006). *Essentials of educational psychology*. Upper Saddle River, NJ: Prentice-Hall.

Parkinson, D. D. (2001). Securing trustworthy data from an interview situation with young chidlren: Six integrated interview strategies. *Child Study Journal, 31*(3), 137–155.

Pinker, S. (1997). *How the mind works*. New York: Norton.

Richards, L. (2005). *Handling qualitative data*. Thousand Oaks, CA.: SAGE.

Rinaldi, C. (2005). *In dialogue with Reggio Emilia: Listening, researching, and learning*. New York: Routledge.

Schafer, R. M. (1969). *The new soundscape: A handbook for the modern music teacher*. Don Mills, ON, Canada: BMI Canada Ltd.

Schirato, T., & Webb, J. (2004). *Reading the visual*. Crows Nest, NSW, Australia: Allen & Unwin.

Siegler, R., Deloache, J., & Eisenberg, N. (2006). *How children develop* (2nd ed.). New York: Worth.

Small, C. (1977). *Music, society, education: A radical examination of the prophetic function of music in Western, Eastern and African cultures with its impact on society and its use in education*. London: Calder.

Small, C. (1998). *Musicking: The meanings of performing and listening*. Hanover, NH: University Press of New England.

Stonehouse, A. (2001). *NSW curriculum framework for children's services. The practice of relationships: Essential provisions for children's services*. Sydney: NSW Department of Community Services.

Turino, T. (2008). *Music as social life: The politics of participation*. Chicago: University of Chicago Press.

United Nations. (1989). Convention on the rights of the child. Retrieved from http://www2.ohchr.org/english/law/crc.htm

Wade, B. C. (2004). *Thinking musically*. New York: Oxford University Press.

Weng-Chung, C. (1967). Edgard Varèse [1885–1965]. Excerpts from lectures by Edgard Varèse, compiled and edited with footnotes by Chou Wen-Chung. In E. Schwartz & B. Childs (Eds.), *Contemporary composers on contemporary music* (pp. 195–208). New York: Holt, Rinehart & Winston.

Wood, E. (2007). Reconceptualising child-centred education: Contemporary directions in policy, theory and practice in early childhood. *Forum, 49*(1), 119–133.

Woodrow, C. (1999). Revisiting images of the child in early childhood education: Reflections and considerations. *Australian Journal of Early Childhood, 24*(4), 7–12.

CHAPTER 9

YOUNG CHILDREN'S FREE MUSICAL PLAY

Musical Behavior and Peer Interaction

Pyng-Na Lee

INTRODUCTION

According to contemporary trends in education, teaching is no longer a means of transmitting knowledge but an induction for students to construct their own knowledge. Play releases children from social expectations, daily routine, and creates a pleasant atmosphere for learning. During play, children freely connect with people, events, and situations to make meaning (Johnson, Christie, & Wardle, 2005). Play is very much part of young children's lives (Van Hoorn, Monighan-Nourot, Scales, & Alward, 2003) and their play parallels cognitive development (Piaget, 1962). Therefore, play in young children's education is highly valued. In music education, research findings point to the significance of free musical playmusical play (Achilles, 1992; Hildebrandt, 1998; Littleton, 1991; Moorhead & Pond, 1978; Ro, 1993; Smithrim, 1997). Achilles (1992) for instance, recommended that young children's music learning should focus more on free musical play along with a reduction of circle time.[1]

Musical Childhoods of Asia and the Pacific, pp. 191–213
Copyright © 2012 by Information Age Publishing
All rights of reproduction in any form reserved.

To fulfill young children's needs for play, in Taiwan, the majority of kindergarten classrooms are set up with four to six play centers: visual art, manipulation blocks, language and housekeeping centers, are frequently seen but rarely a music center (Chang, 2000). In interviewing some kindergarten teachers for their reasons, they replied that a music center would create too much noise affecting the other centers around it. Furthermore, the kindergarten teachers did not think that young children could develop any musical skills through free musical play within a music center. Although previous literature documented the importance of free play, and provided evidence that children could develop skills through interaction with environments, props and people (Vygotsky, 1978), there is little evidence to suggest how children can develop their musical skills through interaction with instruments (props) and peers (people) during free musical play. The current study was thus designed to: investigate children's developmental processes during free musical play; understand how young children might develop musical abilities through interaction with instruments and peers during free musical play, and to document the value of free musical play within the Taiwanese context in early childhood music education.

REVIEW OF RELATED LITERATURE

Children's Musical Behavior During Free Musical Play

The earliest study of free musical play was conducted by Moorhead and Pond (1978) between 1937 and 1940 who observed 2- to 6-year-old children's musical behaviors in an environment set up with musical instruments without adult intervention. Results indicated that free musical play can stimulate children's musical imagination, spontaneous singing and spontaneous movement. However, Moorhead and Pond did not go into the specifics of age differences observed in these musical behaviors. Littleton (1991) conducted a study with 5-year-old children to compare the effects of different environmental designs on children's behavior. It was found that there was more functional and constructive play in music centers and more make-believe play in house-keeping centers. Littleton also found that young children created rhythmic patterns and melodic sequences in addition to sound exploration in the music center, and made various combinations of patterns and sequences to accompany singing and movement. Smithrim (1997) observed 3-year-old children's free musical play and found that children demonstrated long-term concentration on playing instruments, and their musical skills occasionally surpassed what the teacher had taught in the classroom. As a contrast to

Smithrim's observation of children's higher-order musical skills evidenced in free musical play, Rainbow (1981) found that in instructional learning, it is difficult to ask 3-year-olds to imitate rhythm clapping or clap to a rhythm while they are stepping.

In Taiwan, Ro (1993) studied 3- to 6-year-old children's musical behaviors in non-musical environments and found that the majority of musical play happened in group play during which playful situations induced children's musical creativity. Ro also found that singing was the main musical behavior observed in nonmusical environments. Although the contours of children's improvised singing were clear, their sense of tonality was not yet stable as also pointed out by Scott-Kassner (1993) about children at the age of 3 years. Finally, Hildebrandt (1998) mentioned that at free musical play, children created musical fragments in exploration and gradually formed them into rhythmic or melodic patterns woven into a musical structure.

Peer Interactions

Children at different ages demonstrate different levels of social competence. This social competence can be seen in developmental stages, from solitary, parallel, associative to cooperative (Millar, 1968). At free musical play, children naturally collaborate with peers in creative music activities (Moorhead & Pond, 1978), and develop their social competence through peer interaction. Miller (1983) identified that the majority of 3-year-old children's social behaviors were pegged at the solitary and symbolic stage while 4-year-old children engaged in more social imitation.

Two-year-old children often use physical contact and props as mediators to start peer interaction, and soon after they understand the concept of ownership, they start to share or exchange the objects to form a "primitive social contract" (Brownell & Brown, 1985). Furthermore, 2-year-old children can use verbal communication to negotiate their possession rights, and subsequently develop their social communication to compromise (Brownell & Carriger, 1990). Although 3-year-old children frequently imitate each other to facilitate learning, peer instruction is frequently rejected by others (Smithrim, 1997).

When children freely explore instrumental playing, they interact with instruments (props) and peers (people) to develop ability (Vygotsky, 1978). Although there is evidence documenting the importance of free musical play for young children, how children develop their musical ability through the interaction with instruments and peers is lesser known. In Taiwan, preschool[2] teachers do not think that young children can develop any music ability through free musical play, and even believe that older

children such as 5-year-olds at preschools should have instructional lessons instead of free play to prepare for entering elementary school.
Therefore, not only are music centers excluded, but free play time is generally reduced in 5-year-olds' classrooms.

To reiterate, this study aimed to investigate children's developmental
processes at free musical play. Furthermore, considering the lack of
research studies looking at 2-year-olds' musical behaviors and Taiwanese
preschool teachers' negative viewpoints about having free musical play for
5-year-olds, this study was designed with two different age groups in
mind.

METHOD

Design and Participants

To examine young children's musical behaviors and peer interaction at
free musical play, qualitative approaches were employed to investigate the
phenomenon and context. The participants included one class of children aged 5 years at a public kindergarten and another class aged 2 years
at a private nursery school.[3] There were 30 children in the 5-year-old
class and 14 children in the 2-year-old class. The 5-year-old participants
had already had formal music lessons,[4] but the 2-year-old participants
had not except for some singing. During free musical play time, the classroom teachers in both sites did not intervene to scaffold children's musical play, and they were only present in classroom to assist at children's
request.

Sites

This study took place during young children's free musical play which
occurred at the music centers in their classrooms. In the 5-year-olds' classroom, five learning centers: block, language, housekeeping, manipulative, and music centers, had been designed and staged[5] in the classroom.
The props in each center were placed in cabinets which also separated the
classroom into five areas. The music center in the 5-year-olds' classroom
was originally equipped with two castanets, one guiro, three tone blocks,
one set of maracas, two sets of lummi sticks, one tambourine, one set of
cymbals, one gong, two wrist jingle bells, two sets of small brass bells, two
sets of triangles, one keyboard, one set of melodic bells, and a set of resonator bells. Pencils and paper were also included for children to write
down their music. Later, according to children's needs, one xylophone,

one set of finger cymbals, one hand drum, and two piano scores for beginners were added.

In the 2-year-olds' classroom, there were three open cabinets which had musical instruments, manipulative props, and housekeeping props respectively. Unlike the 5-year-old children's classroom with each center separated by short cabinets, the 2-year-old children's classroom was arranged in a more open-spaced manner. Originally, the set of instruments in the music center included two sets of maracas, two sets of lummi sticks, 16 castanets, two tone blocks, one snare drum, one pair of bongos, one hand drum, one music toy, two sets of small brass bells, two sets of triangles, 14 wrist jingle bells, two tambourines, and one set of melodic bells. Subsequently, the instruments were changed according to children's needs. The 16 castanets and 14 wrist jingle bells were each reduced to four, with one toy piano, one set of resonator bells, oneglockenspiel, one washboard as well as a several sticks added to the set.

Data Collection and Analysis

In the 5-year-olds' classroom, observational data were collected over a period of 32 weeks with weekly visits, each of 40 minutes duration. In the 2-year-olds' classroom, data were collected over a period of 18 weeks with 2-3 visits of 30-40 minutes per week. While observing young children's play in music center, this researcher and her research assistant remained unobtrusive to the degree possible in both classrooms. During observation, the researcher took field notes with the research assistant recording children's behavior with a digital video camera. Transcripts were made from recorded video and rechecked with field notes (dated and numbered[6]).

The data were analyzed through the process of constant comparison that included unitizing, categorizing, and filling in patterns (Glaser & Strauss, 1967; Lincoln & Guba, 1985). Unitizing involved the transcripts beingcoded to unitize an independent concept or idea. For instance, Yi-Jun played the melody with clear rhythm and meter on resonator bells (instrumental playing); Zheng-Wei held the maraca to tap castanets, hand drum, and tambourine (instrumental playing); Jun-Kai played a tune on the keyboard (instrumental playing); Wei-Jun tried different fingerings to play *Twinkle, twinkle, little star* on the keyboard (instrumental playing); Liang-Yo showed Wei-Han how to play the rhythm (peer interaction). Those sentences have been unitized and coded; each shows an independent idea.

Categorizing involved grouping similar concepts or ideas together and formulating a title for each category. For instance, Yi-Jun played the melody with clear rhythm and meter on resonator bells; Zheng-Wei held the maraca to tap castanets, hand drum, and tambourine; Jun-Kai played a tune on the keyboard; Wei-Jun tried different fingerings to play *Twinkle, twinkle, little star* on the keyboard. Those four data were categorized together because they are all belong to instrumental playing, and the last (Liang-Yo showed Wei-Han how to play the rhythm) has been categorized as peer interaction.

In the final stage, filling in patterns, various categories were connected through logical relations until the patterns of the relations were shown. Yi-Jun played a melody with clear rhythm and meter on resonator bells (instrumental playing/ improvisation); Zheng-Wei held the maraca to tap castanets, hand drum, and tambourine (instrumental playing/exploration); Jun-Kai played a tune of learned song on the keyboard (instrumental playing/ mastery); Wei-Jun tried different fingerings to play *Twinkle, Twinkle, Little Star* on the keyboard (instrumental playing/reexploration). Although those four statements are all belonged to instrumental playing, the hierarchical relationship of exploration-improvisation-mastery-reexploration is evident. Therefore, the data dates were checked to ensure the logical development, and confirmed the four developmental phases (exploration, improvisation, mastery, and reexploration) confirmed. The analysis process was also coupled with searching for counterevidence as part of ensuring trustworthiness.

Trustworthiness

Strategies strengthening the trustworthiness of the data collected were used throughout this study. Prolonged engagement, testing emerging interpretation with school teachers, and researcher reflexivity occurred during the fieldwork period. Peer review, and reaching for counterevidence occurred during the analysis process, and thick descriptions were employed in writing. Prolonged engagement involves the researcher being submerged in the research sites over a long period to ensure in-depth data collection (Merriam, 2002). In this study, prolonged engagement was realized by 32 visits for data collection. This ensured saturation of data and the emergence of repetitive patterns.

The researcher tested the emerging interpretation with school teachers who also observed the children's activities in the classroom. The teachers' feedback helped guard against researcher bias and methodological deficiencies (Maxwell, 2005). For instance, the researcher's music background tended to position children's instrumental playing as pure "musical behavior"; however, two school teachers pointed to the social function that was hidden beneath this.

Reflexivity involves critical self-reflection by the researcher regarding interpretation, assumptions, theoretical orientation, different thinking, questions, and relationship to the study that may affect the study (Lincoln & Guba, 2000; Merriam, 2002). In this study, the researcher wrote reflective journals for 2 years, noting thinking, crucial change, decision-making, and analysis process. This reflexivity also serves as an "audit trail" (Guba & Lincoln, 1981) to record how the study arrived at the results (Dey, 1993).

Peer review involves examination and discussion with colleagues about the analysis process, the consistency of categorizing emerging findings, and interpretation (Merriam, 2002). This study saw the researcher's colleague, whose specialty is children's play, scan the raw data, sample the findings for checking analytical process, and mutually shape the interpretation with the researcher.

The strategy of reaching for counterevidence involves searching for discrepancies in results throughout analysis (Lincoln & Guba, 1985). That is, analysis is coupled with purposefully looking for incongruence in the findings to challenge the researcher's expectations. For instance, in this study, the researcher found that 2-year-old children showed a tendency to group pulses while they played instruments. To search for counterevidence, each child's instrumental playing was screened, and several children that did not show such evidence were found. Therefore, a conclusion was made that eight out of 14 children showed such a tendency.

Thick description is a strategy to ensure for external validity (Merriam, 2002). Thick description provides rich description to contextualize the study, so the readers will be able to determine whether the finding can be transferred to their own situation (Merriam, 2002). In this study, the study sites of two music centers, participants' music background, and children's musical behavior and peer interaction were described, allowing readers to determine the extent to which their situation matches the study. Finally, while the writing was completed, drafts were sent to the two teachers for reexamination resulting in adjustments to several sentences for better description.

FINDINGS

Musical Behavior

Rhythmic playing. Regularly beating instruments was the most common musical behavior observed in the 2-year-olds, and their pulses frequently show a multiple of a certain number.

Shi-Xian started by using both hands to beat a snare drum with sticks simultaneously 14 times, and then she alternated her hands to beat the bongos seven times. Following that, Shi- Xian had her left hand on snare drum and right hand on bongos and played these two instruments simultaneously seven times. Shi-Xian used both hands to play the snare drum simultaneously 28 times, and then shifted to alternate her hands to play the snare drum 20 times. After a short pause, Shi- Xian again used both hands simultaneously to play the snare drum, seven times (071009).

In this example, pulses of seven are Shi-Xian's basic grouping as 14 and 28 are multiples of seven. In this class, eight out of 14 children showed such a tendency to group pulses. Besides the pulses of seven, four and five were the other common pulses of grouping.

The 2-year-old children's spontaneous rhythmic playing only consisted of quarter notes and half notes which frequently coincided with chanting rhymes.

While Wi-Chee was walking, she chanted the rhyme *Little Monkey* and played the rhythm combined with quarter- and half-notes (Figure 1) on a tambourine simultaneously. The playing rhythm coincided with the chanting rhythm and with her walking pulse (071120).

On the other hand, the 5-year-old children easily produced various rhythmic combinations of quarter- and eighth-notes after a short period of exploration. Furthermore, they expanded the ratio of value from 2:1 to 4:2:1. Occasionally, dotted rhythms were heard from the 5-year-old children.

Mei-Chee shook the maracas to the rhythm (Figure 9.2), and Da-Wei played a wood block to the rhythm (Figure 9.3) (061212, 061219). Jun-Kai used cymbals to play the rhythm (Figure 9.4) and Han-Wei also used cymbals to play the rhythm (Figure 9.5) (061003, 061121). Ya-Mei played gong in the rhythm (Figure 9.6) (061205).

In addition to individual instrumental playing, the 5-year-old children naturally generated small playing ensembles categorized into three types: alternating pulses; accompanying learned melodies; alternating ostinati. In the ensemble of *alternating pulses*, children rotated to play various pulses rather than rhythmic patterns, often with different tone colors created (Figure 9.7 and 9.8).

Figure 9.1.   Wi-Chee's *Little Monkey*.

Figure 9.2.   Mei-Chee—cymbals.

Figure 9.3.   Da-Wei—woodblock.

Figure 9.4.   Jun-Kai – cymbals.

Figure 9.5.   Han-Wei—cymbals.

Figure 9.6.   Ya-Mei—gong.

The ensemble playing of *accompanying learned melodies* was frequently seen in the music center. Children played the instruments with learned songs. Usually, one of the ensemble members played the tune on the keyboard, and the others sang and played their own instruments along with the tune. The instrumental accompaniment played either the pulse or the rhythm of learned songs. In the ensemble playing of alternating ostinati, children rotated to play rhythmic patterns repetitively.

Liang-Yo gave a pair of lummi sticks to Wei-Han, and Liang-Yo himself held the castanet. Liang-Yo showed Wei-Han how to play the rhythm (Figure 9.9.), and Liang-Yo himself played four beats of quarter-notes. They both rotated to repeat the rhythmic patterns several times (061226).

Figure 9.7.   Alternating pulse with cymbals and gong.

Figure 9.8.   Alternating pulse with gong and finger cymbals.

Figure 9.9.   Repeated rhythmic pattern.

Melodic playing/singing. The 2-year-old children were frequently seen singing learned songs at free musical play.

> Shi-Xian sang *Two Tigers,* and the other children next to her started to join the singing. After they finished the song, Shi-Xian restarted *Brother and Father* and the others followed her to sing again. While they were singing, Chee-Cian interrupted with *London Bridge is Falling Down.* Chee-Cian's loud voice overwhelmed Shi-Xian's *Brother and Father,* and the others shifted to follow Chee-Cian's singing of *London Bridge is Falling down* (071002).

The 2-year-old children had learned a lot of songs during transitions.[7] They frequently sang learned songs at free musical play, but the tonality of their singing was not yet stable. As Scott-Kassner (1993) found, they frequently shifted tonal centers as the register was too high or too low for them.

> Yu-Chee sang *Butterfly* and played the tambourine simultaneously. After finishing singing the text "have colorful dresses," she transposed the next phrase "you love flowers and flowers love you" down. While she sang "sweet flowers," she moved this entire phrase up (071006).

Yu-Chee adjusted the interval to her comfortable range. There is a leap of an interval of a minor sixth to C^2 between "have colorful dresses" and "you love flowers and flowers love you." Yu-Chee shrank the interval from minor sixth to minor third. However, when the melodic line was going down, she moved the following phrase up again to adjust to her vocal range. Compared to singing learned songs, the 2-year-old children's spontaneous singing was rarely heard.

Mei-In made up a fish song (080103) (Figure 9.10) with invented text and melody as a counterpart to the learned song (Figure 9.11). The text of the original song is "Little fish, little fish, where are you? Here, here, here we are." Mei-In's invented text reads, "I am not a little fish. I am not a little fish. I am not going home." The original song in a responsorial style was used as a signal for the closure of outdoor play. However, Mei-In's text implies a refusal to go indoors. Comparing the vocal range between *Butterfly* and Mei-In's invented song (Figure 9.10), the vocal range of *Butterfly* is an octave and the range of Mei-In's song is a major sixth. Because the vocal range of an octave is generally beyond 2-year-olds, she adjusted the interval to fit in her vocal range, causing instability of tonality. However, the self-invented song did not show such problems, resulting in stability of tonality. On the other hand, the 5-year-old children rarely sang. Singing learned songs was occasionally heard but no spontaneous songs were heard in their classroom. They played more melodic instruments instead.

The 2-year-old children did not arrange the melodic bells in a row according to pitch order, but the 5-year-old children frequently arranged the melodic bells and other melodic instruments such as resonator bells in this manner before they started to play.

5-year-old Xiao-Zhen played melodic bells one by one, and rearranged the ascending pitch order aurally (061017). Yu-Xiang set up the resonator bells in a pitch tone row according to the size of the resonator bells (061031). Da-

Figure 9.10.   Fish song.

Figure 9.11.   Learned song.

Qian followed the numbers taped on the melodic bells to set up the pitch tone row (061031).

These children set up the pitch tone row in different ways, some aurally, others with visual aids of instrument length and numbers. At the beginning, the 5-year-old children explored melodic instruments without concern about rhythm except for long values at the end of fragments (Figure 9.12). Although the melodies do not show clear rhythmic structure, the tonality is well established. Rhythm was more of a concern later on in their creative process and added to the melodies.

Zhi-Yun played the melodic bells with defined eighth and quarter notes (061114) (Figure 9.13). Yi-Jun played the melody with clear rhythm and meter on resonator bells (061205) (Figure 9.14).

When children added rhythmic elements to the melody, soon the grouping of rhythms was evident. In figure 14, the meter of four is well established except for two measures in three meter. Later on, when children were familiar with pitch, they started to match their inner listening with melodic instruments and gradually played the tunes of learned songs.

Jun-Kai played the keyboard and hit a wrong note (Figure 9.15 final note). He paused for a while and restarted the tune (070403) (Figure 9.16).

The 5-year-old children's instrumental playing can be categorized into four developmental phases: exploration; improvisation; mastery, and reexploration (Table 9.1).

Figure 9.12.   Exploration.

Figure 9.13.   Later focus on rhythm.

rest for a while

Figure 9.14.   Rhythm and meter.

Figure 9.15.   Jun-Kei's error.

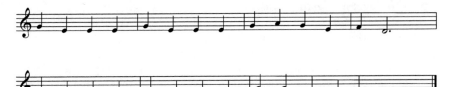

Figure 9.16.   Self-correction.

In the phase of exploration, the time period of playing each instrument is comparatively short, and physical movement occurs before the children think of the sound. The sound production in the phase of exploration is not yet in distinct rhythmic or melodic patterns.

> Zheng-Wei's right hand held a maraca to shake it, and he later picked up a melodic bell on the other hand to shake it with maraca. He held the maraca to tape castanets, hand drum, and tambourine. Afterward, he picked the stick from triangle and plugged in the melodic bell to stir insides for making sound (070417).

Table 9.1. Developmental Phases of
5-Year-Old Children's Instrumental Playing

Exploration	*Improvisation*	*Mastery*	*Reexploration*
Short period of using instruments	Longer period of using instruments	Free improvisation	Return to what was previously mastered to develop playing skills
Children play instruments without inner sound image	Children play instruments with inner sound thinking	Children play familiar tunes or improvisation	
Melodic or rhythmic fragments formed	Melodic or rhythmic patterns made		

In the phase of improvisation, the time period of playing each instrument is significantly longer than the exploration phase and physical movement gradually corresponds with the children's thinking of the sound. Such examples are shown on Figures 9.1–9.9 and 9.12 that clear rhythmic and melodic patterns occur in the phase of improvisation. In the phase of mastery, learned tunes were played on melodic instruments (see Figure 9.16), or improvisations were played (see Figures 9.13 and 9.14). Finally, in the phase of reexploration, in which children mainly played keyboards, various fingerings were reexplored after mastering the tunes to develop playing skills.

> Wei-Jun, who had not taken any piano lessons, sat in front of the keyboard to play the tune of *Twinkle, twinkle, little star.* He used his right hand to play, starting on middle C with his thumb, moving to G and A with his fifth finger and descending with finger 4, finger 3, finger 2 and thumb to complete the first phrase. Then he played the tune with his left hand, beginning with finger 5 and using all fingers in sequence. Afterward, he played the tune again with his left hand, again beginning with finger 5, but this time using a different fingering pattern, including crossing over his thumb with his forefinger to reach the highest note (A) in the phrase. (070320).

At the very beginning, children tended to use the forefinger to play the tune. Later, they put their five fingers on five keys in sequence on the keyboard. While the tune is beyond the five notes, they move their fingers in parallel motion such as the fingering of 5 on G A two notes on the right hand. Later, they save the finger for the note beyond G, and stretched their hand position by using the fingering of 5 2 for the note CG on the left hand. Ultimately, the keyboard technique of the forefinger crossing the thumb has been developed.

In this longitudinal study, the 5-year-old children developed their music ability at free musical play through the abovementioned developmental phases. However, the majority of the 2-year-old children stayed in the exploration phase, and their spontaneous musical behaviors was like a meteoric rise and quickly faded. Later, those instruments had even been transformed into kitchen utensils for housekeeping play.

Body movement. Two types of body movement were observed in the two classrooms. The first type involved moving the body corresponding with the direction of instrumental play.

Two-year-old Ping-Ru shook the maracas, and her body also swung in the same direction as the maracas (071009).

Two-year-old Pin-Xuan beat a hand drum, and then she stepped forward and backward corresponding with her beating pulse. Afterward, she heavily struck the hand drum, and when her hand bounced up from the drum, she raised her hand to make an upright pose. Pin-Xuan struck heavily on the hand drum again, and raised both hands to make another pose when her hand bounced up from the drum. Repetitively, Pin-Xuan struck the hand drum, and each time she created a different pose by changing her hand and foot motion after striking the hand drum (071211).

Five-year-old Yu-Xiang shook the tambourine up and down, and he also moved his body up and down (061121).

Five-year-old Zhang-Zhen held a tambourine to tap on her thigh, buttocks, shoulder and cheek. Afterward, she held the tambourine with both hands and jumped to make the metal on the tambourine vibrate. She later shifted the tambourine to her right hand and lifted it up above her head to shake, and turned circles to make different sounds with it (061226).

The other type of body movement observed was the motions induced by the music from the surroundings.

Two-year-old Wei-Xiong played on an auto music toy. He put the toy on the ground and then he followed the rhythm from the music toy to dance. He jumped and made several circles, and then he bent down to touch the floor. Later, Wei-Xiong propped up his body with his hands and quickly moved his feet forward and backward in the style of a "street dance" (071009).

Five-year-old Pei-An pressed the auto music button on the keyboard and Min-Lun started to dance to the music. Xiao-Zhen followed the music to tap her tambourine and then held the tambourine to dance (061017).

In the 2-year-old children's open plan classroom, the space was designed so that the children could walk around while they played instruments, unlike the 5-year-old classroom where each center was separated by short cabinets and the chidlren's motions were restricted. While the 2-year-olds walked around in the open space, their instrumental playing and singing coincided with walking pulses and three-part rhythms (walking, instrumental playing and singing) that were a natural consequence of their movement.

Wi-Chee sang *Little fish* and played the tambourine while she was walking, generating a three-part rhythm(071108) (Figure 9.17).

Peer Interaction

Children's social behaviors are developed from solitary play (children function in isolation from others), through parallel play (two or more children are neighboring and aware of one another, but there is no interaction between them) and associative play (children play together) to cooperative play (children not only play together but also try to accomplish certain common goals) (Millar, 1968). Although the social behaviors of the 2-year-old children belonged to either the solitary or parallel stage, the instruments seemed to act as catalysts and stimulated more interaction between these children. Brownell and Brown (1985) found that children can share objects to form a social contract after they have the concept of ownership. In this study, it was found that the 2-year-old children's peer interaction frequently centered on instrumental possession rights from which they gradually learn to share, towards an early hint of ensemble playing. Sticks are powerful instruments for the 2-year-olds at musical play. Almost every child liked to have a stick in hand, even though their instruments (e.g., castanets or wrist

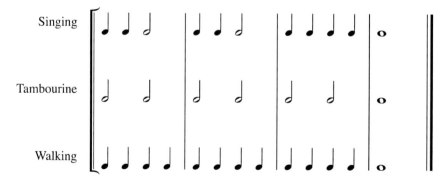

Figure 9.17.   Wi-Chee's "Little Fish" with three-part rhythm.

jingle bells) did not need any sticks. Sticks seemed to function as an extension of hands, and the 2-year-old children used their sticks to play instruments belonging to their peers. Holding a stick seems to be like having the power to play on someone else's instruments.

> Ping-Xuan held a plastic washboard[8] while sitting beside Wei-Xiong. After Ping-Xuan scraped her own washboard several times, she started to use her stick to play Wei-Xiong's drum (071030).

When children used their sticks to play other children's instruments, they were occasionally rejected.

> Chen-Zong held two sticks to play bongos. Shi-Xian came close and used her stick to play Chen-Zong's bongos, and later Wei-Xiong joined Shi-Xian and also used his stick to play on Chen-Zong's bongos. Chen-Zong picked up his bongos and left (071009).

Because Chen-Zong was not willing to share his bongos with others, he took the instruments and left. However, as soon as the "stick holder" successfully joined, a higher level of social interaction was evident, gradually forming the associative stage.

> Yi-Wen had a washboard in hand and Kai-Li, holding two sticks, sat in front of Yi-Wen. Kai-Li used her two sticks to scrape Yi-Wen's washboard, and later Kai-Li gave Yi-Wen one of her sticks. Yi-Wen and Kai-Li scraped the washboard together (071101).

> Ping-Ru used her stick to play Ping-Xuan's snare drum, and they both played together. Ji-Xiang pushed his bongos close to Ping-Xuan, and joined them. Chen-Zong heard the sound and also beat his hand drum to join. The others gradually held their own instruments, came close and joined in (071106).

A beginning glimpse of a drum ensemble was gradually formed in this last example. However, the 2-year-old children's drum ensemble did not show any related rhythmic pattern except for repetitively beating with crescendo and accelerando.

The 5-year-old children were more mature in their social behavior, and through interaction, they mutually facilitated music learning and formed simple ensembles. Peers appearing in the same area created a positive atmosphere for musical playing.

> Yong-Xuan leisurely used his index finger to punch the keyboard. While Guan-Lin stood behind Yong-Xuan to wait his turn, Yong-Xuan became positively engaged in playing the keyboard (061128).

The 5-year-old children facilitated their music learning through imitation, peer instruction, and peer demonstration.

> Pei-Yun used to play melodic bells by shaking them. Once she saw Wei-Jun pressing the bells, Pei-Yun began to press the melodic bells as well instead of shaking them (060919).

> Chi-Yun played the learned tune of *Guest is coming* on the keyboard, and Pin-Wen stood beside her to look. Chi-Yun said to Pin-Wen, "See, I can play this. I'll show you how to play." Chi-Yun stood up and let Pin-Wen have her seat, and Chi-Yun started to explain the finger position and point the notes on keyboard for Pin-Wen to play the tune (061212).

Pei-Yun learned another way of playing melodic bells by imitating Wei-Jun's playing, and Pin-Wen learned to play a tune through Chi-Yun's demonstration and instruction. Furthermore, the 5-year-old children challenged their peers to accomplish certain things together asshown in the following example.

> Yi-Jing used her forefinger to play *Twinkle, Ttwinkle, Little Star*. Ren-Ping brought her a piano score and set it on the keyboard stand. They turned the piano score to *Twinkle, Twinkle, Little Star* and Ren-Ping pointed to the notes while Yi-Jing played. Later, they turned the piano score to *Eagle Grabbing Chickens* and Ren-Ping pointed to the notes and read out the fingerings for Yi-Jing to play (070327).

Through peer collaboration, the 5-year-old children tried to read the music notation and play the tunes from music scores. The 5-year-old children's peer interaction not only facilitated music learning, but also created small ensembles as mentioned before. Therefore, children's social ability influences their musical behavior and music learning at free musical play.

DISCUSSION

Interaction With Instruments

This study found that 5-year-olds developed their musical abilities at free musical play through four developmental phases: exploration, improvisation, mastery, and re-exploration. However, the 2-year-olds mostly remained in the stage of exploration, and after a certain period of time, their musical behaviors faded. Although the 2-year-olds did not demonstrate such developmental phases as the 5-year-olds, their musical behaviors of playing grouped pulses, instrumental playing, singing, and body movement are valuable. The ability to group pulses may pave the way for further learning about meter. Their chanting rhythms and instrumental playing naturally coordinated with walking pulse functioning as the basic beat, and created the duration ratio of 2:1 (see Figure 9.1). As soon as children can make a rhythm comprised of a half note and a quarter note in the ratio of 2:1 on stable beat, it will not be difficult for them to extend such ability to a quarter note and an eighth note as well as an eighth note and sixteenth note. Rainbow (1981) found that in instructional learning, it is difficult to ask 3-year-olds to imitate rhythm clapping or clap to a rhythm while they are stepping, however, in this study, at free musical play children naturally demonstrated such ability. Imitation and free play represent different notions in children's learning. Imitation, mechanical repetition, is not built on children's personal character and it restricts children's free exploration. However, free play gives children chances to connect with people, events, and situations to make meaning (Johnson, Christie, & Wardle, 2005) as well as to display personal experiences. Free play represents a different aspect of learning from the imitation that can be seen in different instructional environments. Further, as Ro (1993) found, during group play, the playful situations induced children's musical creativity. Children's spontaneous singing employs musical elements of duration and pitch with self-invented text reacting to the playful situation, and children explore those elements for self-expression. Such activity provides clear evidence for the value of free musical play.

When comparing instrument use between the 2-year-olds and the 5-year-olds, the 2-year-olds were more interested in rhythmic instruments than melodic ones while the 5-year-olds preferred melodic instruments to rhythmic ones. The 2-year-olds frequently separated a set of melodic bells or resonator bells and picked up only one or two bells to play as rhythmic instruments. Furthermore, the glockenspiel was played with glissando, with melodic fragments rarely created. The 5-year-olds favored the keyboard, xylophone, melodic bells, and resonator bells, and they created melodic fragments with them. Later, melodies with rhythmic variety were played on melodic instruments. More often than not, the children used rhythmic instruments to accompany the melodic instruments.

Interaction With Peers

At free musical play, peers of the 5-year-olds were able to mutually share, teach and facilitate each other's musical learning, a highly-valued endeavor Although the 2-year-olds have not exhibited such mutual teaching, they used instruments as catalysts to induce peer interaction and form associative play which is in contrast to Millar's (1968) finding about 2-year-olds who belong to the solitary or parallel stage. Brownell and

Brown (1985) found that 2-year-old children use physical contact and props as mediators to start peer interaction. The current study found 2-year-olds to be using instruments, particularly sticks to initiate social interaction.

The 5-year-olds sustained their musical behavior and peer interaction through the entire school year, and their instrumental playing gradually improved through the four developmental stages. However, the 2-year-olds' musical behavior underwent a meteoric rise and almost died out after three months. Reexamining the study sites, they were both under the same conditions of having no adult intervention at free musical play. The 5-year-old participants had prior formal music lessons but the 2-year-old participants did not. Although children's musical behaviors can be mutually shaped by their peers, these children mainly constructed their musical play from their prior musical experiences. This concurs with Piaget's (1962) theory that children construct their play from their prior experiences. The 5-year-olds who received musical experiences from music lessons may extend their learning from music lessons at free musical play. It seems, at least from this study, that the condition of having formal music lessons would have a definite impact on young children's musical free play. This researcher would argue against Achilles' (1992) claim that young children's music learning should only focus on free musical play with a reduction of circle time.

In addition, generally, free musical play focused on instrumental exploration but did not consider song learning and music appreciation. According to the Standards of Kindergarten Curriculum which was issued by Ministry of Education in Taiwan (1987), young children are nurtured in their musical experiences through singing, body movement, music appreciation and instrumental play. How to weave song learning and music appreciation into free musical play to develop a music curriculum which is appropriate for young children is a challenge for music educators and needs further study.

RESEARCHER'S REFLECTION

This longitudinal study was originally designed with weekly observations of two sites in mind, looking at 2-year-olds and 5-year-olds in separate settings. The purpose was to investigate the processes of young children's musical development as well as examining musical behaviors and peer interaction during free musical play. While the data collection in the 5-year-old site went well, the data collection almost ceased at the 2-year-old site as their musical behaviors astonishingly died out. Research studies in this area have not explained this decay of musical behaviors in the younger children, and only one study thus far (Moorhead & Pond, 1978) has involved 2-year-old children as subjects. Even then, Moorhead & Pond did not elaborate the findings according to various age levels.

The original data collection for the 2-year-old children was halted after several weeks due to the lack of musical behaviors observed. Subsequently, another data collection period was set-up for the following year. The re-designed data collection was planned for 2–3 visits a week rather than once a week to understand the 2-year-olds' musical behaviors as well as peer interaction. Although the original goal of understanding how the 2-year-olds would develop their musical abilities at free musical play was not achieved, the observations of their musical behavior and peer interaction were still informative and valuable for music education.

Since data were collected through observation, the roles of the researcher and research assistant were designed as outsiders to avoid interruption of the children's play. Children construct their play and make meaning from their own experiences. It seems from this study that children's music making comes out of functionality rather than music making for its own sake. For instance, they created music for birthdays, weddings, or marches during play. This researcher made the decision of defining herself as a non-participant observer and only observing for musical behaviors and peer interaction. Regrettably, the interesting socio-dramatic play leading up to children's music making was missed or not completely understood. Because the rich content of the play might not be easily comprehended by outsiders, entering the children's world by play-ing and chanting with them would have allowed the researcher and research assistant to better understand the meaning and context of their musical behaviors.

Also, children's musical behaviors can happen in any place and any time beyond the music centers. Any props can be transformed into musi-cal instruments by children to create music. If researchers have the benefit of time and include other play situations within their research observa-tions, a much richer set of data can be collected to delve into children's musical play in depth.

NOTES

1. In kindergarten, young children often sit in a circle for instructional learn-ing. Therefore, circle time means group learning time.
2. Kindergartens and nursery schools all belong to preschools in Taiwan. The majority of kindergartens enroll children from four to six years old, and nursery schools enroll children from two to six.
3. Public kindergartens only enroll children aging 4-6 years old.

4. The five-year-old children have music lessons twice a week, and each lesson lasts about 45 minutes. During music lessons, they learn singing, body movement, music appreciation, and occasionally using rhythmic instruments to accompany singing. Those children can sing several songs by memory, use body movement to react different pitch range as well as create motion for listening music.
5. The art center was arranged outside classroom close to the sink where is convenient for children to get water for water color painting.
6. The number shown on the end of each datum indicates the date. For instance, 071009 means the datum was collected on Oct. 9th, 2007.
7. In kindergarten or nursery school, children's learning activity moves from one to another. The short period between two activities is called transition period.
8. The washboard was used as a substitute guiro.

REFERENCES

Achilles, E. (1992). Current perspectives on young children's thinking. In B. L. Andress & L. M. Walker (Eds.), *Readings in early childhood music education* (pp. 67–74). Reston, VA: The National Association for Music Education.

Brownell, C. A., & Brown, E (1985). *Toddler peer interaction in relation to cognitive development.* Paper presented at the biennial meeting of the Society for Research in Child Development, Toronto, Canada.

Brownell, C. A., & Carriger, M. S. (1990). Changes in cooperation and self/other differentiation during the second year. *Child Development, 61*, 1164–1174.

Chang, C. Y. (2000). *A study of learning centers design and application at public kindergartens in Taipei.* Unpublished master's thesis, National Chengchi University, Taipei, Taiwan.

Dey, I. (1993). *Qualitative data analysis.* London: Routledge.

Johnson, J. E., Christie, J. F., & Wardle, F. (2005). *Play, development, and early education.* Boston, MA: Allyn & Bacon.

Glaser, B., & Strauss, A. (1967). *The discovery of ground theory.* Chicago, IL: Aldine.

Guba, E. G., & Lincoln, Y. S. (1981). *Effective evaluation.* San Francisco, CA: Jossey-Bass.

Hildebrandt, C. (1998). Creativity in music and early childhood. *Young Children, 53*(6), 68–74.

Lincoln, Y., & Guba, E. (1985). *Naturalistic inquiry.* Newbury Park, CA: SAGE.

Lincoln, Y. S., & Guba, E. G. (2000). Paradigmatic controversies, contradictions, and emerging confluences. In N. K. Denzin & Y. S. Lincoln (Eds.), *Handbook of qualitative research* (2nd ed., pp. 163–188). Thousand Oaks, CA: SAGE.

Littleton, D. (1991). *Influence of play settings on preschool children's music and play behavior.* Unpublished doctoral dissertation, The University of Texas, Austin, TX.

Piaget, J. (1962). *Play, dreams and imitation in childhood.* New York: Norton.

Maxwell, J. A. (2005). *Qualitative research design: An interactive approach* (2nd ed.) Thousand Oaks, CA: SAGE.

Merriam, S. B. (2002). Assessing and evaluating qualitative research. In S. B. Merriam (Ed.), *Qualitative research in practice*. (pp. 18–33). San Francisco, CA: Jossey-Bass.

Millar, S. (1968). *The psychology of play*. Baltimore, MD: Penguin.

Miller, L. B. (1983). *Music in early childhood: Naturalistic observation of young children's musical behavior*. Unpublished doctoral dissertation, The University of Kansas, Lawrence, KS.

Ministry of Education. (1987). *The Standards of Kindergarten Curriculum*. Taipei: Ministry of Education.

Moorhead, G., & Pond, D. (1978). *Music of young children*. (Reprinted from the 1941-1951editions.) Santa Barbara, CA: Pillsbury Foundation for the Advancement of Music Education.

Rainbow, E. (1981). A final report on a three-year investigation of rhythmic abilities of preschool aged children. *Bulletin of the Council for Research in Music Education, No. 66/67*, 69–73.

Ro, Y. (1993). A study of young children's musical experiences in play. Unpublished master's thesis, National Taiwan Normal University, Taipei.

Scott-Kassner, C. (1993). Musical characteristics. In M. Palmer & W. L. Sim (Eds.), *Music in prekindergarten: Planning & teaching* (pp. 7–13). Reston, VA: The National Association for Music Education.

Smithrim, K. (1997). Free musical play in early childhood. *Canadian Journal of Research in Music Education. 38*(4), 17–24.

Van Hoorn, J., Monighan-Nourot, P., Scales, B., & Alward, K. R. (2003). *Play at the center of the curriculum*. Columbus, OH: Merrill Prentice-Hall.

Vygotsky, L. S. (1978). *Mind in society: The development of higher mental processes* (M. Cole, V. John-Steiner, S. Scribner, & E. Souberman, Eds. & Trans.). Cambridge, MA: Havard University Press.

CHAPTER 10

WESTERN MUSIC EDUCATION IN POST-WORLD WAR II BURMA/MYANMAR

The Case of a Young Violinist and the Gitameit Music Center

Hideaki Onishi and Kit Young

INTRODUCTION

This chapter recounts heretofore rarely known situations about the early
and general music education in Burma/Myanmar through a social and
cultural lens.[1] Unlike many other chapters in this book, this chapter does
not take the form of a typical research paper in the conventional sense of
the word. The primary reason for this is the scarcity of and limited access
to data, a reality apparent from the very beginning of this project where
statistical study of any sort was out of the question. Since there is little
published or formal documentation on Burmese music education written
in English, the authors have had to rely on fieldwork, interviews,
questionnaires, and background reading in Burmese language magazines
and texts. Most of the information was gathered by Young during her

Musical Childhoods of Asia and the Pacific, pp. 215–235
Copyright © 2012 by Information Age Publishing
All rights of reproduction in any form reserved.

residence in Burma/Myanmar from 2003 to 2008, sporadic trips made between 1987 and 2002, and two additional trips in 2009.

Nonetheless, the very scarcity of data itself tells us something significant as well; it can function as a framework around which stories of individuals might be told and against which these stories take shape. Combining these accounts offers a larger perspective and helps us understand the current state of music education in Burma/Myanmar—a closed society. Hopefully this effort will initiate and encourage a forum to promote positive changes. The stories to be narrated here are of a young violin student who has managed to find a way out to continue his music studies overseas. An interview with the musician was conducted in Singapore by Onishi, who then reconstructed the narrative. Further clarification was made over e-mail. The musician's father also answered a questionnaire.

Personal stories like this risk being on their own and taken out of context. We have tried avoiding this pitfall. There were occasions, however, on which we might have compared situations, decisions made, and actions taken by our subject or subjects with those by other Burmese. Research relying primarily on a few individual narratives cannot achieve the completeness of other comparative methods. In fact, we should feel grateful for having at least *some* data on an individual, data of not so insignificant an amount. Moreover, relating the past can lead us to contextualize the present and begin the groundwork for reframing more detailed studies in the future. The authors hope that these profiles will afford a wide perspective and give hope to young aspiring Burmese musicians, both domestic and abroad. Our main focus is on Western music but mention of traditional music will also be made, as the two musical cultures are interlocked through and around what we see as one central issue.

MUSIC EDUCATION AND THE BRITISH EDUCATIONAL LEGACY IN POST-WORLD WAR II BURMA

Although the Burmese achieved independence from the British Empire in 1947, most of the British educational structures of the colonial period remained unchanged. Irrespective of family religion, the Burmese middle class chose primary and secondary schools that were run by Catholics, Methodists, or Baptists and staffed by Burmese teachers who graduated from the British teachers' colleges. The independent, elected Burmese government of U Nu set up free government schools in the 1950s, catering primarily to lower-income Burmese of various religions. However, the middle class still preferred the mission schools because of their higher educational standards in the English language. Beginning in the Ne Win period (1962–1988), the government schools would decide not to include

English until the secondary level. This neglect was in accordance with the isolationist "Burmese Way to Socialism" set forth by Ne Win himself, who wanted to free his country from all prior foreign influences.

The effort to introduce Western art music during this period was sporadic at best. The curriculum of the mission schools in Rangoon (including St. Francis, American Baptist School, and St. Paul's Institute), Taungyi, and Mandalay did not include music, arts, or theater, although in many of the schools Christian hymns were sung in regular chapel services, regardless of the students' home religions. Some of these American and British schools had a rudimentary band as an extracurricular activity, playing British marching music and Burmese anthems arranged in Western tonal style. At the secondary level, students formed clubs to produce plays, compose songs, and create artworks, but these activities were not officially encouraged. Notable among the mission schools in this regard was the Baptist United Christian High School in Rangoon, since they held annual music competitions. Yet their focus was not on Western music but on classical Burmese singing with the accompaniment of *sandaya* (Burmese piano), *saung gauk* (Burmese harp), and *patala* (Burmese xylophone). In the mid-1950s, the Rangoon State School of Fine Arts hired Karen pianist Doris Htoo, who, with a background in Western music, organized a curriculum of "international music." But this program would be cut in the Ne Win period to come (U Toh, personal communication, August 2009[2]).

Children with the most exposure to the Western idioms of tonal harmony through church music were those from the exclusively Christian communities among various ethnic groups, namely Sagaw/Pwo Karen, Palaung, Chin, Kachin, Anglo-Indian, and some Shan and Mon communities. Burman Christians were a minority. Some of these church communities, with foreign missionary and church member participation, were exposed to Bach and Handel through choral singing. In Rangoon and Mandalay, some of the Buddhist, Hindu, and Moslem children had some exposure to British nursery rhymes, Mother Goose, and other simple folk songs in school, although these groups as well as the Christian groups mentioned above had virtually no contact with Western concert music.

The mostly Christian Karen may be a little different in this regard. With approximately 3.5 million people, the Karen form the largest (as of 2008) minority group in Burma/Myanmar, with 7% of the entire population. In a predominantly Buddhist nation, many of the Karen belong to various Baptist sects introduced by American Adoniram Judson and other missionaries, starting in 1812 (Judson, 1883). After their rebellion in the early 1950s, many southern Karen came to settle in Insein, a suburb of Rangoon, where the rebellion was halted by the Burmese government. With the influx of new residents came the establishment of more Karen churches and strong musical groups; string ensembles and church choirs formed the basis for contemporary church music exposure and Karen language support at the primary level. A common perception of many Burmese is that the Christian Karen are the most experienced in Western music of all Burmese (Daw Hla Than, personal communication, March 2009; U Toh, personal communication, August 2009).

Burmese people had access to Western music of various genres, but this did not come through education. They listened to the Burma Broadcasting Service (fondly called "BBS") or Myanma Athan in Burmese, which had weekly broadcasts of Western music with commentaries. The British, French, and American embassies occasionally hosted musicians from their home countries to hold concerts, the most notable from the United States being Duke Ellington, Marian Anderson, Benny Goodman, Louis Armstrong, and Martha Graham. But no effort was made on the part of the government to assimilate these visits or others in the educational sector.

THE NE WIN AND POST-NE WIN PERIODS

Military strongman and dictator General Ne Win imposed "The Burmese Way to Socialism" in 1964 and began a vortex of isolation and suppression that continues today. The impetus for public dissatisfaction with the military regime burst out in 1974 at Rangoon University, in the mass demonstrations of 1988, and again in 1995 at universities in Rangoon/ Yangon and Mandalay. After 1988, Ne Win "retired" and a council of generals or the State Law and Order Restoration Council (SLORC) became the ruling organ. At the suggestion of Ne Win's astrologers so that he and his cronies could escape a bad karmic debt from the genocide of citizens in the 1988 demonstrations and consolidate their power, the military junta made name changes. Myanmar became the official name of the country, with many cities changing from formerly British nomenclature to local terms, from Rangoon to Yangon, for example.

The regime's response to routing young dissidents in the 1990s radically changed national higher education. Campuses were closed down for most of the academic year. The government instituted a nationwide "distance-learning" syllabus for students in most disciplines, choking the outflow of competent graduates to a trickle. The military colleges in engineering, science, medicine, and technical support remained open to military personnel. With great reluctance, the government kept the University of Yangon Medical School open to civilians. As a matter of fact, it was here at the Medical School that many of the dissidents organized their 1995 activities.

Opportunities to pursue music, arts, or theater have never been a part of the national government curriculum at any level outside of government performing arts schools in Rangoon/Yangon and Mandalay. The people's desire for artistic expression had at least found outlets in clubs and associations that formed civilian on-campus life until 1988, but such options became unavailable when most distance-learning campuses required attendance only during 2 months out of the entire academic year for examination. The situation has become even more grim today, as students in the upper middle class take flight once they reach college age. Options are limited. Outlets for gifted children in music are few in the country, with no conservatories or ensembles (instrumental or secular choral) of Western music available for training. In Rangoon/Yangon and Mandalay a primary/secondary State School of Arts (Pandaya Kyaung) and the University of Culture prepare students primarily for study in traditional Burmese music, arts, and theater. Although the latter has a small department of Western music for strings and piano, no attempt is made to pursue any high standard of performance or developing competence. The Myanmar Institute of Theology and the Judson College Baptist Youth Conference has opened music courses but, again, mainly for a Christian fellowship in Rangoon/Yangon.

There are small music programs in some of the international schools: Yangon International Education Center, Network Primary School, Yangon International School (YIS), International School of Yangon, Modern Language Center, and Horizon Kindergarten. There are Burmese students at these schools but only the rich can afford the expensive tuition. The largest of those is the International Language and Business Center (ILBC), the biggest private primary and secondary school in Rangoon/Yangon and Mandalay, and it has a curriculum music program for Burmese citizens. Individual musicians open private studios in the big cities, though tuition is high since they receive no institutional backup (US$4–10 an hour is considered high by many modest middle-class families). Do Re Mi, for example, is a small music school for toddlers and children up to age 10 run by Yuri Hasegawa, a Japanese music teacher married to a Burmese man. She has classes in rhythm and movement for children of rich Burmese and mostly Japanese and other expatriates. She has trained in Orff techniques and helps several local private kindergarten teachers with Orff-style workshops (see the Appendix for the list of music institutions in Burma/Myanmar).

Burma/Myanmar also suffers from a lack of organized groups and venues engaged in and promoting Western music to attract audiences, even in the big cities. This is unlike most of the surrounding Southeast Asian countries, where a vibrant exchange of traditional and Western music (whether classical, pop/rock, or jazz) occurs. Due to the lack of imported

CDs of classical, contemporary, and jazz music and the scarcity of concerts, in addition to the limited number of music education programs described above, there is virtually no opportunity for Burmese musicians to absorb more sophisticated Western and non-Western musical genres. There is a recording studio and a vibrant pop scene that are commercially supported and sustained by fans all over the nation and abroad. This is the music that most young adults call "music" as they bypass Western classical and jazz as being too difficult to listen to or learn, and dismiss Burmese traditional music altogether.

The popularity of pop music in Burma/Myanmar has often been associated with defiance to the regime. Lyrics for rock and hip-hop are closely monitored and easily censored by the authorities. While overt verbal dissent is impossible, musicians have learned to use metaphor for social and political commentaries through verses that depict the emotional turbulence of love, play loud back beats, shout, work up frantic fret work, and grunt to express frustration, anger, regret, and nostalgia that would otherwise be muted. Htoo Eain Thin, a talented lyricist and singer who unfortunately died in 2004, was able to delicately weave metaphor into his ballads about, for example, the pain of living under the regime, his generation's great respect for the national leader of democracy Aung San Suu Kyi, and the sorrow from the 1988 demonstrations with lyrics that were nominally songs of love, nostalgia, and pain. "Ah May Ain [My Mother's House]" and "Yazawin Mya Ye Thadothamee [Our History as Our Bond]" are some such ballads.

A GLANCE AT THE ROLE OF TRADITIONAL BURMESE MUSIC AS A MUSICAL BACKGROUND

Since there was no official music curriculum in post-World War II Burmese primary schools, the children in the families of professional Burmese musicians or amateur music circles were lucky to be surrounded by adults playing and singing Burmese traditional music. Daw Hla Than (personal communication, March 2009), a popular Burmese music singer from the 1950s, describes one such circle started by her father, who was a businessman as well as an amateur mandolin player. She grew up meeting some of the great Burmese musicians and singing traditional *Mahagita* (Burmese classical canon) songs. But in school the Baptist teachers would teach her class Christian hymns, as discussed earlier. She was aware of the disjunct nature of her musical background, and preferred the Burmese music to the hymns.

Traditional music contexts have these connections already set up. The children of Burmese *hsaing waing* (gong and drum ensemble of up to 13 players) musicians follow their parents around to pagoda festivals and government functions, and learn Burmese repertoire by osmosis. After learning how to play the timekeeper like the bell and clapper, they move on to more complicated instruments, such as the *put waing* (circle drum), *kyi waing* (circle gong), and *kyauk lon bat* (six-drum set). Within Nat (Spirit Worship) *hsaing waing* ensembles, children briefly take over on the simpler instruments from their elders while the latter take a break during nonstop playing sessions from 9:00 A.M. to 6:00 P.M. for 7 days on end. This is also how adult musicians teach responsibility in ensemble performance to children.

There is a government-sponsored annual national competition in traditional Burmese performing arts such as vocal music, dance, puppetry, composition, and instrumental performance called So-Ka-Ye-Ti. This was begun in 1993 and is now held in the new capital of Naypyidaw with contestant age groups from kindergarten all the way up to adulthood in both professional and amateur categories. Western art music in Burma/Myanmar does not have the advantages of these historically built-in social connections within musical groups.

Fewer and fewer children have chosen the path of Burmese music in the last few decades, however. Among the most famous examples of this change is rock singer Zaw Win Htut, whose popularity was at its zenith during the 1990s but now seems to be waning. His mother Hta was a renowned singer of a genre of Burmese popular song referred to variously as *Kala Baw, Khi' Haung*, and *Sit Kyo Khit* from before and after World War II in the traditional style. His grandfather Shwe Taing Nyunt composed some of these songs. In a magazine interview, Zaw Win Htut acknowledged his musical lineage and familiarity with the tradition, but also confessed that Burmese music was not where he felt comfortable expressing his ideas as a professional musician (Baumawka Daw Aye Than, 2004; Zaw Win Htut & Daw Hta, personal communication, June 2007).

The difficult relationship of other ethnic groups to the music of the Burmans is a complicated issue, but must be at least briefly mentioned here. Many of them, including disaffected Burmans, are alienated by Burmese music because it has been promoted by the military government for so long in the media as the "national music." Only token attention is paid to music of the minority ethnic groups by the government and no legitimate research and broadcast of this music is supported or encouraged. There are private commercial recording studios of pop music in Zo (Chin), Shan, Akha, Kachin, Karen, and Mon, among other languages, but older, more obscure or traditional music of these ethnic groups is not widely recorded or sold. And the majority of Burmans don't get to hear it.

PHONG PHONG'S EARLY MUSIC EDUCATION

We have mentioned that it is difficult to gain any kind of exposure to Western concert music in Burma/Myanmar, not to mention to acquire a proper education in it. Yet there is always an exception. In spite of all these circumstances, somebody finds a way and makes the first breakthrough for others to follow. Insofar as the present chapter is concerned, it was San Win Htike, or Phong Phong as he is usually called.

Although neither of his parents was from a musical family, they both have loved music and the arts. U Thein Aung from Ta Da Oo Town, Mandalay Division wanted to learn how to play the guitar when he was 18 or 19 years old as it was popular among friends, but his father (Phong Phong's grandfather) did not give him permission to do so, not being fond of music in particular or believing that it would help his son in his career. This disappointment would eventually become part of U Thein Aung's motivation to have his son learn music. On the other hand, Phong Phong's future mother Daw Khin Khin Aye from Khin U Town, Sa Gaing Division was musically active at Mandalay University, where she majored in the Burmese language. Accompanied by an ensemble of traditional instruments consisting of percussion, harp, xylophone, and other instruments, she used to sing traditional Burmese songs after class. She did not take any formal lessons, but her talent became apparent to many; her singing was quite well known among her classmates, and teachers asked her to sing at various events. She had to stop singing in 1988, though, after her parents had moved to China, her father's home country. She also had a health problem and lost confidence in singing.

Their passion for music was to come in full bloom in the next generation. Daw Khin Khin Aye met U Thein Aung at Mandalay University, where he was also a Burmese major, and they soon became friends. When U Thein Aung decided to open a shop in Mandalay to sell painting accessories and stationeries in 1987, he asked Daw Khin Khin Aye to help him with the business. They worked happily together at the newly opened Rose's Bed, also blooming feelings for each other. They married on January 1, 1989. San Win Htike, their only child, was born in Ta Da O Town on May 13, 1994.

His parents wanted to give Phong Phong what they considered modern education and have him learn a subject or two outside of what was considered a "normal education" (Phong Phong, personal communication, June 6, 2009). Not so long after his son was born, U Thein Aung read in a magazine article that some universities abroad, including those in the United Kingdom and United States, required students to take instrumental lessons. He also learned in another article that music develops human intelligence (U Thein Aung, personal communication, 24 August, 2009). They first considered it beneficial for their son to learn as many kinds of arts as possible, and had him take drawing lessons for 2 years when he was around 5 years old, concurrently with violin lessons (U Thein Aung, personal communication, June 2, 2009). The art teacher mentioned that Phong Phong was talented but Phong Phong found the art lessons somehow boring, as his true interest seems to have been in music from an early age, even before he started violin lessons. He liked music because it made people happy. He enjoyed whatever music he heard, whether it was from Disney or Chaplin films. He could even memorize songs from them and impress his family. He was in need of a more musical environment to match his potential.

When Phong Phong became interested in learning how to play an instrument, U Thein Aung decided on the violin since the piano was inconvenient to carry around (Phong Phong, personal communication, June 6, 2009).[3] He began his lessons in December 1999, when he was only 5 years old, in Ruili, China, with Zhang You Yu, a private violin teacher. Ms. Zhang had graduated from the Music Department of Minzu University of China in 1975 and taught there for 6 years. She had just come back to her hometown in early 1999 and Phong Phong became the second student in her private studio, Yunnan Music School. They would meet twice a week for a 45-minute lesson, but it sometimes lasted an hour. Her teaching was systematic. She began the lesson by giving him rudiments, although this is often not the case in Burma/Myanmar. Burmese people tend to try to begin violin lessons with Suzuki books without learning enough foundation and then face difficulties (Phong Phong, personal communication, June 6, 2009). This is just one of the many problems caused by the lack of systematic education in Burma. In Phong Phong's case, his talent certainly mattered, but learning the basics at the outset was crucial to his success.

When he mastered the basics, he moved on to the actual repertoire. Ms. Zhang gave him music from *The Beginners 100 Days* and the two volumes of *The Production of Primary Etude for Violin* for the first 2 or 3 years of his lessons.[4] They moved to Suzuki books when Phong Phong was 8, and this continued until he was 11. The pieces were mostly from Western classical music, including works by Jacques-Fereol Mazas, Fritz Kreisler, Pierre Rode, Niccolò Paganini, Rudolphe Kreutzer, and Antonio Vivaldi, but there were also some traditional Chinese songs. They were taken from *The Production* as well as " 小提琴演奏（业余）考级 " [*Violin Performance Grade Textbook*].

Ms. Zhang would occasionally include rather unconventional methods of teaching in her lessons, to Phong Phong's surprise. One day she wrote down *Happy Birthday* in the original key of G major and gave it to him. They played it in duet, although not in the usual sense of the word: while the student played the song in the original key, the teacher doubled it a perfect fifth above for the entire piece, creating an effect similar to the parallel organum or polytonality (or one may be reminded of Maurice Ravel's *Boléro*). Although it would be difficult to determine the exact effect of such teaching on Phong Phong's development as a musician, it certainly gave him a strong impression. A dedicated teacher, Ms. Zhang tried hard to make her students learn the repertoire through not only her lessons but also a lot of CDs she brought back from Kunming. She also invited a violinist who played a concert with a symphony orchestra. The guest violinist made a strong impression on Phong Phong, who wanted to be a musician like him.

In terms of balancing between practical work and academics, though, Ms. Zhang was similar to the majority of instrumental teachers. While the lessons focused on the technical aspect of violin performance, relevant theoretical or historical aspects of the repertoire were discussed only cursorily. The emphasis on the technical aspect was indeed prevalent in the private music teaching in Ruili (and possibly beyond); there were very few music teachers who could supplement instrumental lessons. And Phong Phong wanted to learn more music theory.

Phong Phong's dedication and persistence played an important role in his formative period as a violinist, especially in the difficult circumstances that he was under. He only had a 2-hour lunch break on weekdays due to the busy school schedule, but he would walk back home for 15 minutes, warm up for 10 minutes, and then work on the repertoire for half an hour, besides actually eating lunch. After all that, he would walk back to school for another 15 minutes. And this was only during the first year of his violin studies. From the second year until he moved to Thailand in 2007, in order to prepare for the audition in Singapore, the practice was extended to 20 minutes of warm-ups and 1 hour of repertoire.

The support and dedication of his parents (of his father in particular) cannot be underestimated, either. Phong Phong recalls:

[U Thein Aung] was very concerned about my violin studies. Every time I practiced he sat beside me. If I played wrong notes he could tell it even though he [was] not a musician and would stop me and let me practice [until I got it right]. He was just like an assistant teacher. He put his best effort to judge my playing and on my violin studies. (personal communication, June 6, 2009)

In 2001, U Thein Aung's business had to close down because of the renovation of the building that his shop Rose's Bed was in. This occurred when Phong Phong was 7 years old and his talent was just being discovered. Even though U Thein Aung was offered a place in the new building, he declined the offer and gave up his work so he could take his son to many musicians to give him more experience: "Therefore, the best supporter for my violin studies is my father. He is very important to me and my violin studies" (personal communication, June 6, 2009). U Thein Aung also took Phong Phong to a 6-day bicycle trip from Yunnan to Mandalay in January 2006. He wanted to model determination on his part and teach important lessons in life. As he recalls in his journal, he wanted to create goals for Phong Phong: "He will have to rely on his own initiative and imagination when he meets difficulties. How to confront and solve these difficulties in order to gain experiences" (U Thein Aung, December 2005–January 2006).

Phong Phong's parents had no special idea of how he would turn out as a musician. They would support him because they both loved music, but there was no need to think about it too much at the beginning. They told him that persistence mattered and he would need to practice everyday if he wanted to excel, although they did not force him to do so. They gave Phong Phong free choice, but he kept practicing everyday, first for 30 minutes, then 1 hour, then 2 hours, and eventually 5 hours. U Thein Aung just sat and listened to him patiently: "He knew well that if he did not continue he would not get a chance like this again" (personal communication, June 2, 2009).

Phong Phong's exceptional talent did not go unnoticed for too long. For example, he was given a solo piece from *The Beginners 100 Days* when he was age 7 or 8. It was a technically demanding piece and it would usually take a student 1 month to learn it, but Phong Phong mastered it only in 2 weeks. He would often play duets with his teacher and surprise her by playing the instructor's part that was technically more demanding. His sight-reading skill was also found to be exceptional. Phong Phong and his parents became more and more serious about his future as a musician as they learned his potential. The only thing they needed was to find opportunity. In the meantime, Phong Phong diligently continued his lessons with Ms. Zhang.[5] Things finally changed in 2004, when he came across a private institution called Gitameit Music Center. Before moving along with Phong Phong's story, we take a look at Gitameit's history prior to his encounter and involvement with the school.

GITAMEIT MUSIC CENTER

Kit Young, one of the present authors, first became involved with Burma/Myanmar and Burmese music in 1987, when she began her studies of sandaya (Burmese music as played on the piano) with Burmese musicians and the Burmese language at the University of Northern Illinois. After living in Thailand from 1992 to 2002, where she was a piano faculty member of Payap University in Chiangmai and Sri Nakarin Wirot University in Bangkok, Young moved to Burma/Myanmar in 2003 (and would remain there until 2008). When she saw a number of children and young adults eager to pursue classical-contemporary Western music but with no place or teacher to satisfy their aspiration, she decided to found a music center devoted to basic and intermediate musical training with her Burmese musician colleagues who were developing Western musical exposure (in classical and jazz): U Moe Naing, Nay Win Htun, and Burmese traditional violinist U Tin Yi. The center opened in December 2003 in Rangoon/Yangon and was named Gitameit Music Center, after the Pali and Burmese words *Gita* (music) and *Meit* (friendship). Gitameit was a nexus for Young's long engagement with Burmese music and musicians.

Everything started from scratch due to the lack of resources. But as the adults learned sight-singing, instrumental expertise, and choral singing and began their student-teaching practice, the school began to take on more children. The curriculum centered around choral singing and solfège classes with daily practice and monthly concerts. To augment the instrumental teaching, the founders brought in as many guests as possible to do workshops so that students would be exposed to new kinds of music from all over the world. In 2004, for example, Gitameit hosted pianist/singer/performance artist Claudia Stevens, ethnomusicologist Marc Perlman, percussionist Maria Jenner, and ethnomusicologist/composer Anant Nakkong. Gitameit also began a series of music-theater projects to give students hands-on experience of various genres of Western music that involve stage presentation (Broadway musicals, operas, and postmodern theater), giving them stage confidence. To introduce techniques of improvisation in ensemble, Gitameit initiated sessions called "New Directions" with poets reciting in Burmese to music improvised by students. Listening classes were compulsory for students, as were sessions on how to use the library, how to read book titles in English, how to use the Internet, and how to make sight-reading a daily practice. Developing good habits of attention was crucial to helping the students stay motivated.

Among Gitameit's goals was to expose audiences to different genres and new ideas by scheduling many small concerts in Rangoon/Yangon at Gitameit Music Center's small auditorium and concerts at hotels. Introducing a cappella singing through Gitameit vocal ensembles to a country where electric power failure is the norm has also been a crucial way to acquaint performers and audiences with different international music styles, traditions, and languages. Another notable development among Gitameit musicians (such as Sai Win Oo, Gita Lulin Maung Ko Ko, U Moe Naing, and Ko Kyaw Swa) was their interest in the wide variety of a cappella sounds and their excitement in composing and arranging songs in Burmese. Many of the music students coming to Gitameit were interested in learning notation and a higher level of guitar playing because their primary interest was in pop music, but they often had little or no knowledge of other subjects such as musicianship, music theory, music history, music theater, or performance practice in instruments (piano, strings, winds, or even voice). It should be kept in mind that Phong Phong was among the fortunate exceptions as he had taken lessons in China with Ms. Zhang and in Burma/Myanmar with one of the Gitameit cofounders, U Tin Yi, who had some background in Western violin technique in addition to the traditional Burmese violin performance.

From the beginning of Gitameit, these activities were favorably covered by private local weekly magazines and journals, which in turn helped audiences and the government feel unthreatened by Gitameit's existence. Gitameit has consistently grown and attracted hundreds of students in the past 5 years, and developed a core group of musicians from different ethnic groups and regions of Burma/Myanmar. In Mandalay Myoma Music School, an offshoot of Gitameit was begun in 2006 with 12 students by U Parami Shoon, Young's student and a scholarship student to Mahidol University College of Music in Bangkok, Thailand. With Young now living in United States, Gitameit is currently run by U Moe Naing, Director, and Nay Win Htun, Manager. It has received donor funds both locally and from abroad and is currently introducing a certificate program in basic music studies, overseen by Ma Thet Suu, a returning master's student from Mahidol University, and Daphne Wolf, a flutist/musicologist working on a grant from the Goethe Institute. Young is still involved with Gitameit as Artistic Advisor and continues advocacy in locating international scholarships and opportunities for Gitameit students. However, the Gitameit directors and older students are increasingly able to do this for themselves as they navigate the Internet and meet more musicians from abroad—an important step in independence. The organization has grown with workshops in capacity building, outreach, and administrative management, all of which are taken on by the musicians themselves. Gitameit also played a major role in relief activities when Cyclone Nargis devastated the Irrawaddy Delta in Burma/Myanmar in May 2008. Musicians delivered food and supplies, and arranged theater and singing classes in various holding centers for child survivors of the storm.[6]

PHONG PHONG MEETS GITAMEIT

At the outset, in order to fund Gitameit Music Center at least partially, Young took on a job at Yangon International School (YIS) as a choral conductor. She started a community orchestra there, consisting of Gitameit and other musicians, and organized a concert in 2003. This initiated contact among musicians who normally would never perform together in Burmese society: musicians from Myanmar Radio and Television (MRTV), and the Christian churches, expatriate musicians, a small string orchestra led by U Tin Yi, and musicians from the University of Culture, which had no orchestra. In 2004, the Gitameit orchestra participated in another concert titled "Oh! Korea." The concert became one of the crucial events to Phong Phong's musical career, when Young invited him via U Tin Yi to play the second solo part of Bach's Double Violin Concerto in d minor BWV 1043 along with Yu Jin, a sixth-grade Korean violin student at YIS. This was the first time that he interacted with a large body of musicians and audience, and his talent was immediately obvious to all. He played to the amazed international audience, who became aware of the potential of a community orchestra to draw young talent into a public sphere.

On the second visit to Gitameit Music Center during the summer of 2005, Phong Phong played some solo music and impressed the audience again. He was then invited to play in an ensemble of four violins and two guitars in a charity concert for homeless people titled "Good to Go!" organized by Gitameit in February 2006. These concert experiences gave Phong Phong what he had been missing: the dynamics of ensemble playing, and he gained a lot of them through playing in the orchestra and quartet. After the 2006 concert, U Thein Aung also felt that playing with Gitameit musicians would be a better way at this point for his son to get more connections to get ahead, and Phong Phong began spending more time with Gitameit than with U Tin Yi. He would further perform in one or two more charity concerts organized by Gitameit before leaving Burma/Myanmar.

Gitameit Music Center gave him opportunities to perform not only in an orchestra and different sizes of ensemble but also with musicians invited from abroad. Among the visitors to Gitameit was Austrian double bass player and conductor Goesta Moeller from the Innsbruck Conservatorium. He began his annual 1-month summer visit to Rangoon/Yangon in 2005, during which he would conduct a small chamber orchestra. The orchestra consisting of musicians from churches, the MRTV Orchestra, and Gitameit would meet and rehearse at Gitameit Music Center. Phong Phong was among them and played under the baton of Mueller for four consecutive years, from 2005 to 2008, and gained a lot of knowledge of music theory and orchestral music. In fact, Moeller is one of the two musicians that Phong Phong considers the most influential to him to date (the other one is his current violin teacher Alexander Souptel). Phong Phong also met local musician teachers and friends at Gitameit. Piano teacher U Parami Shoon complemented his musical education with lessons in music theory and musical interpretation. Young musician friends, including violinist Saw Win Maw and cellist Saw James Hsar Doe Soe, were equally aspiring. Playing music with them was fun and made him happy, and he became determined to continue the path of music.

TO SINGAPORE, AND THE PRESENT

Young met music theorist Hideaki Onishi, the other author of this chapter, from Yong Siew Toh Conservatory of Music, National University of Singapore during the College Music Society International Conference held in Thailand in July 2007. Onishi had always had a concern for the state of affairs in Burma/Myanmar, but was never able to establish connection with the country. He became immediately interested in Gitameit Music Center and decided to pay a 4-day visit to Burma/Myanmar with his ethnomusicologist wife in early September the same year, which happened to be just 3 weeks before the so-called Saffron Revolution broke out. They met local musicians, observed the "So-Ka-Ye-Ti" competition in progress, and, last but not least, visited Gitameit. They each gave a talk on their respective careers, listened to the choir rehearsal conducted by U Moe Naing, took a lesson in traditional Burmese piano and xylophone, tutored students in music theory, and chatted with them over lunch. Most importantly, they had an opportunity to hear Gitameit's most talented students: three pianists, Nay Myo Aung, Olive, and Bosco (one of the two students from Chin State); and three string players, Saw Win Maw, Saw James, and Phong Phong. Surprisingly, the string players had been learning their instruments without a specialized teacher, with Phong Phong being a notable exception. Impressed with their high musical standard and potential, Onishi told them about the Conservatory and suggested they should consider auditioning for it and/or other schools overseas.

Yong Siew Toh Conservatory of Music proved to be an attractive option for Phong Phong in particular, since it offered the Young Artiste Programme for students under college age. Gitameit teachers also suggested that he audition for it. He and his family discussed the matter and decided in October that he would audition the following year, in 2008. This was his only way out of Burma/Myanmar at that point. All family members were pleased with the decision, except for his grandparents in Mandalay, who did not want him to go far away even to study. In order to work on the audition pieces, Phong Phong and U Thein Aung moved to Bangkok and took lessons with German violinist and Mahidol University faculty member Mathias Boegner. The lessons were extremely intensive: they would meet every weekday for 3 months from October through December. Each lesson lasted at least 1 hour to sometimes even

3 hours. Boegner taught Phong Phong Tchaikovsky's Violin Concerto in D major op. 35, Bach's Sonata No. 1 in g minor BWV 1001, Partita No. 1 in b minor BWV 1002, and Chaconne from Partita No. 2 in d minor BWV 1004, among other works. He also worked on Phong Phong's basic techniques such as bow motion. In addition to this already exhaustive lesson, Phong Phong practiced for 5 hours everyday. U Thein Aung patiently sat through the practice, giving him advice, encouragement, and support.

Father and son traveled to Singapore on December 29, 2007 and continued preparation for the audition there. Violin faculty members of the Conservatory offered him generous help. T'ang Quartet first violinist Ng Yu-Ying gave him some guidance and checked his violin, and Head of Violin Studies Zuo Jun even gave him a 1-hour lesson without charge. The audition took place on January 19, 2008. Phong Phong recalls the day: "I think I did well, because I tried my best to perform. I wasn't sure [if] I would be accepted, but I didn't think too much [about it]" (personal communication, June 6, 2009). As a matter of fact, he did a splendid job. All the faculty members came out of the audition room to congratulate and shake hands with him. However, the acceptance did not come immediately, due to an unexpected reason: the Young Artiste Programme only offers a weekly lesson with the instructor and academic classes on Saturday, and students are expected to attend a secondary school on weekdays on their own. This meant that in order to enroll in the program, Phong Phong would have to find a secondary school in Singapore and obtain a student visa. The Conservatory was unaware of this problem since he was the first international student who auditioned for the programme, which was only 2 years old then. Collaboration with the School of the Arts, Singapore (SOTA) was considered but did not materialize. Frustrated with the situation, U Thein Aung decided to look for a school in Singapore for his son to attend and finally found TMS Educational Group. It was only then when Phong Phong was officially accepted to the Young Artiste Program.

Phong Phong now continues his violin studies with Alexander Souptel, concertmaster of Singapore Symphony Orchestra and faculty member of the Conservatory, while attending a local secondary school. He has been spending fulfilling days: "It is great and wonderful to study at the Conservatory. The violin teacher is very cheerful. All other teachers are also very kind and good at teaching" (personal communication, June 6, 2009). Phong Phong's future plan is to study violin performance for the bachelor's and possibly master's degrees. This is likely to be overseas as there is no school that offers such degrees in Burma/Myanmar, at least at the moment. He would love to share music with those who don't have a chance to study or listen to violin music back home. His friend Saw James has also expressed the wish to do the same with the cello; many Burmese people always think of their fellow countrymen before themselves.

CONCLUDING THOUGHTS

We have narrated in this chapter the current conditions of music education in Burma/Myanmar, against which Phong Phong's musical endeavor was depicted. All he needed was talent, dedication, faith, support of family, and a little fortunate turn of events. The two other string players who played for Onishi at Gitameit Music Center in September 2007 also found a place to study music abroad; Saw James was also accepted to the Conservatory and now studies toward a bachelor's degree under Leslie Tan, the cellist of T'ang Quartet, while Saw Win Maw is a student of Mueller at Innsbruck Conservatorium. Some other students were not so fortunate, though. The three piano students that Onishi heard at Gitameit Music Center were all musically talented and most eager, and yet technically not quite capable of handling the standard repertoire just because they did not have a chance to start playing the instrument earlier. For instruments like the piano, it matters a lot.

Phong Phong's story is an exceptional case. It has to be admitted that the early music education in Burma/Myanmar is weak. Music is not implemented in the curriculum and the children have no time with their schedule full of classes. Since schoolteachers offer extra classes outside the regular class hours to earn some additional income, students have to be at school from 7:00 A.M. to 6:30 P.M. everyday once they reach the second term of the fifth year. According to Phong Phong, this is partly because the government does not pay the teachers enough, but it may also be because they are greedy too, creating a vicious circle (personal communication, June 6 and September 15, 2009).

It is important for a country like Burma/Myanmar to have a music center like Gitameit for a better early music education, at least under the current circumstances. It is equally important that a place like Gitameit will continue and other schools will join with a similar goal in the near future until the government begins to institutionalize music education. This can happen, and is beginning to happen. U Parami Shoon has successfully founded Myoma Music School in Mandalay, something similar to Gitameit in its visions, as discussed earlier, and has sent two violinists to Ms. Zhang in Ruili for further study. In addition, since 2007, 10 Gitameit teachers have initiated a program of choral singing, musicianship, and music appreciation in the International Language and Business Center. The thirst among middle-class parents and children for greater exposure to musical skills and associations is palpable. Their aspiration to engage higher, international standards of music education within Burma/Myanmar is being realized, if slowly.

This leads us to the larger issue of music education and community: without these linkages through Gitameit Music Center, Phong Phong (and Saw James) would not have made it to places like Yong Siew Toh Conservatory of Music. It shows that it takes an organization dedicated to creating internal and external links to offer possibilities and options to young musicians in artistic as well as economic terms. In a society where very few of these links have been established, people do not envision such connections and act on them. However, the connections themselves are nodes for a fuller breadth of contact and experience that would eventually benefit a whole culture of curiosity. Consequently, it was this sobering educational climate or lack thereof that prompted Ambassador Tommy Koh, the leader of a delegation from Singapore, to receive Saw James in audition at a dinner sponsored by the Singapore Ambassador to Burma/Myanmar in January 2008. The delegation could not believe that Saw James was one of about only five cellists in the entire country and was learning the instrument by himself only with the help of some method books, because there was no teacher. A member of the delegation who was on the board of the Yong Siew Toh Conservatory of Music was keen to try to get a scholarship for him. Both Phong Phong and Saw James got a taste of the life of musicians outside their country when Gitameit Music Center sponsored the two of them to attend the Southeast Asian Youth Orchestra and Wind Ensemble (SAYOWE), a 10-day festival at Mahidol University in 2006 and 2007.

Another issue that needs to be addressed here is the sense of class that Burmese people (and others) tend to attach to different kinds of music. If it were not for the great culturally weighted division between "Western" and "Burmese traditional" classical music genres in the consciousness of the Burmese middle class, there would be more acceptance of both genres as paths for music education. But the truth is that each musical tradition is ignored by the other. Because of U Thein Aung's belief that Western music was inherently better for his son as a way to a better life, and because of what he perceived to be a better education, Phong Phong totally bypassed U Tin Yi's knowledge of traditional Burmese music and violin style. By encouraging musicians of both Western classical and Burmese traditional music to work together in a society that is paralyzed by separation, new possibilities in music, both education and creation, could emerge. The fundamental philosophy of Gitameit Music Center to encourage musicality, engagement, and curiosity in the musical home of one's choice is a step toward opening up some of the rigidity that defines today's Burma/Myanmar society.

APPENDIX: A LIST OF MUSIC INSTITUTIONS IN BURMA/MYANMAR

Note: This is by no means meant to be comprehensive. Items are ordered alphabetically in each category.

Myanmar Government Music Institutions

- Myanmar Radio and Television (MRTV), Rangoon/Yangon. Formerly called Burma Broadcasting Service (BBS)
- Rangoon State School of Fine Arts
- School of Arts and Music (Pandaya Kyaung), Rangoon/Yangon. Elementary levels of education in Burmese plastic and performing arts.
- State School of Fine Arts and the University of Culture, Mandalay
- University of Culture, Dagon Township, Rangoon/Yangon

Christian Church Programs in Rangoon/Yangon With Western Music Emphasis

- Judson College Baptist Youth Conference, Alone Township, Rangoon/Yangon
- Kachin Baptist Church (Jinghpaw Wunpawng Hkalup Hpung), Sanchaung, Rangoon/Yangon
- Myanmar Baptist Convention, Alone Township, Rangoon/Yangon
- Myanmar Institute of Theology
- Thamine Baptist Church Choir and String Orchestra program

Private Music Schools and Studios Mentioned in the Chapter

- Academy of Music Violin Studio (U Tin Yi, Director), Hledan Township, Rangoon/Yangon
- Do Re Mi Pre-School and Kindergarten Music Family Club (Yuri Hasegawa, director), Eight Mile Road, Rangoon/Yangon
- Gitameit Music Center, Yankin Township, Rangoon/Yangon
- Gitameit Music Center, Mandalay
- Myoma Music Association, Mandalay

International Schools With Music Programs

- Horizon Kindergarten, Taunmwe Township, Rangoon/Yangon
- International Language and Business Center (ILBC), Rangoon/Yangon and Mandalay
- International School of Yangon
- Network Primary School, Sanchaung Township, Rangoon/Yangon
- Yangon International Education Center
- Yangon International School (YIS)

Others

- Baptist United Christian High School, Rangoon (no longer extant)
- Yunnan Music School, Ruili, China, where Phong Phong learned the violin before relocating to Rangoon/Yangon

NOTES

1. In this chapter, the country under discussion before 1989 will be referred to as "Burma," and after 1989 (when the government changed the name from Burma to Myanmar) "Burma/Myanmar." The same goes with the names of the cities, such as "Rangoon" and "Rangoon/Yangon."
2. U Toh is a retired high school principal, a sculptor at the University of Culture, and a translator.
3. However, U Thein Aung (personal communication, June 2, 2009) recalls that it was Phong Phong who chose the violin.
4. Xiang (1989, 1992).
5. Phong Phong's lessons with Ms. Zhang lasted until June 2007. Yunnan Music School, her violin studio in Ruili, has since grown, currently with about 30 students, including a couple of Burmese brought there by U Parami Shoon.
6. For more information on Gitameit Music Center, please visit their website at www.gitameit.com.
7. They are "Chamber Orchestra Concert" at Myoma Music Association, Mandalay (August 13, 2007) and "The Conductor's Art" at International Business Center in Rangoon/Yangon (August 17, 2007).

REFERENCES

Baumawka Daw Aye Than. (2004, August). Thansin mya hnin ah pyan thin [Music melodies and teaching the next generation]. *Life Style Magazine, 7,* 6–34.

Irrawaddy. (1993–). *Cumulative issues: arts and culture*. Chiang Mai, Thailand: Chotana Printing.

Judson, E. (1883). *The life of Adoniram Judson*. New York: Randolph & Co.

Khin Zaw, U. (1981). *Burmese Culture, general and particular by K*. Rangoon: Sarpay Beikman.

Thein Aung, U. (December 2005–January 2006). Unpublished journal. Translated from Burmese by Kit Young.

Zhang Shi Xiang. (Ed.). (1989). *The production of primary etude for violin* (2 vols.). Shang Hai: Yin Yue Chu Ban She.

Zhang Shi Xiang. (Ed.). (1992). *The beginners 100 days*. Shang Hai: Yin Yue Chu Ban She.

CHAPTER 11

HOW CHILDREN LEARN IN A GHARANA

A Case Study of the Family of Ustad Kadar Khan

Sumita Ambasta and Christopher McLeod, with Ustad Kadar Khan Kalavant

INTRODUCTION

The techniques, practices, and repertoires of North Indian Classical music have been transmitted orally from ancient times to the present day. Both the music itself and the life of the musician comprise a total ethos that imbues every aspect of lived experience. Family life and work, play and daily routines, attitudes and perspectives are all nurtured in the context of musical practice and grounded in a foundational awareness of what it means to be a musician and what music is for.

Musical Childhoods of Asia and the Pacific, pp. 237–266
Copyright © 2012 by Information Age Publishing
All rights of reproduction in any form reserved.

Characteristics of Gharana

The study of North Indian Classical music is undertaken with a master (Guru or Ustad) in a unique setting that has long-established conventions and expectations. The *Guru-shisya parampara* (teacher-student tradition) is the core of the larger sociomusical structure known as the *gharana*. A gharana has been defined as "a loose term that usually refers to a group of musicians who share lineal linkages and a particular musical style" (Arnold, 1999, p. 465).

Ustad Kadar Khan (Ustadji) is both a collaborator on and a subject of this chapter. His school, the Kalavant Center, is based in New York. He describes musical gharanas as consisting of seven primary characteristics:

1. Coming into the home.
2. A set of protocols and values.
3. Existence of dialogue and relationship.
4. Protocols determining daily behavior, including interactions, food, clothes, traditions, and relationship to elders and younger people.
5. Modes of exchanges that are peculiar to each lineage. For example, sweets are offered before eating in some gharanas, and after eating in others.
6. What music is to be played at what occasions and times of day.
7. Styles of playing and singing that signify talent, age, and accomplishment.

Though a number of published ethnomusicological studies have described this network of relationships, these traditional pedagogies are scarcely mentioned in the field of education.

Primary Relationship: Guru-Shisya Parampara

The Guru-shisya parampara is a method of teaching that involves a committed relationship between the teacher (Guru) and the student (shisya). In the gharana, the father or the patriarch is first a Guru. In the family, there may be several male members who embody the dual roles of both father and musician. Of these men, one is recognized as the patriarch. The patriarch enters into a formalized relationship with a student,the shisya. The formal ceremony *ganda-bhandhan* is described below. The Guru and shisya mutually contribute to a process of learning that is life long.

Several ethnomusicological studies (Kippen, 1988; Neuman, 1990; Schippers, 2007) examine the Guru-shisya parampara. These, however, exclusively describe the experience of adults in musical training. To understand the nature of the methods adopted in the study of Indian music, this chapter focuses on children within a musical gharana.

In the gharana, children and adults learn in different ways. The etymology of the word gharana is significant. The Hindi word *gharana* is a conjunction of *ghar* (home) and *aana* (to come into). Hence, students who wish to study with a teacher in a gharana have to come into the home. We attempt to describe what this means for children who are born into a musical family and for children who study under a teacher who is part of a gharana. Can the Guru-shisya parampara qualify as a pedagogical method to be studied in a modern context? Does it have any relevance outside the traditional setting of a home? Do the enduring and traditional elements of this method suggest universal values that could benefit music education theory? Where do the intersections of school, home, teacher, and learning occur? How are context and space defined, and do these translate into modern settings of education?

This chapter focuses on one musical family that has successfully adapted its own traditional heritage to a modern setting. The study involves children who are able to carry on the family musical tradition while well integrated into modern educational systems. The role of home or "*ghar*" is emphasized as are family and kinship ties that make study and transmission possible in a continuum, despite relocation or dislocations.

OUR FRAMEWORK

The Guru-shisya parampara is an ancient system of education for which much documentation exists in Indian philosophical sources. Much is known about the Guru as teacher in spiritual contexts or religious situations where students work with a teacher for guidance for meaningful living. Ancient texts like the *Upanishads* refer to the Guru or teacher as the person who helps the student find knowledge of truth.

In the Indian philosophical framework, any area of study is considered a legitimate vehicle to knowledge and truth. This is primarily through a path of immersion and experience. Musical study, then, is considered one among many paths to knowledge.

It is our view that this system is based on certain principles that can have value beyond the Indian culture. Hence, rather than view the system as an exotic "other culture" form of education, we wanted to make an effort to identify guiding principles within this method that can have greater relevance beyond one culture. For this to happen, we recognized that cross-cultural sensitivity and an ability to recognize one's own biases and views would be the first lens through which to view the material and the research findings. Hence, our framework was to describe rather than analyze.

In summary, it was possible to have studied this method with either a Western philosophical framework or with an Indian philosophical framework. It seemed right to us to avoid either, however, and to focus instead on the issue of cross-cultural understanding.

Ustadji speaks of music as a "relationship," and we find this metaphor useful by extension to the entire context of the understanding of the life of this family. Considering the material, we determined that this relational approach was the most appropriate methodological framework for this chapter. This framework of relationship provides a medium to attempt a holistic view of the life of the Kalavant gharana and the children within it. It is also ultimately very practical. We, as researchers, encounter the subjects of this chapter, and they—just as importantly— encounter us. Relationships of trust and mutual endeavor form due to this encounter. Thus, though we approach this study informed by respective backgrounds in sociology and music by the study of theorists and researchers like Dewey (1934), Gardner (1983), Greene (2001), and Jorgensen (2003, 2008) and by available ethnographic and ethnomusicological publications, we feel that our respective experience as parents, our work in the field in different contexts, and our own relationships with members of the Kalavant gharana also provide essential context, cues, evaluative tools, and insight in this study. Moreover, in keeping with the perceptions and values of the subjects of this chapter and attempting to join these to disciplined means of inquiry, we cultivate a dynamic mix of data that is never hierarchical.

Our goal is to study the issue of "relationship" in learning. The educator's relationship to material, as well as to the student, is as critical as the material itself. The relationship to the "other" in cross-cultural situations is also a subject of study, inasmuch this is not an ethnological study, but a way to expand the horizon of learning in the search for universal values.

KALAVANT FAMILY: A CASE STUDY

Lineage: The History of Gharana

Kalavants are families comprised of professional artists. Various musicological texts mention both kalavants and mirasis. The Mirasis, folk singers, were not considered as artistically accomplished as the Kalavants, who were professional classical musicians. The Kalavants embodied the seri-

ousness of art, and find mention in Bhatkhande (1990) as a living example of what music students must aspire to in musicality. The Hindi word
kalavant is a combination of *kala* (art) and *want* (consisting of). The
description denotes artistic accomplishment. Ustadji's family maintains a
centuries-old lineage of music as a vocation. The fact that this family
retains its musical tradition and learning structures in the contemporary
environment of New York City affords a unique opportunity to study how
tradition might be preserved, even while adapting to new demands.

There is a perennial question whether traditional systems of music
must maintain unbending frameworks to survive, or whether they can
flexibly adapt and change with the setting. The research in this study is
informed by this inquiry.

METHODOLOGY

Sumita Ambasta conducted several in-person interviews with Ustadji in
Delhi and Singapore. These interviews took place with his permission in
between lessons, and while observing lessons that he taught. In New York,
Christopher McLeod conducted interviews with five students who are
members of the Kalavant family. Three students based in India were not
available for documented interviews. Their experience and musical education also form part of this study. This is reflected in the narrations of
Ustadji, as well as in the accounts of the New York students.

The interviews with Ustadji were unstructured and were driven by the
ideas that emerged during the lesson at hand. The attempt was to see
what themes and general principles of music education find prominence
in attention and practice. The New York interviews followed a definite
design, which is detailed in the interview overview.

USTAD KADAR KHAN (USTADJI)

Ustadji began study with his father Ustad Reheman Khan at age 7. Ustad
Reheman Khan transmitted to him the knowledge of four different styles
of playing from the four gharanas: Delhi, Ajrada, Lucknow, and Far-
rukhabad. (Ustad Reheman Khan's and Ustadji's relationship to these four
gharanas is diagrammatically depicted in Appendix A.) His family was a
kalavant, or artistic family, that served the royal courts of India. The family
maintains the suffix *kalavant* in their formal name today, which serves to
identify them as professional musicians. Ustad Reheman Khan worked
with All India Radio and is well known in Ahmedabad, Gujarat as an Ustad
(maestro), an authority on tabla. While he generously passed on knowledge

of music to his son, he simultaneously tried to dissuade him from pursuing it as a profession. In the absence of royal patronage, and with the unavailability of enough financial support for their art, Ustad Reheman Khan feared that an adaptation to market circumstances in the pressure of making a living might dilute their traditional art. Ustadji, being the Khalifa, or the successor, displayed a dedication to the art, and forged a new and integral direction. His single-minded devotion to the preservation of the tradition, even while oftentimes living at the vanguard of the tension between tradition and modernity, steadied him. As a result of a series of encounters with the West, he arrived in the United States in 1985 (this was after his school in Ahmedabad, Naad Niket, was burned down during communal riots). He was convinced there was room for the exploration and the study of tradition in the United States. Alive to the various contrasts of life, environment, and culture between his family's ancestral village in Rajasthan, the modern Indian city of Ahmedabad, and New York City, his worldview and musical formation were fortified with new awareness, capabilities, and sensitivities. He proved able both to preserve traditional practice and to adapt to modern circumstances. He established a school, the Kalavant Centre for Music and Dance, in New York City, where he is based at present. His son, along with his nephews, have all grown up in the kalavant musical tradition both in India and the United States, and are the subjects of the interview section of this case study.

Ustadji hopes the next generation will absorb, preserve, and propagate his vocational ethic even as they deal with ever new conditions.

The people who are included in this study as well as their relationships are presented in Appendix B.

ELEMENTS OF MASTERY

In Ustadji's view, a master musician has mastery of four discrete elements: *gayan* (vocal), *vadan* (instrumental), *nritya* (dance), and the solo performing knowledge of his own core skill (i.e., table), in his instance. It is only with mastery of these four skills that he becomes *chomukha* (four faceted). In order to compose skillfully, this entire spectrum of knowledge must be well developed. The entry point of preparation is ongoing exposure to music at a very early age, which develops the foremost musical skill of listening.

THE FAMILY'S ROLE IN MUSIC EDUCATION

To emphasize the need for family involvement, he will encourage the parents of small children who are his students to also take up music so as to form a "musical relationship with the child." For instance, he instructed Sumita Ambasta to learn music, without which, he insisted, her son's musical education could not attain seriousness. To this end, he brought her a sitar, and encouraged her to study with his wife, Bina Kalavant, an accomplished sitar player. The context would not be a lesson-based pecuniary arrangement, but an encompassing relationship driven by music with the goal of creating musicality in the household of the primary student, Siddharth (Sumita's son).

Exposure to music and the creation of a musical environment in the home is essential in this system. The nurturance of a musical atmosphere is an ongoing process for children in musical families. But for other children, music must form a part of the overall framework in which musicality subsequently develops.

Relationship and Recognition

For Ustadji, music education has two salient features: relationship and recognition. The first feature, relationship, is paramount. Trust between the teacher and student takes time to form. Most of early childhood is about creating an atmosphere of love and acceptance, so that an opening takes place. He decides the level of demand to make on a child, based on the level of musicality in the home as well as the child's personality and ability to withstand pressure. Without love and trust, pressure could be counterproductive. He described music as a pathway to human development as well as a craft. In a traditional setting, the teacher controls the space of learning, so that conditions are conducive to learning the craft. In modern settings, this is not always possible, so he encourages the formation of a musical environment in the home to foster musical formation. In this regard, he will play for visiting family members of his students, educate them about the music, and share ideas and views with them. This is to spark the student's curiosity, which is driven by these experiences.

The second feature, recognition, involves understanding the due respect and appropriate place of people, knowledge, and things. An anecdote illustrates this. Once, on his way out, he heard a child use a loud, impatient voice with his mother. He returned to teach the child the following principle: "The child's voice should be two notes below the mother's, and one note below the father's and the Ustad's." This lesson deftly communicated the importance of recognizing protocol in relationships. The mother has the principle role for the child, while both father and teacher have a secondary role, at the same level. Becoming aware of one's own vocal pitch, and listening carefully to determine the pitch of the other, then adjusting the voice accordingly when speaking, would maintain this protocol. He told the child, "Without knowing this basic musical principle of recognition, it is hard to become a musician."

Dynamic Content

The content of transmission during a lesson is dynamic. Lessons do not follow strict curriculum or structure and are improvised depending on the learning environment. For instance, during a workshop he held for elementary school students in an international school, a child, seeing him in an Indian outfit, excitedly asked, "Do you have a snake in the drum?" He asked why she thought there would be a snake in the drum. It appeared she had seen a snake charmer who wore a similar long, flowing shirt. Ustadji then quickly improvised a lesson on the idea of listening through the body, just like a snake. While he played, he asked the children to explore movement and rhythm through their body. This was to underline the fact that music resides in everyone's body. The children moved and danced to the rhythm, and displayed a great ability for attention when he subsequently asked them to be quiet and observe the movements in their bodies. With complete silence the children "listened" to their own bodies.

Thus, he will take musical ideas and make them accessible. He believes that any situation can present an opportunity for instruction, especially with young children. The approach is to encourage play and learning through discovery, rather than to follow structure. The instructional material is not independent of the teacher. Rather, the material, the teacher, and the student are part of an eco-system. The teacher, he maintains, continually learns from the student how to make ideas accessible and easy to digest. A constant refining process occurs. Much, of course, depends on the student, "what he or she takes away."

A student who also studied a number of different musics with other teachers was asked to describe what distinguished his study with Ustadji. He said, "The unique relationship between the teacher and student, where it's not merely the learning of an instrument one plays, but all of life." He also listed the following elements of instruction as characteristics of this study.

- Sitting on the floor
- Learning in many spaces, not necessarily in a classroom or other fixed space
- Conversations about music and life
- Learning orally
- Learning through memory

- Learning focus by using the five senses
- Having fun rather than approach lessons with seriousness

Ganda-Bandhan: The Formal Initiation

There are two phases of musical instruction, which do not coincide with chronological age but with the level of musical development. The first includes that of explorative play, development of a musical sense, and gaining an understanding of the rigor of serious musical study. In the modern setting, this coincides with early childhood development. But this phase is identical for both adults and children who first enter the musical space of a traditional teacher. This time is also used by the teacher to assess the student's worthiness to receive more rigorous instruction, a period that is marked by "ganda-bandhan," or the tying of the sacred thread.

Ustadji described *ganda-bandhan* as a ceremony (*ganda* = thread, *band-han* = tying) that marks the beginning of serious apprenticeship. While one can begin musical education at any time and proceed at a pace of comfort, the student who is invited to perform a ganda-bandhan has been found ready and worthy for it. It is evident from other studies (Kippen, 1988) that the instructional content prior to the ganda-bandhan ceremony is the same both for young children and adults. Ustad Reheman Khan is the patriarch of the kalavant home and still performs ganda-bandhan for the young grandchildren and students who become heirs of the tabla tradition. If students express a desire to learn another musical instrument, then they will necessarily undergo a ganda-bandhan with a master of that instrument. It is the relationship of the family to music that makes these apprenticeships with other masters possible. Hence, for instance, one who studies sitar with a master from a different gharana will identify himself first by that teacher's gharana and then by his own musical lineage. These cross pollinations and integrations continue to take place in a dynamic way.

The ceremony itself is like a feast. Masters from other traditions are invited to bear witness to the commitment the teacher and student make to each other. The teacher's commitment to the student is not a private but a social one: to identify him henceforth as his student, and to withhold anything from him. The student also makes a commitment to recognize the teacher and always give him respect for the gift of learning. A poignant part of the ceremony is when they exchange gram seeds and jaggery to eat. Gram seeds represent beads of iron, and signify the pain involved in digesting hard material. Jaggery signifies the sweetness of musical learning. Both the teacher and the student understand through this exchange that though the process of musical education will bring both pain and joy, they must yet continue. Sometimes, a child younger than 8 will perform a ganda-bandhan (Ustadji did at age 7). But this is rare, and usually signifies musical genius and/or high commitment.

The period after ganda-bandhan is marked by diligent practice or *riaz*. Lessons are intense and demand extensive practice. Much of the material a teacher will impart is secret and comes with the instruction of not sharing it without permission. Riaz takes place on a daily basis and becomes part of a musical way of life. Concentrated periods of meditative study called *chilla* are 40-day periods. The musician sequesters himself in a space apart from the distractions of daily life and undertakes a practice routine of 10–12 hours (or more) a day. It is clear from several sources that this is not possible without familial support—where someone cooks, provides food, and takes care of daily incidentals. This support may come from the mother or from other women of the household. In more modern settings, in the absence of this support, and with the demands of earning livelihood, it is much harder to undertake chilla for 40 days.

Inside the Home: Development of Trust

A central facet of these family traditions that has received little written treatment is the role of women. All women, through their constant proximity to musical activity, learn tabla bols, rhythmic structures, and sing. Since *purdah*, a system of seclusion of women from public life, is generally followed, the women's musical knowledge is usually only known to members of the family. From all accounts, however, mothers supervise practice routines and even sometimes act as teachers in reserve as they monitor and correct mistakes during riaz. The discipline of riaz is made possible due to the familial support of women in the home. The women provide food and care as well as supervision. While these roles and tasks have been underreported, it is clear that the supportive roles of a grandmother, or an aunt, or a mother are critical to musical development. Ustadji's wife, Bina Kalavant, is an exception to this principle of seclusion. She studied dance before her marriage to Ustadji, and subsequently took on the study of sitar after her marriage. As a teacher and performer, her level of leadership and influence in the home is prominent.

"The Drums of War, or How I Met my Tabla Teacher" by Joan Erdman (1999) is a charming account of her own encounter with Ustadji when he was just 18. His version of this meeting includes visits to the family home, which, initially, were not accepted by his father. Only he and his mother hosted Joan Erdman on her first visit. His father refused to meet her. He does not remember the reason for this rejection. It is important to note that it was his mother who exercised influence and eventually convinced his father to host Erdman at home. The idea of "coming into the home" (gharana) had a significance for the family that would probably be difficult to understand in a more modern culture. Acceptance into the family in this way constitutes an essential first step in this culture of instruction. The moment of entrance into the teacher's home signals the formation of a relationship of trust. Teacher and student have embarked together on a path with clearly understood expectations. The teacher will not withhold anything and the student must remain true to the content of the instruction.

Ustadji maintains that improvisation is only possible within set boundaries. The student apprentice must continually leap, as though from a balance beam, with trust that the teacher will hold him. Playfulness and strict attention to rules are the basis of musical improvisation. The foundation of training, however, lies in the relationship of trust between the student and teacher.

THE INTERVIEWS

Overview

The interviews were conducted in New York by Christopher McLeod over a single weekend. Five interviewees, ranging in ages from 12 to 26 years, participated. Zakir and Javed were interviewed on Saturday afternoon; Azam, Imran, and Shakir on Sunday afternoon. It is significant that each of the participants set aside time on a weekend to participate. Also significant was their arrival and departure in groups. It felt something like coming together for small group rehearsal, with the requisite seriousness and focus on the task, but also with the overall sense of ease and relaxation that musicians can enjoy with longtime and trusted collaborators.

Each interview lasted an average of 50 minutes. In each case, the interview developed according to the dynamic interaction between the interviewer and interviewee. To frame the content for the sessions, we developed a questionnaire (Appendix C) that addressed six areas:

- Earliest impressions
- Family life
- Method (method of instruction received)
- Practice
- Performance
- Dreams for my music

Prior to the interviews, we submitted this questionnaire to Ustadji for approval, and he in turn gave it to each of the interviewees so that they could prepare. Though we endeavored to make the questionnaire both detailed and broadly comprehensive, it was intended to be a stimulative and suggestive tool and to provide launch points for discussion. In this, we set a method for our conversations that was generally analogous to a musical improvisation: with stated direction, parameters, and expectations, but also allowing for openness and range as well as the individual nature of each interviewee and the distinctive quality of each combination formed with the interviewer.

The interviews were videotaped for documentation and future review. In preparation for this chapter, the interviews were reviewed separately by each of the authors to record anecdotal data and make observations. To augment, interpret, and enhance the narrative of the interviewees, Sumita Ambasta also viewed each interview with Ustadji, who provided his own responses, further information, and clarifications.

In the balance of this section of the chapter, we detail the findings of the interviews, distributing the narrative according to the content areas of the questionnaire. Quotes are attributed by the first initial of the interviewee.

Dreams For My Music

To establish rapport and to avoid abrupt entry into the recounting of earliest memories, each interview began with discussion about current work and future goals. Beginning in this fashion was also designed to establish a continuum back to early childhood memory with a view as well to fill in the narrative as much as possible.

Without exception each of the interviewees was optimistic about their present circumstances and musical life and looked ahead to a promising future. A. confidently stated his expectation that he "definitely will play at Carnegie Hall," while Z. anticipated a "big future" where he will "work with other musicians globally, love my brothers," and "expand the music." J. expressed the wish to explore musical experimentation in the future, and described a group that is in formation that is trying out different kinds of fusion possibilities. Several of the interviewees spoke eloquently about their desire to transmit what they have to the next and future generations: "What my ancestors did is unique. It's my responsibility to pass it down."

We found the cheerfully assertive attitude and the sense of purpose about the future very attractive and indicative of the solid formation of the interviewees and of their ability to support each other with shared commitments and hopefulness. A., who evinced a charming gift for illustrating his ideas, encapsulated this ethos best by stating, "Trying new things is like a pathway."

Performance

Moving by steps back in time, the interviewees were each asked about recent performances, about their views on performing and audiences, and about the early memories of performance day for their family.

I. detailed a recent performance at New York University where he "tried for the first time" a very tricky "14-beat cycle." His pleasure in sharing this and complete naturalness in speaking about technical questions was evident. S. described a "competition" he joined in at his high school where "the 12th century" was "against the 21st century." His classmates, rendering a verdict, declared that "12th-century music was the best." When it was suggested that this might have had something to do with his remarkable proficiency, he smiled warmly. A. was busy recently as well, having played the previous summer in Bangalore for family and friends and a solo for his elementary school graduation in the spring. A., with characteristic wit, pointed out that the word "play" was a four-letter one.

Both I. and Z. described the day of a performance in their childhood city of Ahmedabad with excitement and vividness, recounting it as "Amazing," "Really exciting—everybody dressing," so much "glamour" with "2,000 people at the first concert." The first performance for I. in Ahmedabad was a competition where he was "nervous" with his "grandfather sitting" and "all the people" near the stage.

It is clear that all the interviewees are active in performing and sharing their music and eagerly seek to avail themselves of opportunities to do so. This energetic pursuit of performing is nurtured from the earliest age by a household and family system that fosters an environment for the preparation, valuation, and celebration of excellence in performance.

Earliest Impressions

For the interviewees, growing up in a household committed to musical enterprise, the most important and imposing presence was the grandfather, Ustad Reheman Khan. The interviewees describe him as "strict," "very serious," and very demanding. Grandfather was the quintessential figure of authority, setting the tone for the family, while mindful of and monitoring the musical development of each "brother." Some of the interviewees remember with fear or intimidation the stature of the grandfather: "I was afraid of grandfather. My whole house was afraid of my grandfather." Each presented their own version of the experience of sitting in their grandfather's room while a lesson was taking place or during his practice sessions. The following description is representative: "My grandfather was known in the city as the best tabla player. He used to sit for hours and hours in his room and play with no fan and no lights on. I would sit in the room with him. Nobody would make any sound when he was practicing. When I got too sweaty I would leave, but then I could come back when I wanted."

Besides the dominant presence of the grandfather, several other factors are mentioned consistently in the description of this earliest musical formation. These include an environment where absorption through listening is constant, sensuous response to the sounds of instruments and the exploration of instruments through touch is cultivated, a sense of play and an ethic of enjoyment and fun in the first years of musical activity is dominant, and the trying out of and experimentation with different instruments is ongoing. The following comments are indicative:

Dad taught me a small piece. I really enjoyed it—it was easy.

I was 3 years old and everyone was playing in the house. I got the instruments and started playing. I don't know what happened, but I could understand what they were saying. I started playing ... it wasn't exactly playing but fooling around.

I tried all the instruments: tabla, sitar, harmonium, and singing.

I would sit in and watch and listen to lessons. This was before formal lessons. Others sat in on the lesson and showed me things too.

Everybody is playing music in the house, in every room.

I would hide in my father's room and play the drum. Everyday he would notice that someone touched the drum. I would just touch the drum and get a good feeling. I would open the case, touch the drum, and get a good feeling.

I was playing with the flute. I've never made any sound on the flute but I was trying it.

Method/Practice

Gharana children are immersed in the musical life of the household and begin to learn by an absorption method that encompasses listening, play, touch, experimentation, and constant exposure to music. Formal lessons, and the inculcation of a daily practice regimen, usually take place after ganda-bandhan.

In our interview complement, Azam was the one exception to this. Azam, whose father is the collaborator on this chapter, Ustadji, began formal tabla instruction at the age of 5 under his father. He has also studied piano since age 7. Though, for our interviewees, they pertain for the most part to years beyond the age of 8, the following comments provide both a flavor of the ethos of musical instruction and the high stress on devoted practice for students who have begun formal training.

> As a kid I would really enjoy the imagination. My grandfather would ask, "Do you know how a flower opens? That is how you learn."

> The process of learning music is like a relationship. You don't jump on a person. You learn slowly. A relationship evolves.

> Dad never pointed out mistakes. Grandfather did. Dad would first talk about the positive.

> I began sitar at 10 years old. At 14, I would practice 6–7 hours a day.

> It is fun to practice everyday. I practice 1–3 hours in a morning session and an evening session.

> I don't like to judge myself, because if I judge myself that will be my limit.

> When two people are practicing they need to be in synch with each other … in synch like magnets…with eye contact. When two people sound like one … they fuse together.

> My grandfather arranged all the pieces—he set it up and I had to practice.

> Lessons…everyday for one hour at a fixed time…. If I'm not there he is not going to teach me for a few days…. Hand position is most important—how to keep your thumb, how to move your finger.

> Practice makes you happy, it's beneficial.

> Grandfather insisted on practice only in front of him. No practice alone.

Family Life

The Kalavant gharana is a joint family unit with a venerable musical tradition. As mentioned above, in addition to a study of the literature, to prepare for this chapter, discussions took place over time with both Ustadji and his wife Bina Kalavant. To come closer to a comprehensive view of the gharana, we have found it essential to consider the interview narratives within the context of the guiding viewpoints of the adults in the household. Alongside the adult viewpoint studied elsewhere in the chapter, the following are some comments that indicate the closeness and mutual support that the brothers feel:

> We are really close and call ourselves brothers.

> There is a cousin who doesn't play and he is lonely.

> There is no competition. We support each other.

> I can't imagine my life without music. I don't know if it would be a very good life, because it is a necessity for us.

> I had a goal when I started to play with everyone in the family.

> … my life without music—I wouldn't know where I would be right now.

CONCLUSIONS

Several recurring themes were found in our original research. These themes are related specifically to early childhood stages of music education and they constitute the core of the narrative.

For beginners, the most important musical skill is listening. It is popularly stated in India that "*Caansen* (master of can = ear) comes before *Tansen* (a legendary Indian musician from the sixteenth century)." Listening is developed through sitting in on lessons, exposure to music throughout the household, and listening to others play.

Absorption rather than acquisition of technical knowledge is paramount in music education. This is repeatedly affirmed by traditional teachers. Beginner musicians are immersed in the values and attitudes of musical life. Technical concerns are secondary. There is a place and time for technical proficiency but it is later and not in early childhood.

For children and beginners, an unstructured environment for study is emphasized. This is to facilitate exploration where music is concerned. It is also unstructured so that the child can respond to the situation, which may be different in different contexts and spaces.

The only principle or structure that guides early education in music is an understanding of relationships. This principle fosters the development of trust and worthiness on both sides in the student-teacher relationship.

Protocols of behavior are inculcated and these also define the boundaries of musical play. Within the music itself, abundant experimentation is encouraged.

Music is considered a part of human development, particularly human spiritual development. It is also an accepted vocation for some. This creates a two-step musical education process. The student must commit to music as a vocation or as a legitimate method of human development or ganda-bandhan will not occur. Ganda-bandhan does not take place in recognition of solely technical achievement. There is a clear distinction between vocational and nonvocational approaches. The first is highly structured and technical, and hence is serious. The second is focused on exploration, with an emphasis on listening. For both steps, the focus is on "learning by doing." "Doing" involves manifesting behavior that reflects the values and attitudes detailed above.

The purpose of music education drives the approaches adopted, in phased stages. This ethic is probably not limited to music education, but may be a defining characteristic of the entire Guru-shisya tradition of teaching. At first, the recognition of the "other" occurs through listening and attention. The development of trust in the relationship sets the stage for the demands of the next step of learning.

The Guru-shisya parampara is the defining principle in the gharana. It emphasizes certain universal values that have relevance to not only music education in particular but educational theory and practice in general. These values in the Guru-shisya tradition are as follows:

- An ethic of relationship between the student and teacher comprises the space for learning. The commitment to the relationship is a prerequisite to learning. In early childhood, the burden of the commitment falls on the teacher. This later gives way to a more equitable relationship (upon the student's attainment of maturity).
- For learning to take place, trust must be established to handle the demands of ongoing instruction and learning.
- Learning is experiential and is forwarded through a process of dialogue and doing.
- Listening to the other is a central value of relationship. Listening is not only embodied, taught, and facilitated by the teacher, but is also required in the process of active engagement with the student. Teacher and student both learn through an ongoing activity of listening.
- Acceptance of ambiguity and tension, which is also related to the value of commitment described above.

These universal values have a place in learning situations beyond the gharana, the home, or traditional situations. Although Ustadji expressed doubt whether these traditional methods had any relevance to modern education, because he doubted the commitment to relationship, we find that there are many possible practical applications from this study. Some of these possible important applications are:

- The relevance of the home environment in creating context and space for learning to occur.

- The development of trust and relationship between the educator and student.
- The recognition of the student's commitment as a necessary requirement for learning to progress.

The teacher also learns through his or her relationship with the student, making the learning process dynamic and nonhierarchical.

While the above is certainly not an exhaustive list, it provides some possible lines of inquiry for further research in educational pedagogy and theory.

RESEARCHERS' REFLECTION

We decided to undertake a case study of Ustadji's family, as it is a rare example of the encounter of tradition and practice with contemporary settings. To discover practices for early childhood, we chose to rely on the narrations and memories of family members, Ustadji himself, and one other student, Siddharth Sachdeva. The methodology included documented (videotaped) interviews.

The questions we posed to the adults were improvised, as we did not want to impose any framework of thought. Research proved that almost nothing has been published that documents the methods of children's music education used in the tradition of North Indian classical music. Research also was conclusive that there has existed a music education system dating back centuries. Hence, we determined that to begin with preconceptions or interpretive templates was unjustified. We could have taken a comparative study or used any of the current accepted music education frameworks to design the questions, but we decided to first collect data and listen carefully for the themes that emerged.

To gather data for early childhood, we observed Ustadji teach children, and also relied on his verbal presentations of his methods. We also conducted interviews with the young musicians of his family, as well as other family members. The interviews involved reliance on memory, which can be incomplete, imprecise, or subject to modification by beliefs. To counter these concerns, the New York interviews were conducted without older family members present. This allowed the subjects to freely present their own memories of early childhood. We cross-checked their narrations with the Ustadji interviews and were able to easily verify numerous details. (Ustadji also reviewed the New York interviews, filling in gaps and answering questions.) This assured us that these narrations were largely accurate. It was clear to the authors that as these subjects were living representatives of an oral tradition, both their ability to remember and to repeat from memory were robust. They correctly described the practices, ideas, and ethos. Yet, each asserted a distinct individuality and was not hesitant to express views that may seem at odds with expectations from a traditional family.

We also studied the published research on the tabla and North Indian musical traditions. Some of these sources were referred by Ustadji. Others we found on our own (detailed in the references). Descriptions of these family traditions and methods featured significant cross- references and coincided with the narrations of the Kalavant family members as well. Due to the concern with deterministic classifications and misrepresentations, there is a powerful reluctance to document within oral traditions. Moreover, these musicians do not usually read ethnographical texts to see how they have been described by musicians or educators from outside the tradition. When they do read ethnographical accounts, they feel the representation is not accurate. We asked Ustadji to collaborate with us on this chapter. It was the only way to meet the ethical concern of recognizing and ascribing the ownership of the knowledge to him and the members of the Kalavant family. Many practitioners of oral traditions fear misrepresentation and withhold information. They are concerned about the potential for disrespect, misuse, or lack of understanding on the part of the researcher or other counterparts. One of the authors has a relationship of trust with the family, as her son is a young student of Ustadji, as well as a contemporary of his son, Azam. She has also studied sitar with Ustadji's wife, Bina Kalavant. She sought permission and cooperation to write this chapter, sharing with them that the process of research has tremendous potential for illumination and can reveal things about study methods that are important to the contemporary study of Indian Classical music. From the conclusions of the chapter, the authors realized that there may be universal values that may also be worth exploring for educational researchers, not only in music education but in all education.

Apart from the personal relationship to the family, the two authors attempted to integrate several different perspectives. Sumita Ambasta's observations of her son's musical study with Ustad Kadar Khan were the primary impetus for this study. She found the methods employed compelling. Moreover, her work as a co-founder of Flowering Tree, a New York–based nonprofit foundation that serves children's education in Asia, made her curious about traditional methods in Asian cultures that might prove adaptable to modern educational settings. The other author, Christopher McLeod, is also a co-founder of this foundation and brings the same interest in educational frameworks. He is a musician in the Western classical tradition, and hence brought an engaged cultural outsider's point of view as well as a musician's awareness and sensitivity to this study. Sumita, apart from her look as a parent and student of music, also brought a sociological lens. Both authors work with children's education and have a vital shared concern to find methods and ideas that can find a large audience and pedagogical interest.

Some accounts describe these oral teaching traditions as unstructured and ignorant. They critique what is characterized as a "mystique" surrounding them. We probed these issues very closely in our questioning. Context, as Jorgensen (2003, 2008) describes, is key in understanding this tradition. We also examined Taylor's (1994) views of cross-cultural understanding exemplified in his image of the "fusion of horizons." Another view we find helpful is that of cultural historian Jacques Barzun. In *From Dawn to Decadence* (Barzun, 2000), he writes about the limitations, for instance, of "abstraction" and "analysis" and of the necessity for more comprehensive evaluations than these tools obtain.

Up until this study, Ustadji has not permitted the filming or documentation of his teaching as he has not been sure how the material would be used and whether it would be misrepresented. This chapter is a unique expression of trust in the sharing of information and in the access to the family. Its single purpose is to further the value of education. The authors have accepted the responsibility of correct representation of facts, and hence have tried to stay with description as far as possible. Our goal has been to represent the case study like the story of a family in an oral tradition, so as to open up questions for inquiry and discussion by other educators.

The demand for synthesis of many voices, viewpoints, and values drove us to explore a philosophical framework especially for this study. This framework has been described in the beginning of the chapter as a study of relationship. We found it useful to use the simple framework of study of relationship to structure some of the writing, and not the research itself, but we also acknowledge that this may not be the only possible framework. Relationship can be studied in both Western and non-Western frameworks. Indian philosophical frameworks have many studies of relationship in at least two traditions: *Adavaita* (nondualism) and *Dvaita* (dualism). It should be acknowledged, however, that the study of these traditions may be too overwhelming for a beginner to Indian philosophy. It may be entirely possible to bring other lenses to study the information and data presented in this chapter, and one does not need to know Indian philosophical frameworks to understand these approaches. We tried to stay with the experiential and practical approaches to pedagogy, with an emphasis on illuminating universal values. We hope that the large context as well as the little details from the childhoods in this musical tradition may bring new understandings to music education.

APPENDIX A: USTAD REHEMAN KHAN'S AND USTADJI'S RELATIONSHIP TO THE FOUR GHARANAS

Please see next page for Appendix A figures

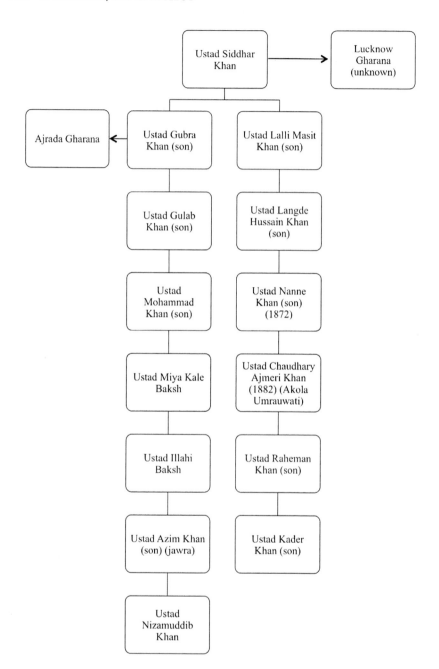

Appendix A.1

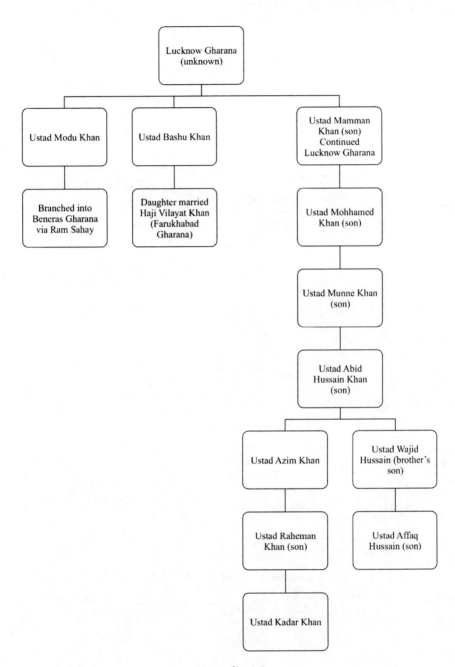

Appendix A.2

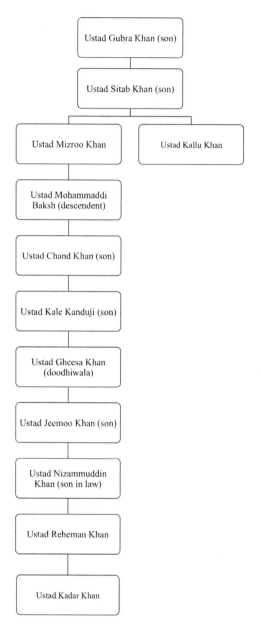

Appendix A.3

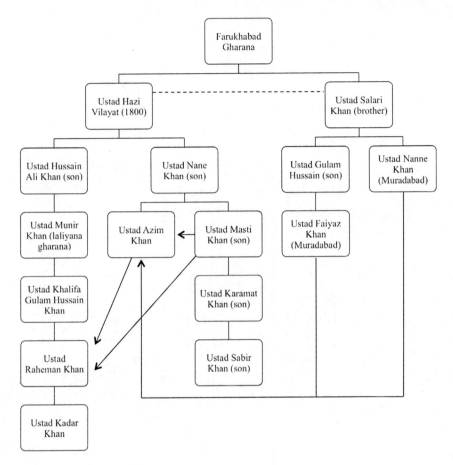

Appendix A.4

APPENDIX B: PARTICIPANTS AND THEIR RELATIONSHIPS

Please see next page for Appendix B figure

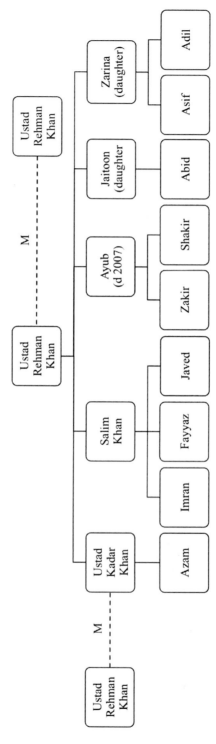

Appendix B.1

APPENDIX C: QUESTIONNAIRE CONTENT AREAS—ALL MEMORIES OF TIME BEFORE 8 YEARS OLD

Earliest Impressions

What are your first musical memories?
What was the first instrument you tried?
Who encouraged you in music: your mom, dad, grandparents?
Did you find you immediately did well in your music, or was it more difficult?
Can you imagine how your life might be different without music?

Family Life (the life of our musical family)

Do you enjoy playing with your mom and dad?
Is there a sense of competition with your siblings? Do you support one another?
How do you see your family as different from other families? The same?
What other things besides music do you like to do as a family?
Who was your primary music teacher?
Who supervised your practice?

Method

What was the first exposure to teaching?
Did you learn the "look ... speak..." method as a child or as an adult?
When do you remember being allowed to touch an instrument for the first time?
When did you formally start learning?
Did you sit in on lessons as a child?
Did you learn by listening? Did you learn by playing? (before the age of 8)
Any specific memory about being a child in a musical family? Elaborate.

Practice

How did you learn how to practice?
Do you like to practice alone or with your siblings? Parents?

264   S. AMBASTA, and C. MCLEOD

Did someone supervise your practice or did you practice alone?
How much do you practice? (Do you need motivation or does it come naturally?)
Do you have an experience of accomplishment when practice goes well? Does this translate to other things you do (in school or other activities)?
(This may not apply to memories before the age of 8, but might put memories in a context about composite musical experience.)

Performance

Do you enjoy performance?
Can you speak about a particular performance that is memorable?
What happens in your family on the day of a performance?
What do you like audiences to experience when you perform?
Would you like to be a performer?

Dreams for My Music

How do you see the future of your music?
Would you like to work with your family in music or branch out on your own?
What are the relationships of your music to other kinds of music you hear in New York? (How would you like to actively engage in exploring these relationships?)
Do you think about how your music relates to technology, media, business?

APPENDIX D: GLOSSARY OF INDIAN WORDS

Aana	To come into.
Bandhan	To tie.
Chilla	A 40-day cycle of practice in confinement. This can have a musical or a spiritual purpose.
Chomukha	Having four faces. A master musician.
Ganda	Thread.
Ganda-bandhan	An initiation ceremony into formal musical instruction in the North Indian musical practice.
Gayan	Vocal music.
Ghar	Home.

Gharana	A household bound together by several characteristics, which are not limited to lineage, but include behavior, traditions, style, etc.
Guru	A teacher who removes the darkness of ignorance.
Kala	Art.
Kalawant	Families of artists.
Khalifa	The named successor in a tradition. The term is only used in Muslim families.
Mirasis	Families of folk singers.
Nritya	Dance.
Parampara	Tradition.
Purdah	Veil. The practice of women not engaging in public life. It consists of protocols of interaction for women.
Riaz	Practice.
Sangeet	Music. This Sanskrit word means "to sing together." Music in India includes vocal, instrumental, and dance.
Shagird	Student of Ustad.
Shisya	Student of Guru.
Ustad	A guru in a Muslim tradition. It can also mean maestro in musical context.
Vadan	Instrumental music. It is derived from vadya, meaning musical instrument.

REFERENCES

Arnold, A. (Ed.). (1999). *Garland encyclopedia of world music: Vol. 5. The Indian subcontinent*. New York: Routledge.

Barzun, J. (2000). *From dawn to decadence. 500 years of western cultural life: 1500 to the present*. New York: HarperCollins.

Bhatkhande, V. N. (1990). *Hindustani sangeet paddhati kramik pustak malika* (K. C. Garg, Trans.). Hathras, India: Sakhi Prakashan.

Dewey, J. (1934). *Art as experience*. New York: Minton, Balch & Company.

Erdman, J. (1999). The drums of war, or how I met my tabla teacher. *Chicago South Asia Newsletter, 23*(1), 3–5.

Gardner, H. (1983). *Frames of mind*. New York: Basic Books.

Greene, M. (2001). *Variations on a blue guitar: The Lincoln Center Institute lectures on aesthetic education*. New York: Teachers College Press.

Jorgensen, E. R. (2003). *Transforming music education*. Bloomington: Indiana University Press.

Jorgensen, E. R. (2008). *The art of teaching music*. Bloomington: Indiana University Press.

Kippen, J. (1988). *The tabla of Lucknow. A cultural analysis of a musical tradition.* Cambridge, England: Cambridge University Press.

Neuman, D. (1990). *The life of music in North India.* Chicago: University of Chicago Press.

Schippers, H. (2007). The guru recontextualized. Perspectives on learning North Indian classical music in shifting environments for professional training. *Asian Music, 38*(1), 124–138.

Taylor, C. (1994). *Multiculturalism: Examing the politics of recognition.* Princeton, NJ: Princeton University Press.

ABOUT THE AUTHORS

Mayumi Adachi is Associate Professor of Psychology in the Graduate School of Letters, Hokkaido University, Japan. She teaches undergraduate and postgraduate courses, and supervises students' research. Mayumi's research interests reflect her interdisciplinary background, including music perception and cognition, musical development, early childhood music education, and the role of music in the lives of mothers and children. She served as an editorial board member of the *International Journal of Music Education*, and is currently on the editorial board of *Psychology of Music, Psychomusicology*, and *Journal of Music Perception and Cognition*.

Sumita Ambasta has a background in Sociology and Human Resource Development. She left a successful career in the corporate world to focus on the development of her two children as an immigrant mother. She lives and works in three countries and has a life long interest in cultural dialogues and in arts and education as a common space to create that dialogue. Sumita and Christopher McLeod founded *Flowering Tree*, the U.S. based not-for-profit organization, supporting children's education and women's development in Asia. She works to integrate arts and cultural experience and awareness through *Flowering Tree's* projects and partnerships.

Patricia Shehan Campbell is Donald E. Peterson Professor of Music at the University of Washington, where she teaches courses at the interface of education and ethnomusicology. Her scholarship and practice concerns children's musical learning and world music pedagogy, and her publishing efforts include *Songs in Their Heads* (1998, 2010, 2nd edition) and

Teaching Music Globally (2004). She chairs the board of Smithsonian Folkways, serves as vice president of the Society for Ethnomusicology, and is president-elect of The College Music Society.

Pamela Costes Onishi earned her PhD in ethnomusicology at the University of Washington, Seattle. Her research interests include diaspora music cultures, youth identity and music, traditional music pedagogy in the schools, Philippine indigenous musical traditions, and the gong and drum traditions of Southeast Asia. She has published on Philippine music hybridities and kulintang improvisations and has presented in various peer-reviewed international conferences and symposia. Pamela is currently a Research Scientist at the National Institute of Education, Nanyang Technological University, Singapore. She handles projects on community arts and arts in education as Principal and co-Principal Investigator at the UNESCO-NIE Center for Arts Research in Education (CARE).

Sonja Lynn Downing is an Assistant Professor of ethnomusicology in the Conservatory of Music at Lawrence University in Appleton, Wisconsin. Her research and teaching interests include Balinese performing arts, music pedagogy around the world, gender and music, and ecomusicology. She has presented at a wide variety of conferences in the U.S. and internationally, and published an article on gender and leadership in girls' gamelans in the journal *Ethnomusicology* in 2010. Sonja has studied gamelan music for over a decade, and has performed with Gamelan Sekar Jaya across the U.S. and in Bali, Indonesia.

Young-Youn Kim chairs the Department of Early Childhood Education at Silla University, Korea. She is a Chief Editor of the *Korean Journal of Music Education* as well as the Korean Representative of APSMER. She has supervised research students and taught in undergraduate and postgraduate early childhood programs. Young-Youn's research interests traverse children's song collection, musical cultures, music education curriculum development for young children from birth, and advice for arts education policy at government level. She is the author of about 40 international and national journal articles and 10 books and book chapters.

Pyng-Na Lee is a professor in the department of Early Childhood Education, National University of Tainan, Taiwan. She supervises graduate research students and teaches in the area of early childhood music education. Pyng-Na's research interests encompass free music play and teacher intervention, young children's self-invented notation, Aboriginal music studies and the investment of early childhood music education in Taiwan.

Chee-Hoo Lum is assistant professor in music education with the Visual & Performing Arts Academic Group at the National Institute of Education (NIE), Singapore. He is also the Director of the UNESCO-NIE Centre for Arts Research in Education (CARE), part of a region-wide network of Observatories stemming from the UNESCO Asia-Pacific Action Plan. Chee Hoo's research interests include children's musical cultures and their shifting musical identities; the use of media and technology by children, in families, and in pedagogy; creativity and improvisation in children's music; elementary music methods and world musics in education.

Elizabeth Mackinlay is an Associate Professor in the School of Education at the University of Queensland, where she teaches Music and Arts Education, Indigenous Education and Women's Studies. Liz completed her PhD in Ethnomusicology at the University of Adelaide in 1998 and continues her work with Aboriginal women at Borroloola in the Northern Territory of Australia. She also completed a PhD in Education at the University of Queensland in 2003. She has published with Peter Lang and Cambridge Scholars Publishing, is the editor of *Music Education Research and Innovation* and co-editor of the *Australian Journal of Indigenous Education*.

Christopher McLeod is an accomplished classical guitarist who has been a student of Michael Newman, Frederic Hand, Rubin Riera, pianist Sonia Rubinsky and others. He has been heard frequently in performances and Master Classes in the New York area. Christopher and .Sumita Ambasta founded *Flowering Tree*, the US based not-for-profit organization, supporting children's education and women's development in Asia. He works to integrate arts and cultural experience and awareness through *Flowering Tree's* projects and partnerships.

Hideaki Onishi earned his PhD in music theory from the University of Washington, Seattle, studying with Jonathan Bernard. His main research interest has been the music of post-World War II composers, and he has presented and published on the works of Takemitsu, Messiaen, and Ligeti. Onishi also collaborates with ethnomusicologist Pamela Costes Onishi in interdisciplinary studies on kulintang (the gong and drum music from the Southern Philippines) and co-directs Sari-Sari Philippine Kulintang Ensemble, actively performing both in and out of Singapore. Onishi is currently assistant professor of music theory and analysis at Yong Siew Toh Conservatory of Music, National University of Singapore.

Peter Whiteman is Associate Director of The Children and Families Research Centre at the Institute of Early Childhood, Macquarie University, Australia. He supervises research students and teaches in undergraduate and postgraduate early childhood programs. Peter's research interests span early childhood music education and musical development, musical cultures, emergent symbol systems and reconstructed childhoods. He is the author of journal articles and book chapters and his research has been presented in a range of international settings.

Kit Young spent the last 20 years performing and teaching at universities and schools in Thailand, Myanmar/Burma and China where her husband was posted to U.S. Embassies. She performs contemporary repertoire, improvisation, and collaborates with musicians and theater artists from these countries informing her compositional material. Her 20-year study of Burmese language, music and *Sandaya* or the unique Burmese approach to the western piano is also a performing interest. Together with Burmese colleagues, Ms. Young started the Gitameit Music Center in Yangon Myanmar in 2003.

CPSIA information can be obtained at www.ICGtesting.com
Printed in the USA
LVOW100713290612

287979LV00002B/22/P

9 781617 357756